BERNARD SHAW: A REASSESSMENT

Colin Wilson

BERNARD SHAW

A REASSESSMENT

 HUTCHINSON OF LONDON

HUTCHINSON & CO (*Publishers*) LTD
178–202 Great Portland Street, London W1

London Melbourne Sydney
Auckland Bombay Toronto
Johannesburg New York

First published 1969

© Colin Wilson 1969

*This book has been set in Garamond, printed in Great Britain
on Antique Wove paper by Anchor Press, and
bound by Wm. Brendon, both of Tiptree, Essex*

09 098010 7

To S. Foster Damon
and to Foster's godson
John Damon Wilson

ACKNOWLEDGMENTS

This book owes its major debt to Michael Bessie, of Atheneum Publishers, who not only commissioned it and made valuable suggestions for rewriting, but who has waited patiently for three years for delivery of the manuscript. I am also indebted to Harold Harris of Hutchinson for patience and for helpful suggestions. Ronald Stevenson drew my attention to comments on Shaw by Beecham, Delius and Busoni. I must also thank the Shaw Trust for permission to quote from Shaw's Collected Works, and Messrs Macmillan and Co. for permission to quote from W. B. Yeats's *Collected Poems*.

CONTENTS

INTRODUCTORY

There can be only one reasonable excuse for another book about Shaw: that it is time for a total reassessment.

At the time I am writing this—eighteen years after Shaw's death—there are signs of a Shaw revival; at least, his plays are again being performed in England and America. But I doubt whether there *is* a Shaw revival in a genuine sense: that is, in the sense of a real understanding of his achievement, a placing of him in historical perspective. The Shaw slump began about forty years before his death, at the beginning of the First World War, and although he still had great successes ahead of him, I think it would be true to say that his serious reputation went into steady decline. Usually, age helps to canonise a writer. Critics discover deeper meanings in his works, overall patterns, and no longer feel embarrassed at using the epithet 'great'. This never happened to Shaw. Even from a fairly early stage in his career there was a tendency to say: 'Oh, Shaw', with a dismissive wave of the hand. And what this meant, translated into more specific terms, was that Shaw was a lightweight, a man of superficial brilliance, but without depth. A kind of monument, perhaps—but the kind that makes you avert your eyes and hurry past, like the Albert Memorial.

This decline was due in part to the attacks of influential writers of the new generation: Eliot, Pound, Wyndham Lewis, D. H. Lawrence, Richard Aldington. And what was most noticeable about these attacks was their lack of critical detachment. Pound wrote about Joyce: 'He has presented Ireland under British domination, a picture so veridic that a ninth rate coward like

Shaw dare not even look it in the face.' Elsewhere Pound refers
to Shaw as 'an intellectual cheesemite'. In Eliot the tone is—as
one would expect—less scurrilous but more deadly. Shaw is
'dramatically precocious and poetically less than immature' and
his 'life force' is merely a 'powerful juju'. D. H. Lawrence
classified Shaw with Galsworthy and Granville Barker as one of
the 'rule-and-measure mathematical folk', and when he writes to
Koteliansky about an article on Shaw for a book called *Scrutinies*
he suggests that it should be done by someone else, as 'slaying
my elders only interests me in spasms'. It is taken for granted that,
whoever does it, it will be a razor job. Aldington echoes Lawrence
when he calls Shaw 'a fanatic of the intellect' in his introduction
to Lawrence's *Apocalypse*. Since Shaw's death, criticism has
become, if anything, more dismissive. Raymond Williams, in a
book on *Drama from Ibsen to Eliot*, calls *Back to Methuselah* 'an
adolescent fantasy', and remarks: 'Shaw's dynamic as a dramatist
is surely weakening, and it seems impossible that it can, as a
major force, survive the period of which he was a victim.' This
is a kind of rock-bottom of dismissal; Shaw is no longer even to
be attacked; only pitied.

On the other hand, Eric Bentley, the author of one of the most
perceptive books on Shaw, admits in his preface:

'I had written two books in which Shaw came to occupy a
central and yet—to me at least—problematic position. I say "came
to" because in the earlier drafts of my first book, Shaw's place
was inconspicuous and, so to say, disgraceful. He was a villain
in a gallery of villains. When the manuscript was revised for the
press, however, he looked like the solitary hero of the collection.
. . . I went on reading him, and seeing him in the theatre, after
finishing both books. Although with the passage of time I was
less and less able to understand him, in the sense of being able to
explain him with a formula, I became more and more aware of
the inadequacy of the formulae which I and others had up to
now made shift with.'

The 'first book' Bentley refers to was *The Cult of the Superman*,
an examination of various writers from Carlyle to D. H. Lawrence, and the most striking characteristic of the book is its
almost pedantic fair-mindedness. It is obvious, for example, that
before attacking Carlyle, Bentley has actually read most of Carlyle

—a feat to which few modern critics could lay claim. And I suspect this explains his change of attitude towards Shaw. He read Shaw, instead of accepting the fashionable critical estimates of him. 'I asked myself: if Shaw is a simple author, why did so many people feel obliged to give their opinion of him, and why did their opinions differ so widely from each other, and why were so many of them complacently shallow?' Bentley's book begins by considering Shaw's theories of political economy—to which Shaw attached the greatest importance; this sets a tone of seriousness that is akin to Shaw's own intellectual world; and it is this, perhaps, that explains why the book is one of the few satisfactory discussions of Shaw as a thinker. I have followed Bentley's example in the present book by devoting considerable attention to 'the economic basis'.

One of the chief problems in writing about Shaw is that his creative life extended over more than seventy years, and he continued to develop and change long beyond the age at which most writers can only repeat themselves. It is difficult to grasp a creative span that goes on for so long. Not that Shaw cannot be reduced to a formula; any consistent writer can be 'formularised'; only the incoherent and inconsistent defy summary. But the formula has to be far more complex than has so far been allowed. To begin with, the development of any major writer needs to be understood from its earliest stages. Joyce provided his own biography, so that it is easy to follow him from childhood to the period of *Finnegans Wake*. And although one may feel that *Finnegans Wake* is an enormous miscalculation, a sort of literary Crystal Palace, it can be read with sympathy because the reader can see how far he has come from the early days. Shaw made his first impact with the public when he was in his forties, with plays that were already as good as anything he would ever write. And although there are a couple of autobiographical prefaces, and the *Sixteen Self Sketches*, he was more interested in forgetting his younger days than in documenting them. It is only in fairly recent years that Rosset's *Shaw of Dublin*, Percy Smith's *The Unrepentant Pilgrim*, and John O'Donovan's *Shaw and the Charlatan Genius* have enabled us to get Shaw's early years into some kind of focus. Shaw's three most distinguished biographers—Archibald Henderson, Hesketh Pearson and St John Ervine—have devoted about one twentieth of their respective volumes to Shaw's first three decades. I have tried to place more emphasis on Shaw's early period in an attempt to show that Shaw's development was as slow and irregular as anybody else's.

My personal attitude to Shaw is explained in the Postscript to this book, and it is, of course, implicit in the whole book. But there are two points that I should make here, because they are central to my conception of Shaw. The first is that he is a romantic. *Arms and the Man* and *The Devil's Disciple* are not anti-romantic plays, or even romantic plays disguised as anti-romantic. They are romantic plays made acceptable to the intellectually fastidious by a certain stripping away of sentimentalism. Shaw was basically as complete a romantic as Shelley or Wagner.

To grasp this is to grasp the essential nature of Shaw's work; but it is not to understand the nature of his greatness. This depended upon his extremely high degree of *objectivity*, and the way he combined this with his romanticism. And this term 'objectivity' requires some further explanation.

It is self-evident that most human beings live in a subjective universe, and that the more protected they are, the more they can ignore the outer world. A baby can close its eyes and forget the outer world, because it is fed and protected by its parents. And in a civilised society most people can ignore the outside world for a great deal of the time because it is the business of civilised society to protect its members. A child can say, in effect: 'The starving children in Asia aren't half as important as my broken toy,' and reality will not contradict him. And since civilised man leads a fairly sheltered life, he can also indulge in this form of subjectivity without being contradicted too often. He can allow his emotions to decide what is real or important; he can choose his private reality to a large extent.

It may be objected that only the rich can afford to ignore reality; the poor are brought face to face with it every day. This is untrue. The poor man's self-chosen reality can be as absurd and trivial as that of the most spoiled social parasite. Any kind of habit has the effect of insulating one from reality, and it makes no difference whether it is a habit of living in a slum or on a millionaire's yacht.

This explains why the most highly developed cultures produce the most pessimism. When we are lulled into somnolence by lack of challenge every molehill tends to become a mountain, every minor inconvenience an intolerable imposition. For a self-chosen reality tends to become a prison. The factors that protect and insulate civilised man can easily end by suffocating him unless he possesses a high degree of self-discipline, the 'highly developed vital sense' that Shaw speaks of. And since clever and sensitive people are inclined to lack self-discipline, a high degree of culture usually involves a high degree of pessimism. This is what has happened to Western civilisation over the past two centuries. It explains why so many distinguished artists, writers and musicians have taken such a negative view of the human situation.

Scientists and philosophers are slightly better off than artists in this respect. They are—at least in theory—concerned with the objective world. Einstein defined his aim as 'to see the world by pure thought, without anything subjective'. C. P. Snow has pointed out that at the time when Europe was convulsed by literary pessimism—in the twenties and thirties—the atmosphere in science was one of excitement and optimism. The scientist may be no more or less sensitive than a poet or painter, but the need to keep an open mind towards the universe means that he is less likely to get trapped in a 'private reality'.

It has always seemed to me self-evident that Shaw's optimism was based upon a high degree of natural objectivity, particularly after socialism had provided a focus for his energies. Very few of the great writers of the past two hundred years have possessed much objectivity—on the contrary, they have usually been notable for the intensity of their subjective vision (Dickens and Balzac are obvious examples). Shaw possessed a higher degree of objectivity than any European writer since Goethe, and it was this that, in spite of his natural romanticism, enabled him to transcend the pessimism and boredom of the romantics.

It also explains his curious insensitivity—for example, his lack of insight into T. E. Lawrence. St Joan remarks: 'Minding your own business is like minding your own body; it's the shortest way to make yourself sick.' For Shaw, Lawrence was simply a man who made himself sick by being too absorbed in his problems and emotions; he was incapable of grasping the kind of self-divided strength that produced the *Seven Pillars of Wisdom*. Shaw had solved the basic metaphysical problem of the nineteenth century without even being aware that he had solved it.

1 WHO IS THEN THE GENTLEMAN?

Shaw was born into the middle of the Victorian golden age. The writer in the England of the mid-nineteenth century could achieve an eminence and authority that he has never achieved since. Dickens and Carlyle, Ruskin and George Eliot, Matthew Arnold and Cardinal Newman were as important as the Prime Minister or the Archbishop of Canterbury. People listened to them seriously; politicians asked their opinions and the reading public paid over enormous sums for their works.

It was also an age that owed its peculiar character to women. There was a woman on the throne, and the morals and manners of the age were shaped by lady novelists: Charlotte M. Yonge, Mrs Henry Wood, Mrs Oliphant, Miss Braddon, Mrs Humphrey Ward—whose audience was again predominantly female. Mudie's circulating library was formed in 1842, fourteen years before Shaw was born, and Mudie's female customers had very definite ideas about what they expected from the three-volume novel. Primarily, it had to be romantic and inoffensive. It had to have the kind of hero who said: 'Miss Mohun, I wonder if I might be permitted to offer you the use of my carriage?', and a heroine who replied: 'Captain Farqueson, I fail to understand how anything in my conduct can have merited your assumption of familiarity.' Oscar Wilde remarked: 'Anyone can write a three-volume novel. It merely requires a complete ignorance of both life and literature.' One of the most eminent members of the Shaw family in the 1870s was his cousin Mrs Cashel Hoey, a writer of three-volume novels.

It takes quite an effort of imagination to grasp what it must have been like to be born into Victorian Dublin—a provincial backwater where most people believed that the three-volume novel offered a true picture of how fashionable ladies and gentlemen behaved. This is an assumption that can be found in Shaw's early novels, and it explains why they are so uncharacteristic. Certainly Shaw had little enough opportunity to discover otherwise; for although his father was a 'gentleman' (which in Ireland was almost synonymous with being a Protestant), his parents were boycotted by the rest of the family for reasons that will appear presently. The Shaw family belonged to the Irish gentry —they had a family seat near Galway—and most of them had that exaggerated interest in social position that is the result of being able to claim marquises and dukes among your third cousins. There was a very odd streak of snobbery in Shaw that has only been recognised fairly recently; he liked to claim to be a descendant of Shakespeare's Macduff; he also claimed Oliver Cromwell among his ancestors, and a sister of the Bishop of York called Mary Markham. Henderson mentions Shaw's 'keen disappointment and chagrin' to discover that the Bishop of York's sister never married. We can note the same snobbery in Shaw's younger contemporaries, Yeats, Wilde and Joyce, so it should not surprise us. Ireland is still a poor country; and, like all poor countries, it has a sharp dividing line between the gentry and the peasantry.

So, as with Joyce, the question of whether he was a gentleman or not was of some importance to Shaw. In 1935 he could describe his own class as 'the Shabby Genteel, the Poor Relations, the Gentlemen who are No Gentlemen'; but that was when he was old and famous. His early novels show that he felt less casual about it in his twenties. James Joyce has described, in *Portrait of the Artist as a Young Man* what it felt like to be the eldest son of an Irish gentleman who drifted steadily closer to bankruptcy; it was a frightening and embittering experience. Shaw was in the same position, and he could not bring himself to be frank about it until he was in his nineties.

In the absence of a fortune the gentleman may be distinguished from the *polloi* by his education. But even this was lacking in the Shaw clan; Shaw recorded that only one of his uncles, the eldest, 'managed to snatch a university education. The rest shifted as best they could without it (rather better than he, mostly).' 'On the whole, they held their cherished respectability in the world in spite of their lack of opportunity. They owed something, perhaps, to the confidence given them by their sense of family. In Irish fashion, they talked of themselves as the Shaws, as who should say the Valois, the Bourbons, the Hohenzollerns, the Hapsburgs, or the Romanoffs: and their world conceded the point to them.' He mentions one of his aunts 'whose conception of the family dignity was so prodigious (the family snobbery being unmitigated in her case by the family sense of humour) that she would have refused an earl because he was not a duke, and so died a very ancient virgin'.

Shaw's father, George Carr Shaw, was a short, unprepossessing man with a cast in his left eye, and a humorous, self-depreciatory manner. Shaw offers the following potted history of his father's business career:

'[My uncles] had an impression that the Government should give them employment, preferably sinecure, if nothing else could be found: and I suppose this was why my father, after essaying a clerkship or two (one of them in an ironworks), at last had his position recognised by a post in the Four Courts, perhaps because his sister had married the brother of a law baron. Anyhow the office he held was so undeniably superfluous that it actually got abolished before I was born; and my father naturally demanded a pension as compensation for the outrage. Having got it, he promptly sold it, and set up in business as a merchant dealing wholesale (the family dignity made retail business impossible) in flour and its cereal concomitants. [The pension was £44 a year; Shaw senior sold it for £500.] He had an office and warehouse in Jervis Street in the city: and he had a mill in Dolphin's Barn, on the country side of the canal. . . . Early in its history, the bankruptcy of one of its customers dealt it such a blow that my father's partner broke down in tears. . . . My father, albeit ruined, found the magnitude of the catastrophe so irresistably amusing that he had to retreat hastily from the office to the empty corner of a warehouse, and laugh until he was exhausted. The business struggled on and even supported my father until he died, enabling him to help his family a little after they had solved a desperate financial situation by emigrating to London: or, to put it another way, by deserting him. The last years of his life were soothed and disembarrassed by this step. He never, as far as I know, made the slightest movement towards a reunion: and none of us ever dreamt of there being any unkindness in the arrangement. In our family, we did not bother about conventionalities or sentimentalities.'*

At the age of thirty-seven—in 1851—this short, cross-eyed bachelor with the humorous manner began to escort a twenty-one-year-old girl to social functions. She was Lucinda Elizabeth Gurly, a ladylike, highly educated young woman who had been brought up by a dragon of a great-aunt and trained to be a concert pianist. Her relatives saw no harm in George Carr Shaw, since he was so obviously ineligible. But what happened was that Shaw, full of 'sanguine illusions as to the future of his newly acquired business . . . was emboldened by her expectations and his business hopes to propose to her just at the moment when marriage seemed her only way of escape from an angry father and a stepmother. Immediately all her relatives, who had tolerated this middle-aged gentleman as a perfectly safe acquaintance with an agreeable vein of humour, denounced him as a notorious drunkard. My mother, suspicious of this sudden change of front, put the question directly to my father. His eloquence and sincerity convinced her that he was, as he claimed to be, and he was in principle, a bigoted teetotaller. She married him, and her disappointed and infuriated aunt disinherited her, not foreseeing that the consequence of the marriage would include so remarkable a phenomenon as myself.

'When my mother was disillusioned, and found out what living on a few hundred a year with three children meant, even in a country where a general servant could be obtained for eight pounds a year, her condition must have been about as unhappy and her prospects as apparently hopeless as her aunt could have desired even in her most vindictive moments.'†

* Preface: *Immaturity*.

† Apparently Mrs Shaw was not much liked by her husband's relatives either. '. . . though they quarrelled between themselves, [they] combined against my mother, who one day, calling on one of my aunts, overheard her exclaiming to the servant who announced her "Oh, that bitch!". After that we all boycotted one another. . . .' Shaw's preface to Winsten's *Salt and his Circle* (1951).

According to Shaw, his father's drunkenness was the cause of their being dropped socially, 'because if you asked him to dinner or a party, he was not always quite sober when he arrived; and he was invariably scandalously drunk when he left. Now a convivial drunkard may be exhilarating, in convivial company. . . . But a miserable drunkard—and my father, in theory a teetotaller, was racked with shame and remorse, even in his cups—is unbearable. We were finally dropped socially.'* Shaw adds that his father finally became a teetotaller in practice 'when a mild fit, which felled him on our doorstep one Sunday afternoon, convinced him that he must stop drinking or perish'. But this was too late to save them socially.

All this sounds straightforward enough, but there is reason to suspect that Shaw is not telling the whole truth. One of Shaw's biographers, John O'Donovan, discovered that Sir Robert Shaw of Bushy Park—regarded as the head of the family—continued to receive far boozier members of the family than George Carr Shaw. And Shaw's cousin Charles, who wrote *Bernard's Brethren*, said that his researches among relatives had not confirmed the story that George Carr Shaw was a hopeless drunkard. All that now seems certain is that the marriage started badly. Mrs Shaw later told her son that she found a wardrobe 'full of empty bottles' in their Liverpool hotel room, and decided to leave her husband immediately. She ran from the house to the docks, intending to ship as a stewardess, but some longshoremen who offered some 'personally tendered compliments' frightened her so much that she hurried back to her husband.

The story is a puzzling one, and has never been adequately investigated. How many bottles of whiskey could a man drink on his honeymoon without his bride noticing his breath? And if he smuggled bottles into the room what was to prevent him from smuggling them out again? And surely a man on honeymoon has other things to occupy his mind besides alcohol? A possible

* In *Sixteen Self Sketches* Shaw claims that his father had been conscience-stricken all his life because he had once allowed his dog to chase and kill a cat; Shaw senior apparently told his son that anyone who committed such an act 'did not merit nor would he ever obtain any success or happiness'. In the same passage Shaw mentions that his father was given to muttering damns and self-reproaches under his breath.

explanation turns up in some biographical notes that Shaw made
in his twenty-fifth year, in which he mentions that his father
drank whiskey, brandy, champagne *and stout*; in fact, says Shaw,
he was so fond of the latter that he sometimes made himself ill
on it. The stout mentioned would presumably be Guinness, and
one of his legends attached to Guinness is that it increases male
potency. Is this the answer to the question of why Shaw's father
should want to drink on his honeymoon? If so, it seems typical of
his bad luck that his bride failed to appreciate that his motives
were relatively disinterested.

The majority of Shaw's biographers have accepted his description of his father as a hopeless drunk—although Shaw's own
teetotalism should have put them on their guard. No doubt they
felt there was no reason why Shaw should exaggerate in such a
matter. But a reason does emerge in a chapter of *Sixteen Self
Sketches* called 'Shame and Wounded Snobbery', written when
Shaw was ninety; and it was later investigated thoroughly by
John O'Donovan. At the age of thirteen, Shaw was sent to a
Roman Catholic school for six months, at the instigation of a
music teacher called Lee. Catholics, being largely poor, were not
'gentlemen'. Shaw was so ashamed of his period in a Catholic
school that he kept the secret until he was ninety—even from his
wife.

Now it is a curious fact that although Lee was one of the major
influences on Shaw's boyhood, Shaw waited until he was eighty
before writing about him in the preface to *London Music in 1888–
90*. There is no mention of Lee in the autobiographical preface
to *The Irrational Knot* (1905), or even to *Immaturity* (1921), which
tells the story of Shaw's family and boyhood at some length.
Shaw writes in *London Music*:

'In the street next to ours, Harrington Street, where the houses
were bigger and more fashionable than in our little by-street,
there was a teacher of singing, lamed by an accident in childhood
which had left one of his legs shorter than the other, but a man of
mesmeric vitality and force. He was a bachelor living with his
brother, whom he supported and adored, and a terrible old
woman who was his servant of all work. His name was George
John Vandaleur Lee, known in Dublin as Mr G. J. Lee. Singing
lessons were cheap in Dublin; and my mother went to Lee to

learn how to sing properly. He trained her voice to such purpose that she became indispensable to him as an amateur prima donna. For he was a most magnetic conductor and an indefatigable organiser of concerts, and later on of operas, with such talent, vocal and orchestral, as he could discover and train in Dublin. . . .'

Shaw describes at some length Lee's great discovery of a method of voice training that involved relaxing the jaw, keeping the tongue flat, 'breathing' instead of 'blowing' and rounding the pharynx and soft palate. This method, Shaw said, had been learned or deduced from the voice production of an Italian baritone named Badeali, who still had a perfect voice at eighty. This system was known simply as The Method by Lee's disciples. Shaw goes on:

'I have to dwell on The Method . . . because my mother's association with Lee, and the *ménage à trois* in which it resulted, would be unpleasantly misunderstood without this clue to it. For after the death of Lee's brother, which affected him to the verge of suicide, we left our respective houses and went to live in the same house, number one Hatch Street, which was half in Lower Leeson Street. The arrangement was economical; for we could not afford to live in a fashionable house, and Lee could not afford to give lessons in an unfashionable one, though, being a bachelor, he needed only a music room and a bedroom. We also shared a cottage in Dalkey, high up on Torca Hill, with all Dublin Bay from Dalkey Island to Howth visible from the garden, and all Killiney Bay with the Wicklow mountains in the background from the hall door. Lee bought this cottage and presented it to my mother, though she never had any legal claim to it and did not benefit by its sale later on.' (He adds: 'I still remember the moment when my mother told me we were going to live there as the happiest of my life.')*

And so, when Shaw was seven, Lee moved in with the family, and Mrs Shaw found a new centre of gravity for her life, having

* B. C. Rosset, in *Shaw of Dublin*, has pointed out that this passage requires a few corrections. Cesare Badiali (not Badeali) was born in 1810, and was heard by Lee in 1859; he was forty-nine at the time and not eighty. (He died at fifty-five.) Lee *rented* Torca cottage and was therefore in no position to give it to Mrs Shaw. When referring to Lee, Shaw consistently misspells his name Vandaleur instead of Vandeleur. Lee was christened George John, and adopted the 'Vandeleur' in 1872, after his move to London.

lost all interest in and patience with her husband. But, Shaw adds, 'although Lee supplanted my father as the dominant factor in the household, and appropriated all the activity and interest of my mother, he was so completely absorbed in musical affairs that there was no friction and hardly any intimate personal contacts between the two men; certainly no unpleasantness'. The association with Lee naturally raises in the reader's mind the speculation that Lee's relationship with Mrs Shaw may have been more than platonic. In fact, Lee *could* have been Shaw's father, since he met Mrs Shaw more than a year before her son's birth. Shaw dismisses the idea emphatically, declaring that his mother was 'the sort of woman who could be matron of a horse guards barracks and emerge without a stain on her character'. Frank Harris pointed out that Lee seems a more likely candidate for the fathering of a genius than George Carr Shaw; but since there is no proof either way, speculation is pointless.

But on one point Shaw told a great deal less than the truth. Speaking of Lee's Method, Shaw wrote that 'it became a religion for him; the only religion, I may add, that he ever professed'. Now this happens to be flatly untrue, and Shaw knew it was untrue. The researches of John O'Donovan revealed that Lee, like the great majority of his singing pupils, was a Roman Catholic. Whether he was a true believer or not, he certainly professed his religion, and was a regular churchgoer who was on excellent terms with the clergy. His music society performed in Catholic churches. The only extant photograph of Lee—which includes Shaw's mother and father—shows him with several pupils whom O'Donovan identified as Catholics.

Here, then, is the more likely reason that the Shaws were dropped by the rest of the family; for all practical purposes, they seemed to have become Catholics, and in doing so, had lost caste. They were living in a *ménage à trois* with a Catholic singing teacher and Shaw's mother and sister sang in Catholic churches. Shaw himself was sent to a Catholic school at Lee's suggestion. And this was certainly more serious than Shaw senior's fondness for Guinness.

So George Carr Shaw's alcoholism must remain an open question. That he drank is not in question; neither is there any doubt that he was sometimes drunk. To Mrs Shaw—who had

been brought up with exceptional strictness and little love—
it must have seemed obvious that he was an alcoholic. Shaw
describes how he came back from a walk with his father, and
whispered in his mother's ear: 'Mamma, I think Papa's drunk.'
'She turned away with impatient disgust and said, "When is he
ever anything else?" ' This tells us nothing about George Carr
Shaw's alleged alcoholism, but it tells a great deal about the
strained relations between the husband and wife. There is a clear
dividing line between even heavy drinking and alcoholism, but
it would not be apparent to Mrs Shaw, who was in no mood for
fine distinctions.

There was one other small matter connected with Lee upon
which Shaw was not entirely frank. He asserted that Lee was
totally uninterested in sex. O'Donovan discovered that Lee
was making advances to Shaw's sister Lucy in 1884, and that this
was probably the real reason that Mrs Shaw broke with him—not,
as Shaw says, because Lee had become a charlatan. It is known
that Lee caused something of a scandal among his upper class
pupils in London when he tried to pass off his housemaid as one
of them (an incident that sounds like the origin of *Pygmalion*).
O'Donovan's investigations all seem to indicate that Lee was
something of a Don Juan. The exact nature of the scandal that
made him leave Dublin has never been cleared up; but it *was* a
scandal, and not, as Shaw claims, 'a desperate financial situation'.
Shaw's sister Lucy had a reputation of being anything but a virgin
in Dublin. (O'Donovan quotes an Irish lady as saying, 'Poor girl,
she has only had four lovers.') Shaw, may, of course, have been
unaware of Lee's Don Juanism, and of his attempt to take
advantage of Lucy's easy virtue. Again, one has to allow Shaw
the benefit of the doubt.

Lee is important for two reasons. First, because by moving
to London when Shaw was seventeen he was the indirect cause
of Shaw's own move three years later. Second: he, and not
George Carr Shaw, was the dominant figure of Shaw's boyhood.
George Carr Shaw was an easy-going, good-natured man, held
in low esteem by the female members of the family—Shaw had
two sisters—and regarded as a failure and a drunkard. Shaw liked
him, but could hardly admire him. Lee was a different matter.
'We never felt any affection for Lee; he was too excessively unlike

us, too completely a phenomenon, to rouse any primitive human feeling in us. When my mother introduced him to me, he played with me for the first and last time; but as his notion of play was to decorate my face with moustaches and whiskers in burnt cork in spite of the most furious resistance I could put up, our encounter was not a success, and the defensive attitude in which it left me lasted, though without the least bitterness, until the decay of his energies and the growth of mine put us on more equal terms.'

Lee was a 'phenomenon', a man driven by a spring of disinterested passion for music. He was not only the object of Bessie Shaw's admiration but of a whole circle of female disciples. Since he had no interest in children or understanding of them—like Shaw himself, according to Miss Patch—there was no chance for familiarity to breed contempt in the young Shaw. In a sense Lee is the archetypal model for a character who dominates Shaw's novels and plays—the disinterested man; Owen Jack, Edward Connolly, Sidney Trefusis, Caesar, Andrew Undershaft, Peter Keegan; a type that keeps reappearing down to Isaac Newton and George Fox in *Good King Charles*. That Lee himself later turned out to have feet of clay was irrelevant; he was still the first man of Shaw's acquaintance to embody the 'intellectual passion'. And this may be why Shaw, at eighty, preferred to forget the Don Juanism.

This is the point to say something more about Shaw's mother. She has a great many points of resemblance to Charlotte Payne-Townshend, the woman Shaw later married, and this in itself indicates that Shaw's relationship to her was a close one, even though he wrote of her 'technically speaking, I should say she was the worst mother conceivable, always, however, within the limits of the fact that she was incapable of unkindness to any child, animal or flower'. Bessie Shaw's childhood had been made miserable by 'strict and loveless training', by 'constraints and tyrannies, scoldings and browbeatings and punishments'. So her idea of bringing children up was to leave them alone. It never occurred to her that children 'needed guidance or training, or that it mattered in the least what they ate or drank or what they did, as long as they were not actively mischievous'. She was 'a thoroughly disgusted and disillusioned woman . . . suffering from a hopelessly disappointing husband, and three uninteresting children grown too old to be petted like the animals and birds she was so fond of'. The latter is interesting: Mrs Shaw *was* apparently capable of expressing affection, but not towards her children. She was kind but uninterested, and Shaw liked her 'because, on the one occasion when she buttered my bread for me, she buttered it thickly instead of merely wiping a knife on it'. He adds: 'Her almost complete neglect of me had the advantage that I could idealise her to the utmost pitch of my imagination and had no sordid or disillusioning contacts with her.'

So the two most important people in Shaw's childhood—his mother and Lee—were aloof and relatively uninterested in him. There was no very close relation with either of his two sisters— both his senior—although he seems to have been fond of the younger of the two, Agnes, who died when she was nineteen. His attitude towards Lucy seems to have been an indifference that was tinged with dislike.

As to Shaw's father, he may have been a self-effacing nonentity, but he bequeathed Shaw at least one important gift: the sense of anti-climactic humour. When he took 'Sonny' for his first dip in the sea he delivered a short lecture on the importance of learning to swim, ending: 'When I was a boy of only fourteen, my know- ledge of swimming enabled me to save your Uncle Robert's life.' Then, after a pause, he added confidentially: 'And to tell you the truth, I was never so sorry for anything in my life afterwards.'

In the same way 'when I scoffed at the Bible, he would instantly and quite sincerely rebuke me, telling me with what little stern- ness was in his nature, that I should not speak so; that no edu- cated man would make such a display of ignorance; that the Bible was universally recognised as a literary and historical master- piece; and as much more to the same effect as he could muster. But when he had reached the point of feeling really impressive, a convulsion of internal chuckling would wrinkle up his eyes; and (I knowing all the time what was coming) would cap his eulogy by assuring me, with an air of perfect fairness, that even the worst enemy of religion could say no worse of the Bible than that it was the damndest parcel of lies ever written.' Shaw senior's attitude to Christianity in general seems to have been irreverent, for Shaw also tells how they were once visited by a Unitarian named Haughton, and Shaw later asked his father what a Unitarian was. George Carr Shaw explained that a Unitarian was one who did not believe that Jesus was crucified, in that he was observed running down the far side of the hill of Calvary.

In the same preface (*Immaturity*) Shaw goes into detail to demonstrate that his comedy is an inheritance from the Shaw's, not the Gurly's: 'My mother, I may say here, had no comedic impulse, and never uttered an epigram in her life.' There follows the classic story of Uncle William ('Barney') Shaw, whose drinking was so heavy that 'a man who made a bet that he would produce Barney Shaw sober, and knocked him up at six in the morning with that object, lost his bet'. Uncle Barney suddenly became a teetotaller, and devoted himself to the ophicleide, a monstrous wind instrument. He also became religious, and used to sit with a bible on his knees and an opera glass to his eyes, watching the ladies' bathing place at Dalkey. It was Uncle Barney who later went insane, 'alleging that he was the Holy Ghost', and tried to commit suicide by closing a carpet bag on his neck, which resulted in his death from heart failure. From Shaw's comment that Uncle William was 'a fine upstanding man and a gentle creature' one would infer that his father's side of the family was not remarkable for strength of character, whatever may have been its virtues. Shaw's imagination, apparently, came from his mother, 'who really lived in it and on it'. He also mentions the influence of his mother's brother Uncle Walter, who was a surgeon on an Atlantic liner, and whose conversation was Rabelaisian and profane. 'Falstaff himself could not have held his own with my uncle in obscene anecdotes, unprintable limericks, and fantastic profanity; and it mattered nothing to him whether his audience consisted of his messmates on board ship or his schoolboy nephew.' Since presumably Uncle Walter's upbringing was as constrained as his sister's, it seems likely that all this was a healthy reaction against the religion of his childhood, a sort of deliberately assumed mask of Mephistophelean impiety. 'His efforts were controlled, deliberate, fastidiously chosen and worded. But they were all the more effective in destroying all my inculcated childish reverence for the verbiage of religion, for its legends and personifications and parables. In view of my subsequent work in the world, it seems providential that I was driven to the essentials of religion by the reduction of every factitious or fictitious element in it to the most irreverent absurdity.'

Shaw senior provided the humour; Uncle Walter the shock tactics. And even Lee provided certain typical elements of the Shavian personality. 'He said that people should sleep with their windows open. The daring appealed to me; and I have done so ever since. He ate brown bread instead of white, a startling eccentricity. He had no faith in doctors, and when my mother had a serious illness, took her case in hand unhesitatingly and at the end of a week or so gave my trembling father leave to call in a leading Dublin doctor, who simply said "My work is done" and took his hat.' Lee became the model for that favourite Shaw character, the man whose 'madness' consists in being sane and reasonable, whose abnormality consists in being perfectly normal. ('I got a clue to my real condition from a friend of mine, a physician who devoted himself specially to ophthalmic surgery. He tested my eyesight one evening, and informed me that it was quite uninteresting to him because it was normal. I naturally took this to mean that it was like everybody else's; but he rejected this construction as paradoxical, and hastened to explain to me that I was an exceptional and highly fortunate person optically, normal eyesight conferring the power of seeing things accurately, and being enjoyed only by about ten per cent of the population, the remaining ninety per cent being abnormal.')*

The advent of Lee in the Shaw household was one of the most fortunate accidents of Shaw's life. He would certainly have been exposed to a certain amount of music, even if his mother had never encountered Lee; but it was through Lee that music became one of the dominating influences in his life. By the time he reached his teens he could 'sing and whistle from end to end leading works by Handel, Haydn, Mozart, Beethoven, Rossini, Bellini, Donizetti and Verdi'. Lee was also responsible for the awakening of Shaw's interest in the visual arts: 'His richer pupils sometimes presented him with expensive illustrated books. He never opened them, but I did.' And the education thus began was completed in the Dublin National Gallery 'where I learned to recognise the works of the old masters by sight'. Shaw also mentions the importance for him of the natural beauty visible

* Preface, *Plays Unpleasant*.

from Torca cottage, speaking of 'clambering all over Killiney Hill, looking at the endless pictures nature painted for me'.

Still, the impact of Lee was not altogether for the good; in fact, a case could be made for the view that he was one of the most baleful influences Shaw ever encountered. He was a man who impressed by sheer personality. He was greatly disliked by the other music teachers in Dublin, and Shaw explains this by saying that he was a man of authentic genius who was naturally hated by dry academics. But O'Donovan's researches revealed that even in his Dublin days, Lee was regarded as a mountebank and an imposter—particularly by Sir Robert Stewart, who was the leader of Dublin music life at the time. When Lee went to London— apparently driven out of Dublin by Sir Robert Stewart—he took a house in Park Lane, waxed his moustache, and became Vandeleur Lee, who promised young ladies that he could make them sing 'like Patti' in twelve lessons at a guinea a lesson. He was highly successful for a time, until his charlatanism became obvious even to his rich pupils, and the guineas stopped flowing in. He dropped dead one day, and the post mortem revealed that his brain had been diseased for a long time. Shaw charitably assumed that this could have been the cause of the deterioration of his character; he remained friendly with Lee to the end, and drafted his circulars for him.

Lee was the dominant male influence on Shaw's childhood, and he was a 'personality', a charming, energetic and very 'Irish' personality. All of which Shaw himself became in due course. Lee's reputation declined, as we have noted, because it became obvious that he was a charlatan. But was not the eventual decline of Shaw's reputation due to much the same cause? The Shaw personality made him famous in the first decade of this century. But in the age of film, radio and television, we are suspicious of 'personalities', since anyone with the least perception can see how little actual talent it takes to become one. All the later criticisms of and attacks on Shaw could be reduced to one accusation: that he bulldozed his way to fame with his personality, like an actor or a disc jockey.

Eric Bentley's point, in the passage quoted in the introduction, is that when he ignored the Shaw personality and concentrated upon what he had to say—which might be labelled the 'impersonality'—he became aware of Shaw's complexity and subtlety. Which gives grounds for the view that, without the flamboyance imitated from Lee, Shaw's artistic impact might have been enormously greater and more long-lasting.

This raises a point of central importance to the understanding of Shaw, and it should be discussed before we go further. I am speaking of the role that self-dramatisation, the 'self-image', plays in the development of talent.

I have tried to point out that there is a contradiction involved in the words 'artistic personality'. Personality is a protective skin designed to make social life tolerable and enable us to get through the repetitive business of everyday living. But the purpose of art lies in the opposite direction: to free human beings from the personality, from the narrowness of the here-and-now, to remind them of the existence of other times, other places. The purpose of art could be defined as 'escape from personality'.

But the contradiction could be over-emphasised. For one method of escaping from the constriction of the personality is to make it bigger, so that there is more room inside it. People who feel most trapped in their personalities are those who would strike other people as being colourless, and the contrary is also true; a man who feels free from his personality, who wears it lightly and casually, would strike other people as having a strong personality.

What is even more important is that self-dramatisation—day-dreaming at its simplest level—plays as active a part in mental development as vitamins in the body's development. There can be no self-development without understanding what you want to become; at least, a clear, imaginative self-image can halve the work.

Having said this, we come very close to the heart of the complex 'Shaw problem'. For it is impossible to read Shaw without becoming aware of his lifelong preoccupation with a persona, an ego with which he can confront the world. He took a great deal of trouble to develop 'G.B.S.' And once G.B.S. had been developed, he tried hard to give the impression that it had always been there. Tanner says to Ramsden: 'Look at the effect I produce because my fairy godmother withheld from me this gift of shame,' and this is the effect that Shaw is determined to produce—although, in 'Shame and Wounded Snobbery', he admits that he has kept the secret of his Catholic schooling for seventy-seven years. Joyce, Proust, Mann, Lawrence, Virginia Woolf, even H. G. Wells, dwell on the miseries and humiliations of the artist's childhood. Shaw goes to the opposite extreme: 'A boy who has seen "the governor" with an imperfectly wrapped-up goose under one arm and a ham in the same condition under the other (both purchased under heaven knows what delusion of festivity), butting at the garden wall in the belief that he was pushing open the gate, and transforming his tall hat into a concertina in the process, and who, instead of being overwhelmed with shame and anxiety at the spectacle, has been so disabled by merriment (uproariously shared with the maternal uncle) that he has hardly been able to rush to the rescue of the hat and pilot its wearer to safety, is clearly not a boy who will make tragedies of trifles instead of making trifles of tragedies. If you cannot get rid of the family skeleton, you may as well make it dance.' But it is interesting to note that his Rabelaisian Uncle Walter was present on this occasion to encourage Shaw to treat it as a joke. Hesketh Pearson's chapter on this period—which consists largely of quotations from Shaw—is called 'A Devil of a Childhood', and implies that young Shaw was a miniature G.B.S. On prayers: 'I had been warned by my nurse that warm prayers were no use, and that only by kneeling by my bedside in the cold could I hope for a hearing; but I criticised this admonition unfavourably on various grounds, the real one being my preference for warmth and comfort. . . . [Besides] I did not care whether my prayers were answered or not: they were a literary performance for the entertainment or propitiation of the Almighty; and though I should not have dreamt of daring to say that if He did not like them He might lump them (perhaps I was too confident of their quality to apprehend such a rebuff), I certainly behaved as if my comfort were an indispensable condition of the performance taking place at all.' On the other hand, we have Tanner telling Ann in *Man and Superman*: 'A sensitive boy's humiliations may be good fun for ordinary thick-skinned grown-ups; but to the boy himself they are so acute, so ignominious, that he cannot confess them—cannot but deny them passionately', which seems to indicate that Shaw was a fairly normal, sensitive boy, and not at all a miniature G.B.S. 'I wanted to brag to you to make myself interesting. And I found myself doing all sorts of mischievous things simply to have something to tell you about. I fought with boys I didn't hate; I lied about things I might just as well have told the truth about; I stole things I didn't want; I kissed little girls I didn't care for.' And in the preface to Davies' *Autobiography of a Supertramp* he writes: 'I suppose every imaginative boy is a criminal, stealing and destroying for the sake of being great in the sense in which greatness is presented to him in the romance of history. But very few get caught. Mr Davies unfortunately was seized by the police, haled before the magistrate; and made to expiate by stripes the bygone crimes of myself and some millions of other respectable citizens. That was hard luck, certainly. It gives me a feeling of moral superiority to him; for I never fell into the hands of the police—at least, they did not go on with the case (one of incendiarism), because the gentleman whose property I burnt had a strong sense of humour and a kindly nature, and let me off when I made him a precocious speech—the first I ever delivered—about the thoughtlessness of youth. It is remarkable what a difference it makes, this matter of the police; though it is obviously quite beside the ethical question. Mr Davies tells us with admirable quiet modesty that he begged and stole and drank. Now I have begged and stolen; and if I never drank, that was only an application of the division of labour to the Shaw clan; for several members of it drank enough for ten. But I have always managed to keep out of the casual ward and the police court; and this gives me an ineffable sense of superior respectability. . . .'

Now begging, stealing and incendiarism are not activities that can be indulged in in a Shavian frame of mind. They are preceded and accompanied by a feeling of guilt; the same goes for 'lying about things I might just as well have told the truth about'. Such a childhood may lack the Proustian note of self-pity, but it is still a long way from being the non-stop vaudeville turn described by Hesketh Pearson. It was a healthy instinct in Shaw that made him minimise the shame and humiliation, but he overdid it. In the *Immaturity* preface he explains he has not risen to the top by effort but by 'gravitation', and he tells a story to underline his point: how a fellow clerk remarked that every young chap thought he was going to be a great man. 'On a really modest youth, this commonplace would have had no effect. It gave me so perceptible a jar that I suddenly became aware that I had never thought I was to be a great man simply because I had always taken it as a matter of course.' This may well be true; constant association with Lee offered Shaw an example of naturally achieved eminence. But to complete the picture, one must take into account his admission: '. . . I was painfully shy, and was simply afraid to accept invitations, with the result that I very soon ceased to get any.' 'Clever sympathetic women might divine at a glance that I was mortally shy; but people who could not see through my skin . . . may well have found me insufferable, aggressive and impudent.' But the whole aim of the G.B.S. personality was to prevent people from seeing through his skin, to convey the impression that he was as invulnerable and resilient as a solid rubber ball. Since he was forty when he achieved recognition, his own version of his development seemed plausible enough to his contemporaries. It imposed on them so well that he came to be considered some kind of a monster. Beatrice Webb called him a 'sprite'; Yeats compared him to a sewing machine; Wells called his mind 'a chaos of clear ideas'. It all amounted to the same thing; he was less than human, a freak.

The evidence would seem to suggest, then, that the young Shaw was naturally shy and introverted, and that he developed the *persona* called G.B.S., who eventually became his Franken-stein's monster and the chief cause of the decline of his reputation. It was, I think, Eric Bentley who pointed out that Shaw died a disappointed man. Shaw once said: 'I have solved every major problem of our time, and people still go on propounding them as if they were unsolved.' This lack of real, active influence—in the way that Ibsen or Tolstoy had influence—can be laid at the doorstep of the G.B.S. monster.

But that is only half the story. Shaw's development is an almost perfect example of a concept I coined elsewhere:* the rope trick. Its starting point is Nietzsche's recognition that 'the great man is the play actor of his own ideals'. That is to say, the great man becomes great by erecting an imaginative self-image, and then 'acting up' to it. But in traditional existentialist thinking, this kind of 'acting' is another name for self-deception, Sartre's

* *Beyond the Outsider,* Appendix 2.

'*mauvais-foi*', and can only lead to inauthenticity. This view is contrary to the facts. All greatness—certainly all artistic greatness —is achieved through the imaginative self-image. Man throws a rope into the air—some notion of his inner-being and destiny— and then climbs it, like the Hindu fakir. According to Sartre, the rope cannot be climbed, because it is pure self-deception, and has no objective support. But the Sartre view—which can also be found in Kierkegaard and Heidegger—is based on a misconception of the nature of imagination, and a failure to understand its powers. The rope *can* be climbed. Thurber's Walter Mitty is a symbol of this misconception; Mitty's grandiose daydreams *separate* him from reality, make him incapable of achievement. The alternative view—the rope trick—is expressed by Shaw in *Back to Methuselah*: 'the serpent said that every dream could be willed into creation by those strong enough to believe in it'.

The rope trick involves an act of choice. The interesting thing about Shaw is that he made his act of choice so late. The decision to become a writer seems to have been taken fairly casually after he arrived in London. During his Dublin period he considered becoming a painter and a musician. Earlier still, his ambitions were apparently connected with swords and fighting; he mentions that he had daydreams in which he saw himself as D'Artagnan and Rob Roy. There may also have been some vague idea of becoming an actor, for he speaks about his admiration for an actor of the old heroic school called Barry Sullivan, whose 'stage fights . . . appealed irresistibly to a boy spectator like myself. I remember one delightful evening when two inches of Macbeth's sword . . . broke off and whizzed over the heads of the cowering pit . . . to bury itself deep in the front of the dress circle'. Rosset devotes several pages in *Shaw of Dublin* to describing Shaw's childhood fantasies—that he was the disinherited son of a duke, Alnaschar the magician, and so on.*

* Rosset, like most of Shaw's biographers, including Ervine and Pearson, seems to have no idea who Alnaschar was. He is to be found in the *Arabian Nights*, in 'The Barber's Fifth Brother'. Alnaschar inherits a hundred pieces of silver and invests them in glassware, from the sale of which he proposes to make a fortune. He daydreams of immense riches, and of being married to the Vizier's daughter, whom he spurns with his foot—and accidentally kicks over the basket containing all his glassware: he is a symbol of the danger of counting your chickens before they are hatched.

B

Some of Shaw's most interesting pronouncements on the question of daydreaming are to be found in his remarks about Algernon Sidney Potts, in the *Major Barbara* preface. Potts is hero of a novel by Charles Lever, *A Day's Ride, A Life's Romance.* '[*A Day's Ride*] was published by Charles Dickens in Household Words, and proved so strange to the public taste that Dickens pressed Lever to make short work of it. I read scraps of this novel when I was a child; and it made an enduring impression on me. The hero was a very romantic hero, trying to live bravely, chivalrously and powerfully by dint of mere romance-fed imagination, without courage, without means, without knowledge, without skill, without anything real except his bodily appetites. Even in my childhood I found in this poor devil's unsuccessful encounters with the facts of life a poignant quality that romantic fiction lacked.' 'Where, then, was the novelty in Lever's tale? Partly, I think, in a new seriousness in dealing with Potts's disease. Formerly, the contrast between madness and sanity was deemed comic. . . . In Lever's story, there is a real change of attitude. There is no relenting towards Potts: he never gains our affections like Don Quixote or Pickwick . . . But we dare not laugh at him, because, somehow, we recognise ourselves in Potts. . . . His author is not throwing a stone at a creature of another and inferior order, but making a confession, with the effect that the stone hits each of us full in the conscience. . . .'

Most of Shaw's biographers mention his debt to Lever; but none of them seems to have read the book. I did so some years ago because I am an admirer of Lever's other novels, which are light, anecdotal, and unfortunately neglected today. *A Day's Ride* is, in fact, quite unlike the sketch of its plot offered in the *Major Barbara* preface. To begin with, there is no evidence that Lever shortened it because it was unpopular; it is as long as his other novels. But more important, there is no sign at all of the 'seriousness in dealing with Potts's disease' that Shaw discerned. It is a light romantic novel of the picaresque *genre*, that has the normal happy ending. It is also an attempt to make comedy out of a theme that Stendhal had already treated tragically in *Le Rouge et le Noir*. Algernon Sidney Potts is the son of a well-to-do Dublin apothecary, whose father intends him to take over the business. But he is also a devotee of German romantic novels, and one day he decides to leave home in search of adventure. It sounds as if Lever intends to produce a kind of nineteenth-century *Don Quixote*; but his intention is not so serious. He is a romantic novelist, who knows that his readers like to identify with the hero. So, in fact, Algernon Sidney Potts has a fairly comfortable and amusing time of it. He wants to be taken for some kind of romantic hero, or at least for an aristocrat. And almost immediately, he meets a group of aristocratic sportsmen who mistake him for one of themselves. Comedy ensues; he loses his hired nag at cards, and follows its trail across England and the Continent; becomes involved in a number of absurd adventures, and is mistaken for the son of a duke by a despotic old lady. The situations are comic; but Potts is the narrator, and he never loses his dignity or his seriousness.

Now obviously, it is untrue to say that Potts never gains our affections like Don Quixote or Pickwick. The author is plainly on his side, and after a few chapters, so is the reader. Which raises the question: how did Shaw come to misread the book? Did he really think Lever had written a novel about Potts's dissociation from reality, a kind of Irish *Madame Bovary*? This is unlikely. He was too good a critic.

No, the far more probable explanation is that Shaw's critical faculty was warped by his self-identification with Potts. Shaw also felt he had been born into the wrong place in life, a natural aristocrat in a family of 'downstarts'. Like Potts, he felt that the future held enormous but vague promises. He must have felt a certain sympathy for Potts when he protests: 'The man who contracts a debt is never called a cheat until his inability to discharge it has been proven clearly and beyond a doubt; but he who enters into an engagement with his own heart to gain a certain prize or reach a certain goal, is made a mockery and a sneer by all whose own humble faculties represent such striving as impossible.' And this sentence points to the basic theme of the novel—and the reason why Shaw found it memorable. 'An engagement with his own heart to gain a certain prize. . . .' But what prize? The whole point about Potts, as about Walter Mitty, is that his daydreams are of the sort that can hardly be translated into terms of definite goals. He simply has an inner conviction that he is someone of importance. And underneath the comedy

Lever is asking the question: Can we definitely state that this is untrue? Do we take the side of 'the world' and laugh at Potts because he is a liar and a *poseur*? We may do so; the author leaves us this alternative. But Shaw is right when he says the author is making a confession; Lever is on Potts's side. He is saying, in effect: Appearances may be against him; there may be no evidence at all that Potts is anything more than a daydreaming apothecary; and *still* Potts may be right and the world wrong.

And this is why 'the story of the day's ride and life's romance of Potts (claiming alliance with Pozzo di Borgo) caught me and fascinated me as something strange and significant, though I already knew all about Alnaschar and Don Quixote and Simon Tappertit and many another romantic hero mocked by reality'. Because in this vital respect Potts differs from Alnaschar and Don Quixote and Simon Tappertit; his author is on his side, not on the world's side. Since Potts there have been a great many more comic daydreamers in fiction, including Kipps, the heroes of Aldous Huxley, Thurber's Walter Mitty and Amis's Lucky Jim. (Even Mr Bloom of *Ulysses* might qualify.) Potts remains the only one whose author understood 'the rope trick', that 'every dream can be willed into creation by those strong enough to believe in it'. Potts is 'poignant' because neither he nor his author were strong enough to will dreams into creation. (Lever was a cheerful, easy-going Irish doctor who became British Consul at La Spezia, and who wrote many of his novels to pay off gambling debts.) But the possibility is there, underlying the comedy of *A Day's Ride*. Shaw made a note of it, and in due course willed the dream into creation.

Shaw entered the office of the land agent Uniacke Townshend when he was fifteen, and remained there for five years, giving considerable satisfaction to his employer. This may seem surprising—particularly since Shaw admitted he disliked the job. 'Behold me therefore in my twentieth year, with a business training, in an occupation which I detested as cordially as any sane person lets himself detest anything he cannot escape from.' In spite of this, when the cashier absconded, Shaw was given the job as a stop-gap, and proved so successful that his employers stopped looking for a replacement. But there are two factors to be taken into account in explaining Shaw's efficiency. One is that a Dublin land agent's office of the 1870s would not be a disagreeable place for an intelligent youth with vaguely artistic ambitions; pressure of work was not great, and Shaw spent a great deal of time out of the office, collecting rents—an experience he later turned to account in his first play. Second—and more important—there was the spectacle of Shaw's father to spur the naturally idle apprentice. In the eyes of his family, George Carr Shaw was a failure and a drunkard who became poorer year by year. His son may have disliked business, but he disliked the idea of being like his father even more. Unlike Lee, George Carr Shaw was a nonentity. And when Lee decided to move to London in 1873 Mrs Shaw found life with the nonentity intolerable, and followed Lee, taking her two daughters with her. According to Shaw, 'we did not realise, nor did she, that she was never coming back and that, except for a few days when my father, taking a little holiday for the first time in his life within my experience, came to see us in London, she would never meet him again. Family revolutions would seldom be faced if they did not present themselves at first as temporary makeshifts.' The Hatch Street furniture was sold, except for the piano, and Shaw and his father moved into a smaller house nine months after her departure. Mrs Shaw returned to Dublin several times to see they were well during the next two years. She was living in a house in Victoria Grove (now Netherton Gardens), off the Old Brompton Road. She was not badly off. She received the income from an inheritance of £1,500, and George Carr Shaw sent her a pound a week.

In a house without music Shaw taught himself to play the piano, his first exercise being the overture to Don Giovanni. The future must have looked depressing. He was a young man without an education, and his only prospect seemed to be a lifetime as a book-keeper. 'To this day, my sentimental regard for Ireland does not include the capital. I am not enamoured of failure, of poverty, of obscurity, and of the ostracism and contempt which these imply.' With Lee and his mother in London, Dublin must have seemed barren enough. 'James Joyce in his *Ulysses* has described, with a fidelity so ruthless that the book is hardly bearable, the life that Dublin offers to its young men, or, if you prefer to put it the other way, that its young men offer to Dublin. . . . A certain futile derision and belittlement that confuses the noble and serious with the base and ludicrous seems to me peculiar to Dublin. . . .' and Larry Doyle sounds the same note in *John Bull's Other Island*: 'And all the while there goes on a horrible, senseless mischievous laughter. When you're young, you ex-change drinks with other young men; and you exchange vile stories with them; and as you're too futile to be able to help or cheer them, you chaff and sneer and taunt them for not doing the things you daren't do yourself. And all the time you laugh! laugh! laugh! eternal derision, eternal envy, eternal folly, eternal fouling and staining and degrading.' All of which explains why Shaw rejected a rise in wages, and decided to join his mother in London, and why, thirty years later, when he returned to Ireland, 'a curious reluctance to retrace my steps made me land in the south and enter Dublin through the backdoor from Meath'. The smell of failure was too strong.

And so, at the age of nineteen and three quarters, Shaw 'packed a carpet bag; boarded the North Wall boat; and left the train next morning at Euston, where, on hearing a porter cry, in an accent quite strange to me (I had hardly ever heard an h dropped before), "Ensm' faw weel?" which I rightly interpreted as "Hansom or four wheel?" I was afraid to say hansom, because I had never been in one and was not sure that I should know how to get in. So I solemnly drove in a growler through streets whose names Dickens had made familiar to me, London being at its spring best. . . .'

2 THE LONG APPRENTICESHIP

The London in which the shy, beardless youth arrived in 1876 was very much the 'London by gaslight' of Sherlock Holmes. Dickens had only been dead five years, and most of the great Victorian literary figures were still alive—Ruskin, Carlyle, Newman, Tennyson, Browning, Trollope, George Eliot. But it would be a mistake to think of it in terms of Scrooge and Sherlock Holmes. Europe was hurtling at top speed towards the twentieth century. A symbolic event had taken place in 1856, the year of Shaw's birth. For three years the Crimean War between Russia and the 'Allies' had dragged on, and it centred on Sevastopol, where great stone forts threatened the assembled warships of England, France, Turkey and Sardinia. (A young officer named Tolstoy made his first literary success by describing life in the garrison.) It seemed a stalemate. But Napoleon III had stripped three small ships to the waterline and covered them with armour-plating. They were so heavy that their engines could only move them at two miles an hour—they had to be towed to the Black Sea. These odd looking monsters left the Allied fleet—to the amazement of the Russians—and struggled and lurched towards the forts. It looked like suicide. The Russian guns pounded them. But the ships came on, untouched. They stopped, and the engines died. And then, for six hours, they bombarded the forts until only heaps of rubble remained. The Crimean War was over—and the modern age had begun.

Ten years later Alfred Nobel invented dynamite, and Edison and Bell simultaneously conceived the telephone. In the year

Shaw came to London, Edison was brooding on the idea of recording sound on a revolving cylinder, and twelve months later the phonograph was born. A mere two years later came the electric light; the age of gaslight was over.

And so the age into which Shaw was born was not the stable, solid Victorian period we like to imagine; it was as much an age of uncertainty and transition as Shakespeare's England—or our own space age. Darwin's *Origin of Species* was published when Shaw was three, and when he came to London clergymen were still arguing hotly against the idea that man is descended from a monkey. (Darwin never said so; but in 1876 this was still regarded as the basic assertion of Darwinism.) Volume one of Karl Marx's *Capital* had appeared when Shaw was eleven, and when he arrived in London, Marx was a forgotten man living in Maitland Park Road, Hampstead.

Mrs Shaw was living with her eldest daughter Lucy off the Fulham Road, which was still a semi-countrified area. The other daughter, Agnes ('Yuppy'), had died earlier that year of tuberculosis, at Ventnor, on the Isle of Wight. Her death at least eased the financial burden on the household, and now Shaw proposed to increase it again. Lucy, who was just starting a career on the stage, regarded her brother without a great deal of affection; and if we are to judge by the portraits of actresses in his novels, his feelings towards her were equally cool. Mrs Shaw was making ends meet by teaching singing, and Shaw was later to write: 'I did not throw myself into the struggle for life: I threw my mother into it.' But this is exaggeration; Shaw was due for his portion of a bequest that came from his mother's grandfather, Whitcroft, the capital of which—£4,000—had been divided between Bessie Shaw and her brother Walter. Her portion could be 'realised bit by bit as her three children came of age'. Shaw's share was no doubt very small; the autobiographical hero of his first novel receives £40 a year as interest on 'Mama's £800'. But in 1876 the average tradesman's wage was ten shillings a week (beer was a penny a pint), and the Shaws' basic family income—just over £130 a year, without counting Mrs Shaw's earnings as a singing teacher or Lucy's as an actress—should have been more than adequate for three people to live on, even in London. And during his first year in London, Shaw actually made a living wage by his pen, ghosting articles for Lee, for a publication called *The Hornet*, at a guinea each. Shaw's accounts show that in the three months at the beginning of 1877, he was paid £19 9s 8d—more than a pound a week.

The next decade, from Shaw's twentieth to his thirtieth year, is in some ways the most important of his life. And it is very nearly as badly documented as his teens. His biographers pass it over with generalities about his poverty, and usually manage to contradict one another— Pearson stating that Shaw 'scarcely put his nose outside London' and Henderson mentioning that he had to flee to the country for peace to write.

This is an absurd situation, for obviously the third decade of anyone's life is of central importance, and in the case of a writer it is usually crucial. Keats, Shelley and Rupert Brooke were dead before they were thirty. Milton had produced all the major poems that preceded *Paradise Lost*; Dickens had written all the books by which he is best known; Byron had almost nothing left to write by that time. Glance at almost any standard biography of a literary figure, and note the amount of space devoted to the third decade—and then compare with any Shaw biography. Pearson has less than twenty pages out of 422; even J. Percy Smith, whose *Unrepentant Pilgrim* is a study of Shaw's development, devotes well under a third of his book to it.

Shaw's literary apprenticeship was a very long one, one of the longest on record; he could not be described as fairly launched until his thirty-fifth year—the year of the publication of *The Quintessence of Ibsenism*. Among his contemporaries, only Arnold Bennett was such a late starter. The ten years after he came to London must have been the slowest of his life To dismiss them in a few pages is to see Shaw completely out of perspective. And to really understand their importance a biographer would need to devote half his volume to them. This is impossible here, because of lack of documentation, but I propose to consider them as fully as possible.

What do we know of the character of Shaw before he came to London? To begin with, that contrary to the accepted notions,

he was an affectionate sort of person This is a deduction from
two known facts: that his mother had no very deep feelings about
him, and that he adored his mother. 'I never knew love when I
was a child', he told Ellen Terry. 'My mother was so disappointed
in my father that she centred all her care on my younger sister,
and she left me to fend for myself.' Percy Smith has argued
convincingly that he not only idolised his mother but that all the
women in his plays from *Candida* on are mother figures. Shaw
made no great tragedy about the lack of maternal affection
(Henderson's statement that he was 'permanently embittered' by
it has no foundation), but it certainly needs to be taken into
account in trying to grasp his personality at nineteen.

I would suggest it is arguable that, just as an excess of mother
love may produce homosexual tendencies in talented sons, so a
certain deficiency—provided it is not too marked—may produce
the opposite effect: intellectuality, enthusiasm for ideas. Wells's
relations with his mother were curiously similar to those of Shaw
with Bessie Shaw. Other names that come to mind in this connection are Russell, Whitehead, Einstein, Beethoven, Shelley and
Joyce. And this suggests another point that is relevant to Shaw.
Most of the names mentioned above discovered their first intellectual passion in science—even Shelley. Science is the epitome
of the 'intellectual passion', the ideal focus for expanding mental
energies. Once such a focus has been achieved, real personal
development becomes possible. In Shaw's case there was no such
focus until he discovered Socialism in his late twenties. This may
explain his extremely long period of 'immaturity'.

Shaw's literary ambitions may have been awakened by his
friendship with a bank clerk named Matthew Edward McNulty,
whom he had known from schooldays. McNulty's decision to
become a writer—he later produced three novels of Irish peasant
life—had been taken fairly early, and in their teens Shaw apparently looked upon McNulty as the one who might possess
literary genius. (McNulty, incidentally, was in love with Lucy,
and proposed to her at one point.) In his late teens Shaw was a
literary amateur of the clumsiest kind. A letter written to Lucy
when he was seventeen hardly shows signs of genius, or even of
the normal ability to punctuate:

'I am sorry to say that I have read your letter. I shall take especial care not to do so again for you really are worthy of your parent in the matter of verbosity and far more personal. Your remarks are most offensive. Let my nose alone, better a bottle than a peony. Did the Mar mention that the cat has got mange as well as Paddy. It has no hair at all on its head which adds to its already prepossessing appearance. . . .'

A year later, in a letter to his mother, the style has become less awkwardly pretentious, although this may be because Shaw had been dragged into a family quarrel between his mother and sister. (For some reason Lucy was under fire from Vandeleur Lee and an impresario called Major V. Carpenter, as well as from her mother.)

'I told [Lucy] all! All! ALL! I trust you may not catch it on her return to the maternal bosom. I trust you have not caught it already. I trust that no profane language rises involuntarily to your lips as you peruse these words. I know that you will love me as you never did before for my straightforward conduct. I feel that even now you are wishing you could kiss me.'

To judge by Shaw's early letters to his family, it seems a safe inference that this verbose way of talking was part of the family ritual. The mature Shavian style is based upon it: 'My dear Tavy, your pious English habit of regarding the world as a moral gymnasium built expressly to strengthen your character in, occasionally leads you to think about your own confounded principles when you should be thinking about other people's necessities.' Or Lady Britomart Undershaft being sarcastic: 'Not since she was a little kid, Charles, as you express it with that elegance of diction and refinement of thought that never seem to desert you.' One can imagine a sentence like that being fired at Shaw senior when he came in with a slightly unsteady walk. It would be natural for Shaw to pick up this rather literary, intimidating manner of speaking and try to improve on it. It is also natural that most of his early attempts should fall flat. His first published work is a letter to a Dublin newspaper written when he was nineteen, taking up a critical attitude towards the hot-gospel evangelists Moody and Sankey. He expresses doubt that the size of the audiences indicates a religious revival: 'Predominant was the curiosity excited by the great reputation of the evangelists, and the stories, widely circulated, of the summary annihilation by epilepsy and otherwise of sceptics who had openly proclaimed their doubts of Mr Moody's divine mission.' 'The unreasoning mind of the people is too apt to connect a white tie with a dreary church service, capped by a sermon of platitudes, and is more likely to appreciate the "gift of the gab"— the possession of which by Mr Moody nobody will deny—than that of the Apostolic Succession, which he lacks.

'Respecting the effect of the revival on individuals, I may mention that it has a tendency to make them highly objectionable members of society, and induces their unconverted friends to desire a speedy reaction, which either soon takes place or the revived one relapses slowly into his previous benighted condition as the effect fades. . . .'

This is hardly sparkling prose. Dickens is, of course, one of the worst stylists in the English language, and he has a lot to answer for. Any writer who has been through a Dickens phase looks back on it with shudders of embarrassment, remembering painful hours spent in trying to torture sentences into the right degree of humorous orotundity. I speak from experience when I say that it leads to a powerful reaction of self disgust. And self disgust, if it goes on for long enough, leads to certain consequences; to a run-down physical condition, and to the feeling that nothing is really worth the effort. Percy Smith, who studied Shaw's unpublished letters and diaries in the British Museum, comes up with these interesting observations:

'There is little to suggest the impoverished but self-sufficient and singleminded recluse, turning his back on society and working his way daily along the shelves of the British Museum reading room. . . . What the record reveals is less impressive . . . a young man of unusual ability and great charm *who simply does not know what to do with himself* [my italics]. . . . Throughout this period one sees him to be a person with an almost hypochrondriacal concern for his health, eccentric in his diet and irregular in his habits, subject to endless colds, neuralgia, headaches, toothaches and general depression. . . . [He] carries on an interminable battle against physical laziness, with the aid of alarm clocks. . . . Eccentric though his habits are, he has an almost neurotic dependence on society—especially the company of women . . . [p. 25].'

The diaries that Smith refers to date from 1885, when Shaw

was twenty-nine. So there can be no possible doubt that everything in the above paragraph also applies to the previous nine years. The apprenticeship was long and dreary, and for a very long time showed absolutely no results. A year after his arrival in London he wrote a 10,000-word letter of advice to a (presumably) imaginary child, Dorothea, 'a practical system of moral education for females'. The style is still leaden, and the advice by no means as revolutionary as one might expect from Shaw. Although Dorothea is told never to listen to religious instruction, and that schoolmistresses are natural enemies, she is also advised to be polite and patient, to do her duty, and to avoid pride and vanity. And one paragraph expresses a disillusionment that sounds strange coming from Shaw:

'It may surprise you, but there is no such thing as contentment in the world. You must not place too much faith in grown-up people. They are always pretending to be better than they are. Aunt Tabitha is not really and truly contented. She is unhappy because she is not married. If she were married, she would wish herself single again. Your godpapa is always wishing for more money. I confess to you that I am discontented' (p. 30).

He had reason to be discontented. After a month at Ventnor in the Isle of Wight—where he went to see Yuppy's grave—he returned to London, and tried half-heartedly for a number of clerical jobs. He even took a cram course in Excise with the idea of becoming a civil servant, but apparently abandoned the idea. Lucy called him a parasite and advised their mother to throw him out of the house. Then, luckily, Lee was able to offer him work, ghosting music articles for *The Hornet*, and this lasted a year. Shaw also played the piano at some of Lee's social gatherings, and thus gained a nodding acquaintance with English society. Painting continued to be one of his chief interests, and he spent a great deal of time at the National Gallery. But altogether it must have been a boring, frustrating life, and one that would lead inevitably to 'endless colds, neuralgia, headaches, toothaches and general depression'. He did not even think of writing novels until he had been in London for two years. Then, in 1878, he planned a work called *The Legg Papers*; it got no further than a sketch—although some of its material seems to have turned up in a short story, *The Miraculous Revenge* (1885). One can guess why he gave it up from the names of some of the characters: Epaminondas Gentleflower, Newcastle Legg, Jupiter Beedleby; clearly, it was another attempt at the Dickensian style. *Immaturity*, based on autobiographical materials, was begun in March 1879, nearly three years after his arrival in London. The *Hornet* employment had terminated in 1877; according to Shaw, his criticisms were so severe that the owner sacked Lee (under whose name they were appearing), Lee having become 'one of the most unpopular men in London'; the paper itself collapsed shortly afterwards. For the next two years he stopped trying to find work, and did nothing in particular except—by his own account—read Shelley, study counterpoint, and write a few unsuccessful articles. Shaw's own comments on this period are frank enough in acknowledging his shyness and gaucheness, but they are fundamentally misleading in that they make no mention of the 'Oblomovism', the nervous depression and sense of defeat and pointlessness revealed in the Diaries. 'I found myself invited to visit the Lawsons, who were at home in Cheyne Walk every Sunday evening. I suffered such agonies of shyness that I sometimes walked up and down the Embankment for twenty minutes or more before venturing to knock at the door: indeed, I should have funked it altogether, and hurried home asking myself what was the use of torturing myself when it was so easy to run away, if I had not been instinctively aware that I must never let myself off in this manner if I meant ever to do anything in the world. Few men can have suffered more than I did in my youth from simple cowardice or been more horribly ashamed of it. I shirked and hid whenever the peril, real or imaginary, was of the sort that I had no vital interest in facing; but when such an interest was at stake, I went ahead and suffered accordingly. The worst of it was that when I appeared in the Lawsons' drawing room I did not appeal to the good nature of the company as a pardonably and even becomingly bashful novice. I had not then tuned the Shavian note to any sort of harmony, and I have no doubt the Lawsons found me discordant, crudely self-assertive, and insufferable.' An aphorism that turns up in *Fanny's First Play* sounds as if it originated in this period: 'You cannot learn to skate without making a fool of yourself. The ice of life is slippery.' But the way Shaw expresses it—'I had not then tuned the Shavian note to any sort of harmony'—somehow denies what he is admitting. When W. B. Yeats admits the same kind of thing, it has somehow a more honest ring:

> 'What matter if I live it all once more?
> Ensure that toil of growing up;
> The ignominy of boyhood; the distress
> Of boyhood changing into man;
> The unfinished man and his pain
> Brought face to face with his own clumsiness;'

Or:

> 'Things said or done long years ago,
> Or things I did not do or say
> But thought that I might say or do,
> Weigh me down, and not a day
> But something is recalled,
> My conscience or my vanity appalled.'

Shaw confers on his own admissions the knowledge of hindsight, the understanding that comes in retrospect:

'When a young man has achieved nothing and is doing nothing, and when he is obviously so poor that he ought to be doing something very energetically, it is rather trying to find him assuming an authority in conversation and an equality in terms which only conspicuous success and distinguished ability could make becoming. Yet this is what is done, quite unconsciously, by young persons who have in them the potentiality of such success and ability. . . . The truth is that all men are in a false position in society until they have realised their possibilities and imposed them upon their neighbours. They are tormented by a continual shortcoming in themselves; yet they irritate others by a continual over-weening. This discord can be resolved by acknowledged success or failure only; everyone is ill at ease until he has found his natural place, whether it be above or below his birthplace.' And later in the same preface: 'When I had to come out of the realm of imagination into that of actuality, I was still uncomfortable. I was outside society, outside politics, outside sport, outside the Church. If the term had been invented then, I should have been called The Complete Outsider.' But the point about the

Outsider—a term I was to borrow from Shaw—is that he is unable to slap himself on the chest and call himself The Complete Outsider. As soon as he has achieved this much self-consciousness, he is already ceasing to be an Outsider. Shaw did not cease to be an Outsider until he was in his mid-thirties.

I am underlining this point, not because I think that Yeats's twinges of agonised vanity are the 'right' attitude, and that Shaw's dismissal of his immaturity as an irrelevancy is the wrong one. This is a matter in which I happen to agree with Shaw. If an artist's life is a fight to 'escape from personality', to become totally absorbed in something *other* than himself, then the miseries of immaturity are no more important than the mumps and measles to which children are subject. Living is a continual act of choice, and the clumsy and immature have more choices to make than other people, since every defeat, every humiliation, suggests the alternatives that Shaw felt outside the Lawsons: to ignore it and press on, or to run away. In the twentieth century, it has become the fashion to run away, and then write about it at length. Proust's way—leading to a cork-lined bedroom and increasing slovenliness of dress—was ultimately the way of defeat, no matter how impressive the literature he made out of describing his life of defeat. (The *Recherché* is a great novel because of its descriptions of *other* people—Charlus, Swann, the Guermantes—not on account of its hero.) The same is true of Thomas Wolfe; even of Joyce. The point is raised explicitly by Shaw in an interesting exchange of letters with Henry James about the latter's *Owen Wingrave*, a story James had turned into a play. It is about a young pacifist who is expected to follow the family tradition of soldiering; he defies his relatives and confronts the family incubus (which haunts one of the rooms), then dies of heart failure. Shaw had to write to James about the play on behalf of the Stage Society, and he urged him to rewrite it so that Owen wins the encounter with the ghost. 'What the play wants is a third act by your father,' said Shaw, who certainly felt more sympathy for the religious mystic, Henry James senior, than for his 'artistic' son. Shaw said it was a damnable sin to create a 'houseful of rubbish' with such art, to bring on the hero carrying a torch, and then calmly announce that the rubbish has choked the hero. This is to preach cowardice, said Shaw, and to perpetuate 'the fatalism that broke out so horribly in the 1860s at the word of Darwin'. 'People don't want works of art from you; they want help,' he concluded. In a long reply James pleaded that his imagination, 'absolutely enjoys and insists on and incurably leads a life of its own, for which just this vivacity itself is its warrant', and says that a play designed to help people would 'more likely than not . . . be shallow and misleading'. But this kind of plea for 'freedom of imagination' is casuistry. The imagination is not 'free'; if it tries to operate on uncongenial material, it ceases to operate, or loses most of its vigour. The imagination's role is largely a 'compensatory' one. The body cannot live and grow without food, but the mind *can* live and grow without experience—at least, without the coarse, repetitive kind of experience that makes up everyday life. The more creative a man is, the more vital the role his imagination plays. Shaw, who knew that 'every dream can be willed into creation', felt that James's poetic defeat-fantasy was the waste of a vital faculty. It was not a matter—as Leon Edel suggests—of an artistically insensitive socialist trying to turn a 'work of art' into a Shavian comedy. As far as Shaw is concerned, it is *the* fundamental and vital question upon which he is disagreeing with James, and the view he advances is the essence of Shaw, the most important thing he had to say.

But this consideration of Shaw's early London period raises another question which was equally crucial for Shaw. It could be argued that he survived his enormously long and discouraging apprenticeship because of his sense of humour, which prevented him paying too much attention to his conscience or his vanity. Equally important was his sense—which increased as he grew older—of his uniqueness; in fact, of his genius. The danger—for his artistic and intellectual development—lay in the combination of these two. This can be seen, for example, in a letter he wrote to a mistress, Florence Farr, when he was thirty-six:

'Now listen to me, will-less girl. When you tell me that I best know what I am, I assent, not with humility, but with towering head striking against every star and raising great bumps on them; so that astronomers reel amazed from their telescopes. Cubits high and fathoms deep, I am the noblest creature you have met in this wood of monkeys where I found you straying. . . .'

He goes on to tell her:

'There are two sorts of genius in this world. One is produced by the breed throwing forward to the god-like man, exactly as it sometimes throws backward to the apelike. The other is the mere monster produced by an accidental excess of some faculty—musical, muscular, sexual even. A giant belongs properly to this category: he has a genius for altitude. Now the second order of genius requires no education; he (or she) does at once and without effort his feat, whatever it may be, and scoffs at laborious practice. The first order finds it far otherwise. It is immature at thirty, and though desperately in need of education (being less a child of Nature by so much more as it is advanced in evolution) can find nothing but misleading until it laboriously teaches itself. I am a genius of the first order; and so are you; but I know my order and the price I must pay for excellence, whereas you are always appealing to the experience of the second order to justify your own self-neglect.

'You are wrong to scorn farcical comedy. It is by jingling the bells of a jester's cap that I, like Heine, have made people listen to me. . . .'

In the first paragraph we have Shaw using his old trick of disarming by exaggeration, as in the early letter to his mother: 'I feel that even now you are wishing you could kiss me. . . .' In the second he is completely serious, except in including Florence Farr in his category of 'godlike' geniuses. He believes every word he says, and what he says has a great deal of penetration. 'G.B.S.' is in abeyance; it is Shaw himself speaking. In the final paragraph, while believing himself to be still completely serious, G.B.S. has edged back in again, and the result is the questionable assertion about the value of farce. The comparison with Heine points to the unsoundness of the argument. Heine was one of the greatest of German lyric poets, in the sense that lyric poets can be great; but if poetry is to be judged by the standard of epic greatness—of Dante, Goethe, Milton—then he is a minor poet, and does not belong to Shaw's first order of genius. The second, it will be remembered, comes about through 'accidental excess of some faculty—musical, muscular, sexual even'. He may have had Mozart in mind as the musical example (Bax and Britten would be good examples among more recent composers). And if Mozart fits, Heine certainly does.

Shaw is clowning when he tells Florence Farr 'I am the noblest creature you have met in this wood of monkeys', but in another sense, he is quite serious, as he is also serious about his head striking the stars. He had a deep and very powerful awareness of his genius and potentialities. And if we think in *these* terms—and not of his actual achievement, which was certainly very considerable—it is clear that he fell a long way short of realising his potentialities. Tolstoy was later to tell Shaw that his flippancy endangered his reputation: 'the problem about God and evil is too important to be spoken of in jest. And therefore I will tell you frankly that I received a very painful impression from the concluding words of your letter: "Suppose the world were one of God's jokes, would you work any the less to make it a good joke instead of a bad one?" ' Tolstoy may sound humourless, but his intuition went to the point. If we think in terms of the achievements of some of the great figures of the nineteenth century— Beethoven's symphonies, Balzac's Human Comedy, Tolstoy's *War and Peace*, Wagner's *Ring*, Hegel's System—it is quite clear that Shaw left no comparable monument. *Back to Methuselah* is a great work, but if we ask why it is not as unarguably great as Wagner's *Ring*, the answer is that Wagner's stock in trade was melody, and Shaw's was humour, and some of the bad jokes of *Back to Methuselah* detract from its total impact far more than some of the bad music of the *Ring*. In his argument with James, Shaw was right because he was basically more serious than James; in his argument with Tolstoy, Tolstoy was right, because he was fundamentally more serious than Shaw. The Shaw sense of humour served him well through the 'long apprenticeship', but it was to become a dubious ally in his later years.

But to return to the Shaw of 1879—the beardless youth of twenty-three (he grew his beard after a bout of smallpox in 1881), with a round, childish face, which looked rounder and more childish under the bowler hat he sometimes wore, and prominent ears; this Shaw wore his hair parted in the middle, and looked younger than his actual age; in fact, in most of the half-dozen photographs that exist of this period,* he looks little more than an overgrown schoolboy. He has a strong Irish accent; and since

* All to be found in *Bernard Shaw through the Camera* by F. E. Loewenstein (London 1948).

most of the Irish in London are servant girls and day labourers, Londoners are somewhat inclined to look down on him, failing to perceive that he is a member of the class of Protestant gentry. His sister Lucy is fully mature, very attractive, and has had several lovers; her brother is clever enough, but in comparison with her, feels he lacks weight and personality. And in their not infrequent disagreements, she enjoys pointing out that cleverness is no substitute for experience. He is aware that changes are taking place inside him, but they seem to be invisible to his family. (Jack Tanner later complains: 'to be treated as a boy was to be taken on the old footing. I had become a new person; and those who knew the old person laughed at me. The only man who behaved sensibly was my tailor; he took my measure anew every time he saw me, whilst all the rest went on with their old measurements and expected them to fit me.') And so he takes to spending as much time as possible alone, and wandering around London at night. He is obviously at a loose end, but can find nothing he wants to do; he cannot even be bothered to write to his father, who calls him 'an ill-natured cur' for his neglect. And now, after three years of enduring Lucy's sarcasm and his mother's puzzled incomprehension, he decides that it is time he made a token gesture of embarking on a career: he will write a three-volume novel. So one day in March 1879 the twenty-two-year-old aspirant sits in the British Museum reading room and writes:

CHAPTER ONE

'At four o'clock in the evening of the shortest day in the year 1878 a young man passed from the main street in Islington into a quadrangle through an arch, over which was an iron plate inscribed *Dodd's Buildings.*

'*Dodd's Buildings* enclosed a flagged square of which each side was only sixty feet long; yet the square contained eleven severely respectable houses. It was a quiet spot in a noisy neighbourhood, and conveyed an impression that Dodd, though unimaginative as an architect, was a strictly pious man.'

Not a very good beginning. How did Dickens get around these stupid physical details?—sixty feet long, eleven houses. Eleven into sixty won't go, but if you make it sixty-six, it adds another word to a sentence that already sounds too pedantic and mathe-matical. . . . Novel-writing is certainly not as easy as music criticism. A music criticism can start off with a flourish: 'The *Hornet* regrets to have to inform its readers that it has been getting some grievous knocks lately, owing to its unreasonable tendency to be honest. . . .' That has a certain snap, a panache. In the novel you have to stay in the background and present your material. Even that bit about Dodd being strictly pious is a transgression of the rules. . . . He stares at his opening two para-graphs, decides he had better leave them alone, heaves a deep sigh, and grinds on:

'The young man, when he had despondently surveyed the court for some time, turned to the left, and knocked at the door marked No. 3. (Of course, a door isn't marked No. 3; it's just marked 3; damn these details. . . .) After an interval, a voice within screamed "Rose!" It was the voice of a woman losing her temper; and from this most unpleasant of all sounds the visitor shrank. . . .' A thousand words and three pages later he has finally got his hero alone in his room, and his flagging interest begins to revive:

'Robert Smith, sitting alone before the fire and ruefully stroking his shins, was a youth of eighteen, with closely cropped pale yellow hair, small grey eyes, and a slender lathy figure. His delicately cut features and nervous manner indicated some refinement; but his shyness, though fairly well covered up, shewed that his experience of society was limited, and his disposi-tion sensitive.' There, that was better. Refined, sensitive . . . not very positive virtues in a hero. Still, he could introduce another hero later. . . . And now he has got the hero alone, Smith can start unpacking his boxes. And he unpacks in minute detail for the next two pages: a Shakespeare, a Bible, a photograph album (McNulty's parting gift when Shaw left Dublin), paper collars and linen collars, shirts and hand-knitted socks. ('Other under-clothing he had none.') And having unpacked, Smith proceeds to do a sum. He has £92, and various expenses (all written down in full) come to £70 15s 4d. That leaves £21 4s 8d for his hero to live on. . . .

And at that moment, there is the clanging of the hand bell that announces the Museum's closing time. It has taken the apprentice novelist five hours to write ten pages, and he feels stiff and slightly headachey. But the novel is begun. And if anyone wants to know why it is so ordinary and pedestrian the answer is that this is his intention. As he later told one of the eleven publishers who rejected it: 'In writing it, I did not propose to save it from appearing dull to a reader who should seek for excitement in it. The design was, to write a novel scrupulously true to nature, with no incident in it to which everyday experience might not afford a parallel. . . .' Thirty-five years later James Joyce would begin a novel with a similar purpose; but Joyce faced up to the fact that if the incidents are 'true to nature' and everyday life, then the real interest of the book must lie in the style. Shaw failed to see this, or rather, he could see no way around it. But he was aware of the other major problem that also arises in Joyce: the problem of the hero who is more sensitive and intelligent than the other characters. For what can you make such a hero *do*? You can only try to set him off against other characters who lack his 'refinement'—in *Ulysses* it is Mulligan and Haynes. Shaw tries this method in the opening pages of *Immaturity*. There is a knock on Smith's door.

' "Come in," said Smith.

'Immediately there entered a young man of dissipated appearance, whose dirty-fine dress and manner displayed the combination of shabbiness and pretence characteristic of the sort of poor dandies who are naturally slovens . . . His eyes were watery; his blotched complexion was an unwholesome yellow; and he bore himself with the feeble swagger of one who made it a habit to be as insolent as he dared, and who durst but little.'

There; the idle apprentice to act as foil to the industrious one. . . . But it still didn't solve the problem of what the hero ought to *do*. It would be easy if he was one of those heroic heroes of Scott and Byron—Smith's boyhood favourites, we are told—but he is only a sensitive and immature young man. And then Shaw might take a leaf out of Lever's book and make his hero a slightly comic figure, daydreaming of romance and being continually brought down to earth. But reducing his stature would be as dishonest as magnifying it; Shaw's self-belief was too strong for that. And so the problem remains. Before the end of the first chapter, Smith has decided to leave the house of the draconian Mrs Froster. Then the doorbell rings, and Smith answers it, to find a pretty Scots girl on the doorstep. And 'from that time he thought no more of leaving Mrs Froster's house'. That sounds promising ... Smith is rather young, but that shouldn't prevent a delicate, intellectual romance. But all that happens is that Smith teaches her French, and they remain 'just good friends'. Besides, Harriet is the first of the Shaw heroines: 'Smith was fascinated by the sweetness of her smile, and awed by the impression of power that he received from her fine strong hands and firm jaw.' Which raises the question that Robert Louis Stevenson was later to ask: why did Shaw create such women? The answer should be clear enough by now. Shaw was used to strong women, and had no fear or dislike of them. It was important to his self-respect to believe that women could be as strong as men. Male protectiveness towards women formed no part of Shaw's personality. He felt at ease with down-to-earth, unromantic women. He felt thoroughly ill at ease with 'womanly women', and found it impossible. to believe in their sincerity. He believed that under the surface, all women were realists and well able to take care of themselves; but it suited some of them to look helpless and soft, to dupe 'manly males' into taking care of them. Over a span of seventy years all the women Shaw created fall into these two types (with, perhaps, a small third division for 'dragons'): the romantics and the non-romantics, the sirens and the realists. In Shaw there are no 'womanly' heroines like Ophelia or Elizabeth Bennett or Anna Karenina. (Perhaps it was this lack of male protectiveness that made Beatrice Webb call him a sprite and say that it would be impossible for a woman to fall in love with him.) Shaw's women never *give* themselves. One could almost believe that he was unaware of the existence of women whose existence needs to be complemented by a man, basically 'faithful' women, like Peer Gynt's Aase. Yet his sister Agnes had been one of these gentle, patient women. As far as one can gather from his rare references to her, Shaw seems to have rationalised himself into an oddly detached attitude about Agnes. She had been his mother's favourite, he told Ellen Terry. Agnes had died of consumption, which she caught off a servant girl in the days when the disease was believed to be non-infectious. Her death was therefore not a tragedy; merely the outcome of carelessness, and the hopeless incompetence of doctors. It was simply another reason for his distrust of the medical profession. And Agnes could be forgotten.

The three Shavian types of female all appear in *Immaturity*. Harriet Russell is the real heroine, the realist. There is the siren Isabella, the daughter of an Irish M.P. who engages Smith as a secretary, who is flirtatious and dishonest. And there are one or two 'dragons', notably Mrs Froster and Lady Geraldine Porter, a younger and more amiable Lady Britomart Undershaft. The man who eventually marries Harriet is a painter called Cyril Scott, based on Cecil Lawson (who died in 1882), Shaw's second hero. (He told Macmillans that he had originally intended to call the book *A Quadrille*, and the two heroes and heroines would change partners several times.)

The Irish M.P. is one of the best characters in the book, and the scenes in which he appears show how much Shaw had learnt from Charles Lever. The scene between Woodward (the M.P.) and his Irish servant is typical:

' "If you plaze, sir, Miss Izzabella sez youre going out to dhrive in the phaytn wid her afther lunch; and she wants to know wont you come up and ate a pick furst."

' "Tell her I'm too busy," said Woodward.

' "But she bid me not to come back widhout your honor," persisted the footman coaxingly. "Arra, do, sir; come up and have a bit. What's the good o' killin yourself over them ould letters?"

' "Very well; very well: tell her I'll be up in a minute," said Woodward resignedly.

' "God bless yer honor," replied Cornelius briskly, and retired.

' "Well certainly," thought Smith, who had expected to see the man discharged on the spot for his familiarity, "these Irish. are the most extraordinary people." '

It is interesting to note that Smith is English; Shaw had already decided he preferred the English to the Irish. Woodward asks his secretary: 'You're an Englishman, aren't you?' 'Smith admitted his nationality with a misgiving, lest the gentleman, who was evidently an Irishman, should regard a Saxon secretary with envy and hatred.'

In rejecting the book, the Macmillan's reader commented: 'It is dry and ironic in flavour. . . . Recognising all these things, I ask myself what it is all about: what is the key, the purpose, the meaning of a long work of this kind without plot or issue?' He had put his finger on the book's central failing. Long before the reader is halfway through its 420 pages he is seized with a suspicion that Shaw has no idea of where he is going. Incident follows incident; the quadrille goes on; but all to no particular end. Perhaps this would not matter too much—after all, Lever's novels are equally plotless—if Shaw had only tried to write about the kind of thing that interested him, the affairs of his central characters. But *Immaturity* has a defect that is to be found in all the five novels: he feels that a novel should involve a large cast of characters, and that they should all get their fair share of the action. And so for a great deal of his time he is writing about people for whom he feels not the slightest sympathy—conventional social types who can be found in any other Victorian three-volume novel. He plodded on, setting down page after page of conventional dialogue. His persistence is incredible when one considers how it must have bored him. But he had decided that he had better be a writer, chiefly because he could think of nothing else that appealed to him. He had nothing in particular to say as a novelist, and this must have been apparent to him after writing the first ten pages of *Immaturity*. But there was no alternative.

Immaturity was finished on the 28th of September 1879, and revised during the next month. On the 8th November it went off to its first publisher, Hurst and Blackett, who rejected it with such promptitude that it was on the way to its second—Kegan Paul—five days later. They rejected it on the 25th. Shaw's family were in financial difficulties, and his cousin, Mrs Cashel Hoey, suggested that Shaw might take a job with the Edison Telephone Company of London. He was given a job on a commission basis—to persuade people to allow the Company to put up its poles on their roofs; Shaw was to receive half-a-crown for every permission. By the end of the year he had earned exactly half-a-crown, and a letter resigning from the company led to better terms, a salary of £48 a year, which was increased two months later to £80. But work, 'that sin against my nature', was uncongenial to Shaw. He might not know what he wanted to do—he must have known he was no novelist—but he had a very definite sense of what he didn't want to do. The Edison telephone was not a success, 'being nothing less than a telephone of such stentorian efficiency that it bellowed your most private communications all over the house instead of whispering them with some sort of discretion', and when it was merged with Bell's National Telephone Company all employees were given notice and invited to reapply for employment; Shaw hastily slipped away. This was in July 1880. *Immaturity* was still being rejected regularly, but Macmillan's took an interest in Shaw, and George Macmillan recommended him to John Morley, editor of the *Pall Mall Gazette*. Shaw tried writing several articles and reviews for them, but their tone was too harsh, and Morley advised Shaw to get out of journalism. A story, *The Brand of Cain*, met with as little success.

No, it looked as if the answer lay in the novel. But it would have to be quite different from *Immaturity*. And what was wrong with *Immaturity*? Even Shaw could see that the trouble lay in the hero's character, or, rather, complete lack of character. Smith was a hermit and an intellectual. What was needed was a new style of hero, something closer to the man of action. Besides, the first requisite of a novel is that the hero should get the girl; in *Immaturity* Smith only kisses Isabella once. This would also have to be remedied. And so shortly after leaving the Edison Company —and after one more half-hearted attempt to get a clerical job— Shaw decided to utilise his experience of electrical engineering in a new novel. This was written during the remainder of 1880, at a steady rate of five pages a day, according to Shaw's preface to *The Irrational Knot*. And it certainly showed an enormous advance on *Immaturity*. It is shorter, it has a real hero, and the plot outline is firm. Shaw put his finger on its chief fault in his preface: 'I had . . . the classical tradition which makes all the people in a novel . . . utter themselves in the formal phrases and studied syntax of eighteenth century rhetoric. In short, I wrote in the style of Scott and Dickens.'

By far the most interesting thing about *The Irrational Knot* is Shaw's choice of a hero, the inventor and electrical engineer, Edward Conolly. For one realises with sudden clarity why Shaw continued to write novels throughout five years of total failure. It was not simply that he wanted literary success; there was something more basic involved. The novels served an important purpose in his development as an individual, for they record his *search for a hero*. They were *mirrors*. The shy, awkward young man from Dublin wanted to know what he ought to do with his life; that is, what sort of a person he wanted to become. Robert Smith was a fairly accurate self-portrait, a long look at himself. But it told him nothing. The novel is inconclusive. This can be seen if one compares it, for example, with Joyce's equally colourless self-portrait as 'Stephen Hero'. But Stephen Dedalus ends with the knowledge that it is his 'destiny' to be an artist, 'to forge in the smithy of my soul the uncreated conscience of my race'. (Admittedly, this is in *The Portrait of the Artist as a Young Man* and may be hindsight; but the comparison holds, none the less.) In the last paragraph of *Immaturity*: 'As Smith recrossed the bridge, he stopped and stood in one of the recesses to meditate on his immaturity. . . . At last he shook his head negatively and went home.' And what will Smith do now? One can only guess that he will become a highly efficient chief clerk—he has just passed his business examinations—but apart from that, his future is opaque. The qualities Shaw has given him—intelligence, imagination, the power of seeing things clearly—do not point to any obvious destiny. And they were Shaw's own qualities. The Shaw hero must possess these qualities; but if he is to be dynamic rather than static, then he needs some others too. What others? Edward Conolly is an attempt to answer the question. 'There was no cloud of vice or trouble about him: he was concentrated and calm, making no tentative movements of any sort (even a white tie did not puzzle him into fumbling), but acting with a certainty of aim and consequent economy of force, dreadful to the irresolute.' This is certainly a more promising hero than Robert Smith. He sounds almost like the hero of a cartoon strip; you can imagine the big square jaw, the clean-cut features. . . .

The plot of the novel can be quickly described. Conolly meets Marion Lind at a concert. (Like Shaw, he plays piano accompaniments.) Socially speaking, she is 'above' him. She nevertheless accepts him when he proposes to her, and marries him. But she is a romantic young lady, and finds his quiet efficiency disappointing. She runs off with an old admirer—suitably ardent and romantic, but a weakling. He deserts her in New York, and

Conolly comes to fetch her back. But there is no reconciliation; they stay separated. There the novel ends.

There is a secondary plot concerning Conolly's actress sister, who also falls in love 'above' herself. She refuses to marry the young man, but they live together. He is also a weakling and allows her to support him; finally, she leaves him, takes to drink, and dies an alcoholic.

It can be seen from this brief outline that the aristocrats come off badly. In fact, just about everybody comes off badly except the dedicated and self-controlled hero. It is clear that the book has a moral, and the moral is typically Shavian: that in this life, the only really successful and happy people are those who are dedicated to something beyond themselves. As to the aristocrats, Shaw may not yet have been a socialist, but his feelings about them are already quite definite: 'These aristocratic idle gentlemen will never be shamed out of their laziness and low mindedness until the democratic working gentlemen refuse to associate with them instead of running after them and licking their boots.' Conolly's sister Susanna is certainly superior to her aristocratic paramour Marmaduke, but she also has a basic failing: lack of seriousness. As her brother watches an audience clapping enthusiastically, he remarks: 'That sort of thing, from a woman of her talent, is too cheap to say thank you for.' Nine years later Shaw said very much the same thing about his sister Lucy, who was playing the lead in an enormously successful operetta called *Dorothy*:

'The female of the species has not yet developed a conscience: she will apparently spend her life in artistic self-murder by induced Dorothitis without a pang of remorse . . . "Dorothy" herself . . . sang without the slightest effort and without the slightest point, and was all the more desperately vapid because she suggested artistic gifts wasting in complacent abeyance.'

This outspoken review was published in the *Star*. Lucy's biographer, H. G. Farmer, cites it as an example of Shaw's bad manners. This may or may not be justified, but it is certainly an example of his consistency.

All in all, *The Irrational Knot* is probably Shaw's best novel, if one makes allowance for the usual fault—the number of boring characters who add nothing to the action. Artistically, it is a very fair success. And from the point of view of Shaw's search for a hero it is more than that. It is a definitive statement of his philosophy. Robert Smith of *Immaturity* was hardly likely to win converts for the gospel of efficiency and self-control. But Conolly reveals its positive side. And this is because he is shown in the conventional love relationship, and gives Shaw the chance to express some of his fundamental misgivings about this relationship. After all, what is history but a series of love stories? And what is so pointless and futile as history? Paris and Helen elope and Troy is burnt down, men rant about religion and burn heretics, kings march their countries to war over an insult; everyone wallows in emotion, and the result is that life seems to be 'a tale told by an idiot'. A vital instinct in Shaw insisted that life is *not* tragic by nature. Like Nietzsche, he could say: 'I have made my philosophy out of my will to health.' His novels may be bad *as* novels, but they are important because they are Shaw's attempt to answer the question of 'nihilism', of whether life is tragic by nature. The tragedy in Shakespeare's plays springs out of 'fatal flaws' in his heroes. Shaw decided to create heroes who possess self-control and a sense of purpose, and see whether life seen through their eyes still looks like a 'tale told by an idiot'. In *The Irrational Knot* he argues convincingly that it doesn't. When he finished *The Irrational Knot*—sometime around Christmas, 1880— he must have known that he had justified his belief that he was a writer with something worth saying.

All the same, Conolly is not the end of the Shavian search for a hero. To a lesser degree he has the same flaws as Robert Smith: that is, his character is such that it does not lead to action. This is not noticeable in the first half of the novel, where Conolly falls in love with Marian, proposes to her, and overcomes the objections of her family. (There is an excellent scene where Marian's father—who is also Conolly's employer—sends for him with the intention of browbeating him, and ends by being browbeaten; Shaw is at his best at this sort of thing.) But once they are married the old problem arises. What now? Marian ought to be perfectly happy to be married to a man like Conolly, and that should be the end of it. In fact, her elopement with her aristocratic ex-admirer is completely out of character. But the purpose of the novel is to show the character of the 'superior man' under adversity as well as success. And so his wife has to leave him. He is completely indifferent, of course, absorbed in his work. And when his wife is deserted by her lover, he immediately goes to New York and offers to take her back, unperturbed by the disgrace or the fact that she is pregnant. When she asks if he would not rather be free, he says: 'Freedom is a fool's dream. I am free. I can divorce you if I please; if I live with you again, it will be by my own choice. You are free too: you have burnt your boats, and are rid of fashionable society, of your family, your position, your principles, and all the rest of your chains forever.' She still demurs, and Conolly says goodbye. The novel ends with a brief flash of Shavian romanticism:

' "Good-night," said Marian rather forlornly, after a pause, proffering her hand.

' "One folly more," he said, taking her in his arms and kissing her. She made no resistance. "If such a moment could be eternal, we should never say goodbye," he added. "As it is, we are wise not to tempt Fortune by asking her for such another."

' "You are too wise, Ned," she said, suffering him to replace her gently in the chair.

' "It is impossible to be too wise, dearest," he said, and unhesitatingly turned and left her.'

This is certainly a better ending than the previous novel's. But it cannot make up for the weakness of the second part of the book. It would have been more convincing if Shaw had learned something about the work of inventors, and given an account of Conolly's struggles, or showed him in conflict with the businessmen who will utilise his inventions, as Sinclair Lewis did later in *Arrowsmith*. But instead of trying to show Conolly at work, Shaw wastes time on conversations between the usual boring socialites, and his hero remains slightly out of focus. Shaw still lacks the courage of his convictions. He is too original to turn out a standard three-volume novel, and still not confident enough to attempt anything else. So it falls between two stools.

Perhaps the most interesting thing about *The Irrational Knot* are its clear indications that Shaw was a dramatist. He sets scenes and develops them just as in his plays. This can be observed if we take the opening paragraph and transpose it into the present tense:

'At seven o'clock on a fine evening in April the gas has just been lit in a room on the first floor of a house in York Road, Lambeth. A man, recently washed and brushed, stands on the hearthrug before a pier glass, arranging a white necktie, part of his evening dress. He is about thirty, well grown and developed muscularly . . .' and so on. And on the next page, when his sister comes in, the scene is handled exactly as a playwright would handle it: she takes up a letter that lies on the mantelpiece and reads it aloud, thus informing the audience that her brother has been asked to sing at a concert in Wandsworth; then she reads the programme aloud and comments on it in detail. This same visual way of presenting material had already been present in *Immaturity*:

'Feeling sleepy, he went into the hall, where the reproachful looks of a manservant apprised him that he was the last guest stirring in the house. When he was gone, the domestic extinguished the remaining lights; and, after flitting round the gallery with a single taper, like a liveried ghost, vanished and left the great hall in darkness.' This sounds rather like the ending of *Der Rosenkavalier*; a real novelist would have said: 'He went to bed and fell asleep immediately' or something of the kind, instead of leaving the camera focussed on an empty stage. In *The Irrational Knot* the dramatic element is present all the time. For example, there is a scene in which Conolly's actress sister discovers that the young aristocrat who has been paying her attentions has given her a false name; the following pages could be transferred to the stage exactly as they stand—the violent row ending (inevitably) in the woman twisting the man round her finger. It leaves no room for doubt that if Shaw had started with plays instead of novels he would have made a name a great deal earlier.

The Irrational Knot, written in six months, started off on the usual round of publishers. The Macmillan reader's report described it as 'a novel of the most disagreeable kind . . . the whole idea of it is odd, perverse and crude. It is the work of a man writing about life when he knows nothing of it'. And apart from its faults publication 'is out of the question. There is far too much adultery and like matters.' An American publisher also rejected it on grounds of immorality. As far as a career was concerned, prospects were still bleak. A magazine called *One and All* accepted an article on Christian names in 1879 for fifteen shillings, but rejected all the other articles and stories that Shaw immediately deluged them with. He even tried the device of writing some articles under a female pseudonym, hoping that editors might show more indulgence; no one did. Commissions for Lee brought the occasional £5. He was permanently broke:

'A little past midnight, in the same [evening dress], I was turning from Piccadilly into Bond Street, when a lady of the pavement, out of luck that evening so far, confided in me that the last bus from Brompton had passed, and that she would be grateful to any gentleman who would give her a lift in a hansom. My old-fashioned Irish gallantry had not then been worn off by age and England: besides, as a novelist who could find no publisher, I was touched by the similarity of our trades and predicaments. I excused myself very politely on the grounds that my wife (invented for the occasion) was waiting for me at home, and I felt sure so attractive a lady would have no difficulty in finding another escort. Unfortunately, this speech made so favourable an impression on her that she immediately took my arm and declared her willingness to go anywhere with me, on the flattering grounds that I was a perfect gentleman. In vain did I try to persuade her that in coming up Bond Street and deserting Piccadilly she was throwing away her last chance of a hansom: she attached herself so devotedly to me that I could not without actual violence shake her off. At last I made a stand at the end of Old Bond Street. I took out my purse; opened it, and held it upside down. Her countenance fell, poor girl! She turned on her heel with a melancholy flirt of her skirt, and vanished.'

But being without money when you have a roof over your head and regular meals is, after all, not such an inconvenience. Shaw's 'literary struggles' all took place between a pen and a sheet of paper. This may be the reason that his attitude to money was so paradoxical. Now and for the rest of his life he was capable of returning money that he felt he hadn't earned, as, for example, when Lee sent him £5 for 'expenses' incurred in ghosting the book on voice training. This is not the attitude of a man who has ever had to worry about money. On the other hand, his business sense was so acute that in later years he often created an impression of miserliness. The late Esme Percy told me of how Shaw arrived at a rehearsal one day in the Strand. His car (which he usually drove himself) had broken down, and he had travelled to town by train. The cab driver charged Shaw a shilling from St Pancras to the Strand instead of the usual sixpence or nine-pence. Shaw grumbled about it all through rehearsal, and was still grumbling when he left the theatre in the evening. He always charged newspapers special high rates for articles or reviews, as Miss Patch has recorded. He declined to waive his performing fees for amateur companies. When paying small bills he would often write several cheques—so that, for example, if the bill was for £15, he would write three cheques for £5 each, knowing that his signature was worth more than £5 and that they would never be cashed. It was in order not to devalue the price of his signature that he always refused autographs to strangers. Yet all this was not a miserly concern with money; only another aspect of his obsession with efficiency, the kind of eye-to-business displayed by Vivie Warren and Captain Bluntshli. There are innumerable anecdotes about his generosity. When G. K. Chesterton died, Shaw immediately wrote to his widow to offer her a blank signed cheque, to be filled in for any sum she needed. When word reached him that Doré Lewin-Mannering (who played the Bishop in *St Joan*) was going through a bad period, Shaw immediately sent him a signed edition of his works, which Lewin-Mannering's daughter Betty sold to Heffer's for £400—which was what Shaw had intended.* Shaw's attitude towards money was that of a man who had never needed it urgently to keep him alive, and who could consequently feel quite detached about it. In the days of *The Irrational Knot* Shaw only needed money to post off his manuscripts and take a bus to the British Museum. (And when, on December 23rd, 1880, the Shaw family moved to 37 Fitzroy Street—a descent in the world—he no longer even needed bus fares.)

Three days before he completed *The Irrational Knot* a fellow Irishman, James Lecky, took Shaw to a meeting of a debating group called the Zetetical Society. Shaw had applied for member-

* This anecdote—and the one about Shaw writing several cheques—was told to me by Leonard Hibbs, Lewin-Mannering's son-in-law.

C

ship a few days before, which seems to indicate that he had already decided to turn himself into a public speaker. 'I had an air of impudence, but was really an arrant coward, nervous and self-conscious to a heartbreaking degree. Yet I could not hold my tongue. I started up and said something in the debate, and then, feeling that I had made a fool of myself, as in fact I had, I was so ashamed that I vowed I would join the Society; go every week; speak in every debate; and become a speaker or perish in the attempt. I carried out this resolution. I suffered agonies that no one suspected. During the speech of the debater I resolved to follow, my heart used to beat as painfully as a recruit's going under fire for the first time. I could not use notes: when I looked at the paper in my hand I could not collect myself to decipher a word. . . . I seemed so uppish and self-possessed that at my third meeting I was asked to take the chair. I consented as off-handedly as if I were the Speaker of the House of Commons; and the secretary probably got his first inkling of my hidden terror by seeing that my hand shook so that I could hardly sign the minutes of the previous meeting. . . . My first success was when the Society paid to Art . . . the tribute of setting aside an evening for a paper on it by a lady in the esthetic dress momentarily fashionable in Morrisian cliques just then. I wiped the floor with that meeting; and several members confessed to me afterwards that it was this performance that first made them reconsider their first impression of me as a bumptious discordant idiot.'

Shaw was determined to become formidable, and he took the measures necessary. This also explains the lack of *rapport* between Shaw and the literary generation that followed. The heroes of Proust, Joyce, Lawrence, Aldous Huxley, were oversensitive 'Outsiders' who accepted Outsiderism as an inevitable condition of their relation with society, and also embraced the alienation that went with it. They could not accept society's terms; society could not accept their terms; so there had to be a gap. But Shaw had discovered and proved to himself that the gap can be closed by self-discipline. From then on he had the minimum of patience with anything that sounded like self-pity.

Still, prospects remained discouraging. After Macmillans, *The Irrational Knot* was rejected by Richard Bentley and Sons, Smith Elder and Blackwood's. Shaw wrote more applications for clerical jobs, and was probably relieved when they were unsuccessful. Towards the end of 1881 he was even seriously considering emigrating to America. (Chichester Bell, cousin of the inventor of the telephone, had moved there; it had been Bell who introduced Shaw to Wagner's music in his Dublin days.) The thought of losing his regular meals probably deterred him. Instead, he ground out two more novels, *Love Among the Artists* and *Cashel Byron's Profession*. Since these are no better and no worse than the previous novels, there would be no point in describing them at length. The search for a hero continued, and the hero of *Love Among the Artists* was his most interesting yet, 'a British Beethoven, utterly unreasonable and unaccountable, and even outrageous, but a vital genius, powerful in an art that is beyond logic and even beyond words'. If Owen Jack—the composer—had held the centre of the stage it would have been Shaw's best novel. But most of the novel is taken up with the doings of the various aristocratic nonentities whom Shaw felt it necessary to include. *Cashel Byron's Profession* represents a retrograde step in Shaw's search for a hero. Cashel is the son of a successful actress who (like all Shaw's actresses) cares for no one but herself; he runs away from school and becomes a prize-fighter in Australia.* On returning to England he meets Lydia Carew, a wealthy young lady, and eventually marries her. The novel is simply an account of the ups and downs of their love affair which, as can be imagined, are all connected with the necessity for Cashel to keep his profession a secret from Lydia. Cashel is an amiable simpleton, completely un-Shavian. And since he is the only hero in the novels with whom Shaw is obviously not identifying in any way, he is the least interesting of them. The ironical thing is that this least Shavian of the novels is, from the point of view of conventional storytelling, the best of the six. Shaw records that a reader of *Man and Superman* told him to his face that *Cashel Byron* was

---

* Shaw's interest in pugilism came about as a result of his friendship with Pakenham Beatty, an Irish poet and alcoholic, who was also an enthusiastic pugilist. Shaw received boxing lessons from Beatty's friend Ned Donelly, a celebrated coach who became Ned Skene in *Cashel Byron's Profession*. In 1883 Shaw and Beatty actually applied to enter the Amateur Boxing Championship at Lille Bridge grounds, although Shaw only weighed ten stone (140 lb). They were both turned down.

the best thing he ever did. And it was later to become his first success with the general public, so that he wrote: 'I never think of Cashel Byron's Profession without a shudder at the narrowness of my escape from becoming a successful novelist at the age of twenty-six. At that moment an adventurous publisher might have ruined me.'

There is something in this. For when he was halfway through *Cashel Byron*—in September 1882—Shaw stumbled upon the discovery that would alter the direction of his life and give him the unity of purpose that he lacked. He discovered socialism.

3 THE ECONOMIC BASIS

It happened on the evening of September 5th, 1882, when Shaw happened to attend a lecture by Henry George at the Memorial Hall in Farringdon Street. Henry George was no ordinary economist. Sailor, prospector, printer and journalist, he achieved overnight fame with the publication of *Progress and Poverty* in America in 1879. And if we ask why a work preaching socialism should make such an impact twelve years after the first volume of Marx's *Capital* appeared, the answer is that George was a kind of prophet who wrote with the passion of an evangelist. *Progress and Poverty* asks why, in the age of labour-saving machinery and new inventions, do wages tend towards a bare minimum? And he comes up with the strange answer: because a lot of people make an unfair profit out of *rent*. Workers and industrialists both toil for the good of the community. But when they have created a flourishing city where there was once only a farming village, who benefits most? The men who happened to *own the land* on which the city is built, for its price has now soared. These landowners are the men who batten unfairly on the wealth produced by the rest of the community. And the solution? According to George, it lies in abolishing all taxes except a tax on land. Landowners should pay a tax that amounts to the yearly value of the land. So if a landowner makes a million dollars a year in rent from land in the centre of Chicago that is the amount he should pay to the government in tax on the land. This obviously amounts to confiscating his land and giving it to the community.

George was, to be honest, a crank. He was obsessed by land,

and thought that his 'single tax' would bring about the millennium—universal happiness and prosperity. He thought that trade
cycles—the regular slumps and booms in trade—were due to
speculation in land. He was wrong, but the beautiful simplicity
of his idea made him very influential.

Shaw bought a copy of *Progress and Poverty* for sixpence from
an usher, and the book's effect on him was revelatory. For six
years now he had been struggling in a society that seemed to
have no particular use or place for him. Shelley had made a
revolutionary of him, and for years now he had been thinking
about the conflict between religion and science, the overthrow of
the Bible, the rights of women, marriage and free love. And
all to no effect; the iconoclasm of the novels had been a series of
swipes at the empty air. 'Thus a bee, desperately striving to reach
a flower bed through a window pane, concludes that he is the
victim of evil spirits or that he is mad, his end being exhaustion,
despair and death. Yet if he only knew, there is nothing wrong
with him; all he has to do is to go out as he came in, through the
open window or door.' And here, in *Progress and Poverty*, George
had showed the bee how to get back into the garden. Shaw's
obsession with the conflict between science and religion had been
'a mere middle class business'. 'The importance of the economic
basis dawned on me.' 'Your born Communist begins like the bee
on the pane. He worries himself and everybody else until he dies
of peevishness, or is led by some propagandist pamphlet . . . to
investigate the economic structure of our society.

'Immediately everything becomes clear to him. Property is
theft; respectability founded on poverty is blasphemy; marriage
founded on property is prostitution; it is easier for a camel to
go through the eye of a needle than for a rich man to enter the
kingdom of heaven. He now knows where he is, and where this
society that has so intimidated him is.'

All Shaw's biographers have quoted this statement. None of
them have questioned his assertion that he had somehow found
his 'answer' in socialism. But was it really the answer? Shaw was
the bee on the window-pane, a revolutionary in search of a cause.
His real cause was reason and courage and self-discipline, and it is
summarised in Conolly's closing remark in *The Irrational Knot*:
'It is impossible to be too wise, dearest.' And the 'economic

basis' has very little connection with the kind of wisdom Shaw was interested in. In terms of the central question of human evolution, socialism is a side-issue—an important one, perhaps, but still a side-issue. Why, then, should George's book strike him as so revelatory, when he had already read Shelley, Darwin, J. S. Mill and the rest? The answer is not connected with the ideas contained in the book but with the sense of *practical purpose* that Shaw could derive from them. If he could have derived the same practical purpose from the rights of women or Bradlaugh's Secular Society these would have become his 'revelation'. He was badly frustrated; his novels were getting nowhere; his articles and stories were always rejected. He had been in London for six years and had not made the slightest dent on the capital. What he needed most of all was to *stop marking time*, to have a sense of motion, of getting somewhere. He had too many talents and none of them seemed marketable. He was a novelist, a public speaker, a journalist, a pianist—he even tried song-writing. He wrote bad verses to a girl with whom he had 'fallen vehemently in love', a pretty nurse called Alice Lockett; but the love affair, like his other activities, marked time. He lived in a revolutionary period; the air was seething with social and intellectual changes. But he was a spectator; his own attempts to join in were ignored.

And now Henry George came up with a complete indictment of 'this society that had so intimidated him', and a beautifully simple solution of its problems. It was as if he had placed a large club in Shaw's hands, and then pointed out exactly who deserved hitting. At last Shaw had a practical point of application, a crack into which he could insert his crowbar. Socialism was not an answer to Shaw's *intellectual* problems. It was an answer to the purely practical problem of what to do next.

And now, at last, things began to happen. Two years before, at the Zetetical Society, he had met Sidney Webb, a mild-mannered, erudite young man with a London accent and an air of quiet efficiency, who 'used notes, read them, ticked them off one by one, threw them away, and finished with a coolness and clearness that, to me in my then trembling state, seemed miraculous'. Shaw sized him up as 'the most able man in England'. He was impressed that Webb 'knew more than the lecturer; knew more than anybody present; had read everything that had ever

been written on the subject; and remembered all the facts that
bore on it'. He said later: 'Quite the cleverest thing I ever did
in my life was to force my friendship on Webb, to extort his, and
keep it.' It may have been through Webb he heard about H. M.
Hyndman, a friend and disciple of Karl Marx—who at this time
was still unknown in England. Hyndman had launched a society
called the Democratic Federation, whose meetings Shaw soon
began to attend. When Shaw brought up the name of Henry
George, Hyndman advised him to read Karl Marx. Shaw claims
that he did so, reading *Capital* in Deville's French translation. I
find this hard to take literally, in view of Shaw's well-known
inability to speak foreign languages, and the difficulty of Marx's
text. On the other hand, Shaw would not have to struggle very
far into *Capital* before coming upon one of its central and most
controversial arguments: that the 'value' of a commodity is the
value of the labour that has gone into it. It is upon this assertion
that Marx builds up his whole demonstration of the ultimate
downfall of capitalism. Shaw's immediate response was to deny it,
on the obvious ground that the value of a commodity is not the
value of the labour that goes into it. The value of a diamond is
not the value of the labour it has cost to get it out of the ground;
it is a purely artificial value based on *demand*. And Shaw's contradiction of the labour theory of value was no doubt enough to
get him into argument with Hyndman, as well as with Webb and
Sydney Olivier (another socialist comrade), and to produce
eventually a full grasp of Marx's arguments.

But although Shaw's socialism is not the integral part of his
philosophy that he liked to assert, it was undoubtedly an extremely
important part of his life and character. He started writing and
thinking about it in 1883, and he was still writing and thinking
about it sixty years later. Because most of Shaw's biographers
have possessed the artistic rather than the political temperament,
it has become the least appreciated aspect of his life-work.

It is important to understand that Shaw's interest in social and
political issues had the force of a religious conversion. During
the year 1883 he suddenly began to read political economy—
Adam Smith, Ricardo, Malthus, and Proudhon, as well as Marx
and Engels. Apart from music, Shaw had never studied any
subject so thoroughly. This was the first completely *intellectual*

discipline of his life—perhaps the only one, since he never made a comparable effort to understand science or philosophy. In order to understand the impact it made upon his mind, it is necessary to look at the nature of these theories that influenced him so deeply.

Concerning the following section, I must make a personal confession. Like most people, I find economics rather a repellent subject—in spite of Yeats's story about Pater, who told Lionel Johnson that he had books on economics on his bookshelf 'because I feel that nothing human should be foreign to me'. In my mid-thirties I knew all Shaw's work except the *Fabian Essays*. Eric Bentley's book led me to feel that, in some respects, these may be regarded as the key to Shaw. I settled down to reading the various works on political economy that had sat unread on my bookshelves for ten years or more. And I was amazed to discover that I had never really understood Shaw; this was an aspect of his personality that none of his biographers had bothered to discuss—presumably because they all found economics as dull as I had.

The following section should be skipped by anyone who feels strongly that he does not wish to understand why Shaw was so deeply committed to socialism. For it is admittedly by way of a compromise; anyone who really wants to understand Shaw should read Adam Smith, Ricardo, Mill and Karl Marx.* For those who lack the time and inclination, I must try to sketch in the background of Shaw's economic thinking.

It is generally agreed that the first major political economist was Adam Smith, a contemporary of Dr Johnson, whose *Wealth of Nations* appeared in 1776. Smith was the first great *laissez faire* economist. And his central point was this: Modern society is

* Or at least some of the more readable popularisations of the subject: Robert Heilbroner's *The Worldly Philosophers,* Eric Roll's *History of Economic Thought,* Michael Stewart's *Keynes and After* (Penguin), or Douglas Vickers' *Theory of Money, 1690–1776.*

becoming steadily more prosperous because of specialisation of labour. In a pin factory, ten men each concentrated on a different part of making the pin, and could make forty-eight thousand pins a day; if each man made whole pins, he couldn't make twenty a day. The basic law of political economy (it was not called economics in those days) is the law of supply and demand. And obviously, the more prosperous society gets, the more it can afford to buy. The demand rises, and so does the supply, and thus society becomes more and more prosperous. All you have to do is let it alone.

Smith introduced the labour theory of value, that Marx later took over. But he differs from Marx in that his conclusions are entirely optimistic. There are setbacks, but they are temporary. As society grows more prosperous, the competition for workmen increases, and this acts as a temporary brake, for higher wages means lower profits and less accumulation of wealth. But then the number of workers increase as the higher wages enable them to raise bigger families, and soon there are more than enough. And so the rising spiral continues. . . .

It will immediately be noticed that this kind of argument tends to be absurdly abstract. For example, it is untrue that an increase in the prosperity of workers leads to an increase in their families. Surveys in a number of underdeveloped countries have shown that it is the poorest families who produce the most children, as if poverty has made them fall back on the only available pleasure. The more prosperous the family, the smaller the family unit. The advances in economics—such as they are—usually come about when realistic critics point out the weaknesses of an old theory, and try to put a new one in its place.

This is what happened with Smith's successors. Thirty-two years after *The Wealth of Nations* the Reverend Thomas Robert Malthus produced his *Essay on the Principle of Population*, in which he pointed out that increased prosperity leads to increased population, and that the population increase tends to outstrip the prosperity. Society is not headed up, but down. (Again, in spite of the modern population explosion, the above observations on underdeveloped countries contradict this.)

Malthus's friend David Ricardo, a Jewish member of Parliament, took an even gloomier view. He is the true predecessor of

Karl Marx and Henry George. He agrees with Malthus that the workers will never be any better off, because of this incorrigible tendency to produce more children. And he anticipates Henry George in believing that the capitalists will also find it impossible to improve their lot. For as industry expands, it needs more land; the price of land soars, and only the landowners benefit as the capitalist pays out his profits on more land and rising wages—for as land prices rise, so does the price of grain, and the workers have to eat. Ricardo takes Malthus's gloomy theories one stage further; the society he envisages could be described as 'the rat race'.

Ricardo's ferocious pessimism produced a back-swing into idealistic Utopianism. In the early nineteenth century a young industrialist called Robert Owen set up 'co-operative villages' to demonstrate that society need not be founded on man's exploitation of man, and became highly successful as a businessman. His contemporary Charles Fourier suggested the setting up of 'phalansteres', a kind of co-operative hotel (very similar to the ideas developed by the behavioural psychologist B. F. Skinner in his book *Walden Two* (1948), which has achieved immense popularity among American students in recent years). The Count Claude de Saint-Simon advanced the revolutionary idea that the highest rewards of society should go to its workers, not to the idlers and aristocrats; he died of starvation and discouragement before he explained how this was to be brought about.

Most important of all, perhaps—although half-forgotten today —is John Stuart Mill, whose *Principles of Political Economy* was the first exhaustive textbook in the field. For Mill's central contribution to economics was one extremely simple and yet vital statement. It is true, he said, that society is governed by rigid laws of production, which cannot be evaded or cheated. But *there is no law of distribution*; society can do what it likes with its resources. There is no 'law' that makes society a rat race. It is as if a Martian psychologist were to argue that human beings are basically governed by self-interest, and that as they become more successful, their attitude towards their fellow human beings will become increasingly impolite until all human society is destroyed by conflict. Theoretically, it could be made to sound irrefutable. But a civilised human being merely has to reply: It is true we are governed by self-interest, but we can *choose* not to be dominated by it; we can choose to be polite to people who are not of any immediate use to us; we can choose to help somebody without any particular hope of profit.

It was this view of Mill's that led indirectly to modern 'Keynesian economics': to what is sometimes called 'priming the pump'—that is, for the government to control trade cycles by deliberate government spending to bolster the economy during slumps.

But less than twenty years after Mill's *Political Economy* (1848), with its message of man's free will, came the most rigid and deterministic of economic theories: that of Marx.

Now Marx's whole approach is even more abstract than Smith's or Ricardo's. He claims that he will prove, by the most rigid logic, that the competitive system is bound to destroy itself, and must be taken over by a workers' society. Capitalism must disappear; not because it is evil—Marx claims to be indifferent to moral judgements—but because the laws of economics say so.

Marx's arguments—grossly simplified—can be expressed in this way. The value of a commodity is the amount of labour that went into it. In that case, how much will it sell for? Obviously, everybody will try to get the highest possible price. But eventually, competition will bring prices down until it sells at its actual labour-value. Thus far, the argument is Adam Smith's.

But if it sells at its labour value, no one makes a profit. How can the capitalist make a profit? By deliberately exploiting his labour force. He does not do this out of wickedness, but because he has no choice; he doesn't want to starve. He must create 'surplus value', value over and above that of the commodity. He can only do this by getting the labourer to work for more hours than he gets paid for. The 'value' of the labour that the worker sells is the amount of money he needs to keep himself and his family alive. The amount of work he does *should* be exactly equivalent to the amount of food he and his family consume, the amount of coal and clothing they need, etc. (remembering that every commodity has an exact labour value). The capitalist can only get surplus value by making him work *more* hours than this, and forcing him to work by the threat of starvation.

And so we have the first stage of capitalistic society: lots of capitalists making their profit by exploiting the workers and creating surplus value. This is Ricardo's rat race. And according to Ricardo, the situation is in a kind of equilibrium, for workers tend to multiply their numbers, and so there are always plenty of them for the capitalists to exploit. But Marx simply dismisses this as 'a libel on the human race'. In any case, it makes no crucial difference. For capitalists are soon forced to compete with one another by buying machines, which produce a brief honeymoon period of increased profit as a highly mechanised factory competes with a factory employing more workers. This cannot last, for sooner or later everybody will be forced to use the machines —by the principle of competition—and prices will drop.

And now comes a crucial point in the argument. Machines are a commodity like any other, and sooner or later, competition in the sale of machinery will make it reach its natural price. And what is its natural price? Well obviously, the value of what it can produce. If a machine could produce goods ten times its value, then there would be a rush to buy them which would force up the price, until sooner or later, it is equal to the value of the actual labour it gives. But this means that a machine cannot be exploited like a workman. 'The law that surplus-value does not arise from the labour power that has been replaced by the machinery, but from the labour power actually employed in working with the machinery, asserts itself.' So the profits shrink, and machinery is thrown on the market and bought cheap by bigger concerns, so that the capitalists proceed to eat up one another. 'One capitalist always kills many.' No matter how big the monopolies get, the downward trend continues, for if the workers have been replaced by machines, who buys the products of the machines? Moreover, if the competition motive is weakened because one large firm holds a monopoly, the whole process is accelerated by the increasing laziness and carelessness of the monopoly. (In this, Marx seems to have anticipated Arnold Toynbee's law of challenge and response.) The periodic crises become more and more serious, until the workers, disgusted by the spectacle, decide to take over the means of production.

One might summarise the whole thing by saying that according to Marx, the workers are the first victims of the machines, then the small capitalists, and finally the big capitalists. The whole drama springs out of the combination of the machine with a *competitive society*, a society in which workers are treated as a 'mass' of labour power. The solution comes when true individualism is re-established; individuals work for the good of one another, and the machine ceases to be a juggernaut that destroys men, and becomes a servant of society.

It must be admitted that all this sounds logical enough; but then, so did Smith and Ricardo. It is not difficult to sound logical when you are talking about Society with a capital S; the question is whether these theories really describe the way society operates. Marx's edifice is built on his definition of value as being the amount of labour put into a product. After that, the rest follows logically.

The whole structure is so full of holes that it is difficult to resist the temptation to dismiss it all as a farrago of nonsense. Shaw saw immediately that the labour theory of value is an untenable abstraction; value depends solely on what I am willing to give for a product, and how easy it is to obtain. An economist called W. S. Jevons—who was drowned at Hastings a few weeks before Shaw attended the Henry George lecture—had advanced an alternative theory, which he called the 'utility' theory of value, which is quite simply the amount of satisfaction a person derives from a certain thing, quite apart from its actual 'usefulness'. An obvious example of this is a work of art—a Van Gogh painting, let us say. The price of a gramophone record may approximate to its 'labour value', because any number of copies can be produced. And any number of copies of the Van Gogh can be produced in theory; yet a collector may be willing to pay half a million pounds for the original. Why? His reasons are purely personal; he looks at it and says, 'Ah, this is the painting that Van Gogh actually created.' He can't really tell the difference between this and a clever imitation. He is *conferring* value on it. And Jevons' theory of value is worth bearing in mind as an antidote to the Marx theory; man *chooses* his values far more than Marx will admit.

Perhaps the basic fallacy in Marx is the fallacy about the value of the machine: that a machine cannot be exploited, and that it cannot therefore produce surplus value. A machine *is* an exploitation of the laws of nature. If I use a tube to suck petrol out of the tank of my car into my lawn-mower I am using a simple machine, and the whole point of the machine is that I am using my knowledge of a law of nature—in this case, air pressure—to save myself labour. If I lack a piece of tubing when I want to syphon off petrol its value to me may be considerable—far more than the labour value of the piece of tubing. It is the nature of a machine to produce more than its labour value, and it does this by utilising the untapped forces of nature, like a power station placed at the foot of Niagara Falls. Nature provides the 'surplus value'. A machine—let us say a dynamo—may be easy to manufacture, and its materials may be inexpensive, but the power it can produce is out of all proportion to these factors. Marx's argument that the value of a machine is simply the value of what it can produce is obviously untrue. And what will determine the price of machines on the market is not the value it will yield over its working life, but *what it costs to manufacture*. If a shopkeeper tried to charge me ten pounds for a piece of plastic tube, on the grounds that it will eventually be worth that much to me for syphoning petrol, I shall obviously find another shop where the price is more reasonable.

Oddly enough, Shaw embraced Marx's value theory, and derided Jevons and John Stuart Mill—the latter was Sidney Webb's preferred economist. Although his denial of the value theory pulled away the foundations of *Capital*, Marx was too good an ally to waste. Shaw was intoxicated by the sheer power of Marx's indictment. For the moment, he was unaware of the philosophical consequences of dialectical materialism. In any case, he thoroughly approved of Marx's sentiment: 'The philosophers have only *interpreted* the world in various ways; the point however is to *change* it.' What Shaw liked about *Capital* was that 'it is a jeremiad against the *bourgeoisie*, supported by such a mass of evidence and such a relentless genius for denunciation as had never been brought to bear before'. He found Marx so much more impressive than George that he quickly resigned from the Henry George society (the Land Restoration League) when he found out that it had nothing against capitalism as such. And for a while he was unable to find any practical application for his newly acquired communism. Then he heard of a group called the Fabian Society, which was an offshoot of a highly idealistic group called the Fellowship of the New Life, whose aim was the total reconstruction of society 'in accordance with the highest moral possibilities'.

The group had alliances with spiritualism,* and a number of its more practical members had broken away to form a more purely political organisation. The Fabians had no rigorous economic theory, and they did not accept Marx's notion of the Class War. They were practical socialists, who wanted socialism to become as politically respectable as Liberalism.

Shaw discovered the Fabians by reading their tract *Why are the many poor?* and he attended their next meeting, then introduced Webb to them. This was what they had both been looking for: a group of educated, highly intelligent men with a practical purpose. Shaw was twenty-seven—nearly twenty-eight—when he joined. It was the turning point of his life. Being a member of this dedicated group gave Shaw the feeling he had always needed: of being practical, competent, capable of real work. This seems absurd when we consider that he had written four bulky novels, all on a high level of originality. But the novels, as I have pointed out, are oddly inconclusive; they provide no answer to the question: Where now? Basically, Shaw still felt a lightweight; and indeed, his new colleagues were inclined to regard him as a lightweight. Sydney Olivier (later Lord Olivier), after acknowledging the 'transparent liberality and generosity of his character', writes: 'But Webb and I were university graduates . . . and we often judged Shaw's education and his appreciation of academically and socially established humanities to be sadly defective. . . . On the face of his conversation I thought his appreciation and sympathies in regard to a good deal of the springs of human conduct perversely shallow and limited, and his controversial arguments often cheap and uncritical.' Nevertheless, Shaw was a good member of the team, for he could present an argument with wit and style, and explain the aims of socialism with a clarity that made Webb and Olivier seem elephantine: 'The most striking result of our present system of farming out the national land and capital to private individuals has been the division of society into hostile classes, with large appetites and no dinners at one extreme, and large dinners and no appetites at the other.' This is from the second Fabian tract: Shaw lost no time in adding his weight to the team.

Shaw's basic argument for socialism was a very simple one, and

* Shaw's mother was a spiritualist.

it is derived from Jevons. It is presented with beautiful clarity in chapter 29 of *The Intelligent Woman's Guide to Socialism*, published in 1928. Why, Shaw asks, are private companies not allowed to compete with the Post Office as letter-carriers? 'The reason is that the cost of carrying letters differs greatly as between one letter and another. The cost of carrying a letter from house to house in the same terrace is so small that it cannot be expressed in money. But the cost of carrying the same letter from the Isle of Wight to San Francisco is considerable . . . You would naturally expect the Postmaster-General to deliver a dozen letters for you in the same terrace for a penny, and charge you a pound for sending one letter to San Francisco. What he actually does for you is to deliver the thirteen letters for three-halfpence apiece. . . . Our reason for forbidding private persons or companies to carry letters is that if they were allowed to meddle, there would soon be companies selling stamps at threepence a dozen to deliver letters within a few miles. The Postmaster-General would get nothing but the long distance letters . . . and when we found that the advantage of sending a letter a mile or two for a farthing was accompanied by the disadvantage of paying sixpence or a shilling when we wanted to write to someone ten miles off, we should feel that we had made a very bad bargain. The only gainers would be the private companies who had upset our system.'

But where most important commodities are concerned, says Shaw, this is exactly what *has* happened. For example, some coal is very cheap to produce because the mines are accessible and close to railways or rivers; other coal is more expensive because it may be mined from under the sea, or in some distant and inaccessible place. The owner of this mine will have to charge a high price for it to make it pay. Now the owner of the more accessible mine may try to undercut him to some extent; but he will also take full advantage of the high price to charge the highest possible price for his own coal. This is Jevons, who pointed out that 'the exchange (value) of the least useful part of the supply fixes the exchange value of all the rest'. Obviously, if coal was nationalised, like the Post Office, the cost would be averaged-out, as with stamps, and the housewife would get her coal at something like cost-price. Private ownership in mines has exactly the same effect as it would have in the Post Office: to force up prices.

It is interesting, if perhaps not entirely relevant, to speculate why the nationalisation of the coal mines in England has not produced this fall in the price of coal. At all events, the above is Shaw's central argument for socialism. It is a purely practical one, with no talk of Class War or the labour theory of value. Being reasonable and practical, it had considerable appeal for the English, and explains why the Labour movement in England gained political ascendancy so quickly. The nearest thing to a revolutionary principle in Shaw's socialism is the Saint-Simonian assertion that everybody should work. 'Under modern conditions each of us can produce much more than enough to support one person. If everyone worked, everyone would have a good deal of leisure.' His objections to capitalism have nothing to do with its tendency to destroy itself, but simply with its tendency to produce waste because waste means higher profits. This is the undogmatic socialism of the Webbs. The great Breakages Limited speech in *The Apple Cart* is a dramatisation of the chapter on waste in the Webbs' *Decay of Capitalist Civilisation*.

But even before he had joined the Fabian Society Shaw was utilising his new-found beliefs as material for a novel. It was called *The Heartless Man*, and was started in July 1883 and completed in less than four months. Shaw later claimed that it was intended originally to be a vast work 'depicting capitalist society in dissolution with its downfall as the final grand catastrophe'. This sounds like another typical Shavian exaggeration, for the novel is clearly self-complete, and the tone is too light to lead to such a final catastrophe. When finished it was given the title *An Unsocial Socialist*. For many reasons it is the most interesting of the 'novels of his nonage'.

First, and most significantly, it reveals the end of the Shavian search for a hero. In Sidney Trefusis, the rich socialist of the title, Shaw had finally produced a character that he felt represented his own potentialities. Apart from the immature Robert Smith, no hero of Shaw's novels had been a definite self-portrait. But in all essentials Trefusis *is* Shaw. The fact that he reappears eight years later as Charteris in *The Philanderer*, and then twenty years later as John Tanner in *Man and Superman*, is evidence that Shaw felt he had at last produced a mirror that reflected him faithfully.

Even more significant is the fact that Shaw now felt confident enough to let his immense romanticism out of the bag. It is a schoolboy romanticism that is far from the realism of *The Irrational Knot*, and it goes a long way towards explaining why Shaw still felt himself unformed and immature. Still a virgin at twenty-seven, his daydreams obviously involved love affairs in which he was irresistible to women. But the Shaw of the daydream is no Casanova, but a man driven by a purpose in which women can play no part. All of this is extremely clear in *An Unsocial Socialist*.

The first part of the book takes place in a girls' school, where Trefusis is disguised as a gardener, having fled from his newly-wedded wife. 'For five weeks I have walked and talked and dallied with the loveliest woman in the world, and the upshot is that I am flying from her, and am for the hermit's cave until I die. Love cannot keep possession of me; all my strongest powers rise up against it and cannot endure it.' Under these circumstances it seems strange that he should move into a cottage close to a girls' school where—coincidentally—one of his wife's relations is a pupil. The truth is that Trefusis is an inveterate flirt.

At the boarding school are three young ladies of seventeen: Agatha Wylie (the relative), Gertrude Lindsay and Jane Carpenter. Agatha is the Shavian heroine: intelligent, mischievous and realistic. Jane is plump, good-natured and sentimental. Gertrude is one of Shaw's favourite aversions, the social snob, the slightly underbred girl who never ceases to judge everybody by their breeding. (He even went to the trouble of introducing one into *Cashel Byron's Profession*—as the heroine's companion—although she is completely irrelevant to the plot.) Naturally, they become extremely curious about Smilash—as Trefusis calls himself—and about his barbarous accent, which resembles no local English dialect. Shaw manages to get a great deal of broad Dickensian fun out of Smilash:

' "No lady," said Smilash with a virtuous air, "I am an honest man and have never seen the inside of a jail except four times, and only twice for stealing." '

Smilash's disguise is penetrated when his wife turns up on speech day, but he manages to get her alone and lectures her on socialism and economics at some length, before persuading her to return to London without him. Trefusis's socialism sounds idealistic and utopian: 'I am helping to liberate those Manchester laborers who were my father's slaves. To bring that about, their fellow slaves all over the world must unite in a vast international association of men pledged to share the world's work justly; to share the produce of the work justly; to yield not a farthing—charity apart—to any full-grown and able-bodied idler or malingerer, and to treat as vermin in the commonwealth persons attempting to get more than their share of wealth or give less than their share of work.' After Henrietta has returned to London, Smilash is accused of abducting her, but manages to prove his innocence, leaving the young ladies of the college even more mystified and intrigued.

One can almost hear Shaw chortling with delight as he devises these absurd situations. He was twenty-seven when he wrote the novel; apart from the economics, it reads as if it has been written by a highly romantic youth of seventeen. In the final scene he even takes his revenge on Alice Lockett—the nurse—upon whom Gertrude Lindsay is apparently based. Like every other girl in the book, Gertrude is in love with Trefusis. He gets engaged to Agatha, and Gertrude leaves for London. Trefusis decides to travel by the same train and try to persuade her to marry a young poet. At first he tries common sense: 'Love is an overrated passion,' etc. When that fails, he tries a sentimental speech about renunciation, and how he will always keep a corner of his heart for her. This works. When the train arrives Trefusis remarks to an acquaintance who meets him: 'There goes a true woman. I have been persuading her to take the very best step open to her. I began by talking like a man of honour, and kept it up for half an hour, but she would not listen to me. Then I talked romantic nonsense of the cheapest sort for five minutes, and she consented with tears in her eyes.' Alice Lockett's attitude to Shaw was thoroughly ambivalent. She liked him, but distrusted his flippancy and his intellectualism; so she remained defensively satirical, protesting: 'Some men are so clumsy, instead of drawing forth the most noble part of a woman's hand, they repress it.' And at the end of his reply, Shaw told her: 'Your corner is an adorable place in which to pass the evening of a busy day. You will find all about it and about your dual entity (if you understand that) made the foundation of the most sentimental part of my new book.' It was Shaw's rather unfair way of having the last word. When *An Unsocial Socialist* was serialised in a magazine he made sure that Alice and her sister received the monthly parts.

There is one episode in the novel that has aroused the distaste of practically every writer on Shaw: the death of Henrietta, and the hero's attitude towards it.* Henrietta dies of pneumonia after getting caught in a storm, and Trefusis's response is philosophical: 'What's past cannot be mended. I have much to be thankful for, after all. I am a young man and shall not cut a bad figure as a widower.' When the doctor talks about the feelings of the dead girl's parents Trefusis says: 'Let them spare their feelings for the living, on whose behalf I have often appealed to them in vain. Damn their feelings!' This carries him into a vein of socialistic reflection: 'She had a warm room and a luxurious bed to die in. . . . Plenty of people are starving and freezing today that we may have the means to die fashionably.' When he actually sees his wife's body he bursts into tears, but is ashamed of 'this fraud of grief'. 'I have the mechanism of grief in me somewhere; it begins to turn at the sight of her, though I have no sorrow; just as she used to start the mechanism of passion when I had no love.' After addressing the body for some time on the subject of man's mortality, he quarrels with Henrietta's father, telling him: 'I thought you loved Hetty, but I see that you only love your feelings and your respectability. The devil take you both! She was right; my love for her, incomplete as it was, was greater than yours.' With which he slams out of the house.

This is the kind of thing that Olivier might have cited as evidence of Shaw's 'perversely shallow and limited sympathies'. In fact, it reveals nothing more than that he was an exceptionally immature twenty-seven, highly developed intellectually, completely undeveloped emotionally. His treatment of Henrietta is not 'heartless' because she was never a reality to him. And this explains why Shaw never became a good novelist; most of his characters—with the exception of the heroes—are pasteboard figures, chessmen who are moved according to the needs of the

* This so shocked the editor of the *St James Gazette* that he refused Shaw a job as a book reviewer.

plot. Shaw makes no attempt to 'get inside them', so they are always doing and saying things that are not strictly in character—as in *The Irrational Knot*, when a doting father refers to his baby as 'it'. The texture of *An Unsocial Socialist* is so light that this hardly matters; it bounces along on a level of absurdity, rather in the manner of *The Importance of Being Earnest*. This is the reason that it was the most immediately successful of his novels—being the first to reach print. But when Macmillan's rejected it with the comment that they 'would be glad to look at anything else he might write of a more substantial kind', he was indignant: 'You must admit that when one deals with two large questions in a novel, and throws in an epitome of modern German socialism as set forth by Marx as a makeweight, it is rather startling to be met with an implied accusation of triviality.' He was apparently unaware that the book's lack of substance lay on the emotional and human level, not in its intellectual content.

Shaw made only one more attempt at a novel—four years after *An Unsocial Socialist*; the chapter and a half was published in 1958 as *An Unfinished Novel*. For the sake of completeness this may as well be considered here. Once again we have the typical Shaw hero—quiet, competent and realistic—posed against a background of emotional women and self-indulgent men. Dr Kincaid, a young London doctor, goes to a small country town to become the assistant to Pelham Maddick, an apprentice-trained doctor without a medical degree. Maddick is the typical Shavian weakling, a direct descendant of Frazer Fenwick of *Immaturity*: 'Dr Maddick, it was evident, dressed at being a young, handsome, and dashing man, and had neither youth enough nor character enough nor money enough to be more than a passable counterfeit. . . . His eyes were small and watery, and his assertive nose was large in the wrong places and red at the end.' Maddick's wife, based on Edith Nesbit, the wife of a Fabian colleague, is attractive, self-willed and thoroughly spoilt; she is also dissatisfied with her husband, and pours out complaints about him within minutes of Kincaid's arrival in the house. Then there is Lady Laurie, another spoilt and pretty young woman, who had married an old man for money. She sends for Kincaid, who asks what she has had for dinner.

' "Nothing."

'Kincaid did not accept this as final; and after some questioning it appeared that her meal had consisted of soup, hock, turbot, artichokes, roast beef, champagne, salad, savoury eggs, tipsy cake, custard, ice pudding, curaçao, toasted cheese, coffee, and—medicinally—brandy and soda.'

Kincaid proceeds to bully her—to her secret delight. Then Maddick appears on the scene, and reveals his feebleness of character by petting and humoring her.

' "It is alright," said Kincaid. "She has eaten too much; that is all."

'Maddick turned green, and looked at his unmoved colleague as at a brawler in church.'

It is clear that Shaw has landed himself in a *cul-de-sac*. There is no possible way of developing the situation—short of introducing still another woman with whom Kincaid *can* feel some sympathy. For he is obviously too realistic to get involved with either of the other two ladies. When Mrs Maddick tries to discuss love with him he cuts her short with: 'Perhaps you will excuse my saying that love is the one subject that bores me so intolerably that I cannot as much as pretend to take an interest in it.' So what can happen? Mrs Maddick and Lady Laurie will continue to be pretty and spoilt; Pelham Maddick will continue to be weak and self-indulgent. And Dr Kincaid will stand with folded arms, looking superior and doing nothing. Shaw was back in the situation that had almost wrecked *The Irrational Knot*. And one becomes clearly aware of Shaw's basic weakness as a novelist. All his novels have been full of romanticism disguised as anti-romanticism. They are daydreams of a peculiar kind: the kind in which the dreamer wishes to be simultaneously involved and uninvolved: that is, involved by chance, against his will. It is the kind of daydream that allows you to have your cake and eat it. The Shavian hero wants to remain detached and virtuous, to preserve the picture of the superman who is all drive, inner-direction, purpose, yet who, against his will, keeps finding himself in these delicious romantic involvements in which beautiful young women are captivated while he remains indifferent. It is a basically negative situation. It took Shaw a long time to recognise it, but when he did, he also recognised that he had to give up writing novels. To the second edition of *An Unsocial Socialist* he added an appendix, a 'Letter to the Author from Mr Sidney Trefusis', in which Trefusis ties up some of the loose ends of the novel by telling Shaw what has happened to various characters in the meantime. He ends by advising the author to give up novel writing. 'The poetry of despair will not outlive despair itself. Your nineteenth-century novelists are only the tail of Shakespeare. Don't tie yourself to it; it is fast wriggling into oblivion.' Shaw decided to take his own advice.

4 THE UNFAIR CRITIC

With his discovery of the Fabian Society, Shaw's luck changed. The period of marking time was over.

To begin with, *An Unsocial Socialist* was accepted for serialisation by the Socialist monthly *To-day*, and ran throughout December 1884. Shaw was not paid for it, of course; but in the following February, it was accepted for publication by Swan Sonnenschein and Co, to whom Shaw sent the magazine version. They also printed his story *The Miraculous Revenge* in a magazine called *Time*. And although they no doubt felt they were doing him a favour in accepting his book, his relations with them reveal the highly developed business sense for which he became known in later years. He returned a cheque for three guineas (for the story) and told them he wanted nine. And he declined to assign them the permanent copyright of the novel, arguing that he might want to rewrite it in five years. They ended by compromising—a seven years' lease with a royalty of 10 per cent. At the same time he returned a cheque to another editor—it was an article that was never printed—with a note beginning: 'If you give cheques for nothing, you will ruin yourself as an editor. If I write articles merely for money, I will ruin myself as an artist.' He has no bargaining power—as far as reputation is concerned—but he is nevertheless determined to establish himself in the minds of editors and publishers as a definite personality, not as just another hopeful nonentity.

In 1883 he gave his first public lecture without notes, to an audience of workmen in Woolwich—invited by them, presumably, as a member of the Henry George group. A lecture to the Zetetical Society was less successful; the audience grew impatient with a discourse on socialism, and indicated this so clearly with boos and interruptions that Shaw 'rapidly and apprehensively' changed the subject. He was not always a good speaker, and at this stage was so determined to be serious and informative that he occasionally struck audiences as dull. Dan Rider describes how on one occasion the chairman actually fell asleep. At other times the reaction was more violent, according to Hesketh Pearson,* who quotes Shaw as saying that rotten vegetables were flung at him during open-air meetings, and that on one occasion the contents of a chamber-pot were emptied on his head.

The Irrational Knot and *Love Among the Artists* also found their way into print in a socialist monthly, this time *Our Corner*, edited by the famous atheist and advocate of birth control, Annie Besant. She attended a lecture of Shaw's early in 1885, apparently determined to attack him for his views on the upbringing of children (her own two having been taken away from her by a court order). Either the Shaw personality or the Shaw logic so impressed her that she ended by attacking his opponents. She subsequently became a member of the Fabians—their most important catch so far.

Shaw and the other Fabians also spent a great deal of time at Blackheath, at the house of Hubert Bland, one of the original Fabians. Bland was something of an anomaly as a socialist, for by temperament he was a Tory imperialist, and he looked the part—broad-shouldered, with a monocle and military moustache. Where women were concerned, he had no morals. His wife discovered one day that her best friend—who lived with them—was pregnant, and she was sympathetic and helpful—until she discovered that her husband was the father of the baby. Then she ordered the friend out of the house, and Bland threatened to go too. So the friend—and her child—stayed on, and in due course Bland added another mistress and her baby to the household. When his daughters were teenagers he seduced their school friends. His wife, Edith Nesbit—later famous as a writer of children's stories—presided over this strange ménage with a

* *Extraordinary People,* Heinemann, 1965.

stoicism that concealed masochistic leanings. She became Mrs Maddick in the *Unfinished Novel*.

The serial publication of *An Unsocial Socialist* in 1884 brought Shaw one of the most important friendships of his life—with the poet William Morris. Morris was a remarkable figure, an architect-turned-painter-turned-poet. He was not a good painter, and his poetry is not of the first quality; but he was an idealist who believed that it should be possible to change the world to make it conform with the dreams of poets. It was this aspect of his personality that made such a deep impression on Shaw, as well as on another Morris disciple, W. B. Yeats. Morris had been the youngest member of the Pre-Raphaelite brotherhood, and he made medieval tapestries and printed a beautiful edition of Chaucer at his Kelmscott Press. Now he was one of the senior members of the socialist movement—although only fifty—and his earlier reputation was unknown to most of his comrades. Morris was a socialist because he believed that 'art is the expression of pleasure in labour'. Like many other late Victorians he didn't like the ugliness and smoke of industrial cities; he liked to dream of medieval towns in which craftsmen were also artists. And he saw no reason why English workmen should not once again become craftsmen who worked for pleasure instead of for the enrichment of capitalists. The title of one of his pamphlets, *How We Live and How We Might Live*, reveals the practicality of his approach. Shaw probably had Morris in mind when he wrote in *The Perfect Wagnerite:* 'All this part of the story is frightfully real, frightfully present, frightfully modern; and its effects on our social life are so ghastly and ruinous that we no longer know enough of happiness to be discomposed by it. It is only the poet, with his vision of what life might be, to whom these things are unendurable. If we were a race of poets, we would make an end of them before the end of this miserable century.'

Morris, Hyndman and Shaw were all three members of Hyndman's Democratic Federation for a time. But both Morris and Hyndman were the children of rich parents, and neither could govern their tempers. In the early stages Morris offered to take his orders from Hyndman, and Shaw remarks: 'I smiled grimly to myself at this modest offer of allegiance, measuring at sight how much heavier Morris's armament was; but Hyndman accepted it at once as his due. Had Morris been accompanied by Plato, Aristotle, Gregory the Great, Dante, Thomas Aquinas, Milton and Newton, Hyndman would have taken the chair as their natural leader without the slightest misgiving, and before the end of the month have quarrelled with them all.'* This is what happened with Morris; and although Morris had the majority of the committee on his side, he simply took his majority out of the Democratic Federation and formed his own group, the Socialist League—an action that again impressed Shaw. Morris was not the type to take advantage of his majority to waste time voting down issues on which he disagreed with Hyndman. The Socialist League met at Morris's beautiful house in Hammersmith, in which 'everything that was necessary was clean and handsome; everything else was beautiful and beautifully presented. There was an oriental carpet that was so lovely that it would have been a sin to walk on it; consequently it was not on the floor but on the wall and halfway across the ceiling. . . . On the supper table there was no table cloth: a thing common enough now . . . but then an innovation so staggering that it cost years of domestic conflict to introduce it.' Mrs Morris was very beautiful—she had been one of the favourite models of the Pre-Raphaelites—and very silent; it pained her to see socialist workmen in heavy boots clumping in and out of her beautiful drawing room, but she said nothing.

For Morris the whole venture was an absurd tragi-comedy that took years off his life—he died at sixty. Both he and Hyndman thought the Fabian Society middle class and intellectually snobbish. So it was; but because its members were social and intellectual equals, they got things done. Morris thought that socialism should begin with the British workman, but they only wasted his time and money. His committee ended by voting against Morris's leadership, upon which, says Shaw, 'Morris, who had been holding the League up by the scruff of its neck, opened his hand, whereupon it dropped like a stone into the sea'.

But Morris came to admire Shaw for the same reason that Shaw admired Sidney Webb: for his grasp of the 'economic basis', and he said in the course of one of his addresses: 'In

* 'William Morris as I Knew Him', in Vol. 2 of May Morris's *William Morris, Artist Writer Socialist* (1936).

economics, Shaw is my master.' 'The shock this gave me,' says Shaw, 'shews how far I placed him above myself. I was positively scandalised.' Morris found the grind of practical socialism so demoralising that he turned away from it to 'pour out tale after tale of knights in armour, lovely ladies, slaughterous hand-to-hand combats, witches in enchanted castles changing humans into beasts, lovelorn heroes going mad in the mountains, haunted woods, quests after impossibilities, all under medieval conditions as far as their contacts with anything earthly was concerned'. Meanwhile, the Fabians stuck to their middle-class drawing rooms and discussed economics. And Morris, if he had been well advised, would have stuck to Kelmscott, his medieval manor in Gloucestershire, and to forwarding the cause of socialism with books like his *News From Nowhere* and *The Dream of John Ball*.* He needed solitude and he was condemning himself to endless socialising; it eventually killed him.

In his long preface on Morris, written forty years after the poet's death, Shaw gave details of a romance that has caught the imagination of all his biographers.

'Now it happened that among the many beautiful things in Morris's two beautiful houses was a very beautiful daughter, then in the flower of her youth. You can see her in Burne-Jones's picture coming down *The Golden Stair*. . . . I was a bachelor then, and likely to remain so, for I . . . felt about marriage very much as Jack Tanner does in *Man and Superman*. . . .

'One Sunday evening after lecturing and supping, I was on the threshold of the Hammersmith house when I turned to make my farewell, and at this moment she came from the dining room into the hall. I looked at her, rejoicing in her lovely dress and lovely self; and she looked at me very carefully and quite deliberately made a gesture of assent with her eyes. I was immediately conscious that a Mystic Betrothal had been registered in heaven, to be fulfilled when all material obstacles should melt

* Shaw once attributed the couplet:

> 'When Adam delved and Eve span,
> Who was then the gentleman?'

to William Morris (he quotes it in the first play of *Back to Methuselah*). In fact, it was used by John Ball himself—one of the leaders of Wat Tyler's peasants' revolt (1381)—in his speech at Blackheath to the rebels. Ball was later hanged.

away.' But the mystic betrothal never came to anything, for 'suddenly, to my utter stupefaction . . . the beautiful daughter married one of the comrades. . . . I regarded it, and still regard it in spite of all reason, as the most monstrous breach of faith in the history of romance.' Later still, Shaw needed a rest, and went to stay with the young couple. 'Everything went well for a time in that *ménage à trois*. She was glad to have me in the house; and he was glad to have me because I kept her in a good humour and produced a cuisine that no mere husband could elicit. It was probably the happiest passage in our three lives.

'But the violated betrothal was avenging itself. It made me from the first the centre of the household; and when I had quite recovered and there was no longer any excuse for staying unless I proposed to do so permanently and parasitically, her legal marriage dissolved as all illusions do; and the mystic marriage asserted itself irresistibly. I had to consummate it or vanish . . . I vanished.'

This picture needs to be completed by some further information, which Shaw failed to provide. May Morris was not beautiful; she was a mannish young woman who might have posed for Britannia. Hesketh Pearson was told that May Morris, at forty, was 'tall and masculine, with a moustache', and Shaw, when prompted, agreed about the moustache, only protesting that 'it made a pair of lines so decorative that they would have enchanted the finest Maori tattoo-artist'. In later life she became a lesbian and lived with a Miss Lobb, whom Shaw describes as 'obviously strong enough to take me by the scruff of the neck and pitch me neck and crop out of the curtilage'. The 'comrade', on the other hand, was Henry Halliday Sparling, who appears in a photograph with May Morris and Shaw as being a great deal shorter than either, with a receding hair line and a mild and bookish appearance. The mystic betrothal could never have been consummated, no matter how many obstacles to it were removed. Shaw was romantic enough to admire a Pre-Raphaelite young lady in a pretty dress, but in practice he was a realist who knew exactly what he wanted.

And what did he want? Percy Smith's theory about mother-figures is certainly borne out by the two love affairs in which Shaw got involved that year. The British Museum diaries reveal that Shaw finally lost his virginity on his twenty-ninth birthday, July 26th, 1885. He was not the seducer, but the seduced. The lady in question was a widow, and fifteen years Shaw's senior; her name was Jenny Patterson. He met her at about the same time as Annie Besant. His attitude towards the relation seems to have been almost clinical; his diary for July 10th records: 'Found Mrs Patterson here when I came home. Walked to her house by way of the park. Supper, music and curious conversation, & a declaration of passion. Left at 3. Virgo intacta still.' And the legend that Shaw never 'kissed and told' is disproved by his entry three days later: 'In the evening wrote to E.McN. an account of what had passed on Friday evening.' On the 17th: 'Mrs Patterson came', and Shaw walked Annie Besant home from a Fabian meeting. The following day he was at an Exhibition of Inventions where he saw May Morris; after walking part of the way home with her Shaw went on to Mrs Patterson's, and there followed 'forced caresses'. On the 19th and 20th he called at her Brompton Square home twice, but she was out both times. Then, on the eve of his birthday, the 25th: 'Went back to Brompton Square, where I met Mrs P. and M. [Shaw's mother] returning from Inventions. We walked along Brompton Rd looking for a bus, but they were all full. So on the corner of Montpelier St M. went on by herself and I returned to the Square with J.P. & stayed there until 3 o'clock on my 29th birthday which I celebrated with a new experience. Was watched by an old woman next door, whose evil interpretation of the lateness of my departure greatly alarmed us.'

So on July 10th Shaw was already clear in his mind that Mrs Patterson would be instrumental in getting rid of his virginity; on the next occasion there are 'forced caresses'; then he calls twice, now fairly sure of his quarry. On the evening of his birthday he is so eager for the long-anticipated experience that he leaves his mother to walk back from Fulham to Fitzroy Square in order to return to Mrs Patterson's. (Montpelier Street is close to Brompton Square, so he didn't escort his mother very far.) It is interesting to speculate what excuse he offered his mother for returning to Mrs Patterson's at midnight. Perhaps he told McNulty, to whom he again wrote a full account of the experience a week later; but McNulty later destroyed Shaw's letters at Shaw's suggestion. Shaw also described the experience to Sidney Webb, and received Webb's confidences in return.

So far, Shaw has been the pursuer, forcing caresses on the reluctant widow. Now the affair becomes a Shavian comedy as Mrs Patterson turns round and pursues Shaw, who suddenly recognises that he is not the seducer after all. On August 3rd Shaw has to write Mrs Patterson a 'rather fierce letter', and the following day again: 'Wrote to J.P. in reply to her answer to yesterday's explosion.' The cause of the explosion is not clear, but in view of the later development of the relationship, it seems fair to guess that she was already becoming possessive and jealous. Even in the few pages of the diary covering this three-week period several other ladies occur: Annie Besant, May Morris, Eleanor Aveling and Alice Lockett. On August 5th he has made it up with Mrs Patterson to the extent of having supper at Brompton Square followed by 'love-making until 1.20'. But the affair into which he had strayed casually in two weeks was to drag on for eight years—by which time Shaw was thirty-seven and Mrs Patterson over fifty. During those eight years there were a great many quarrels. One of the earliest was caused by Annie Besant—who was also nine years Shaw's senior. There are no diaries recording the affair with Mrs Besant, and so there is no way of knowing when the Fabian comrades became lovers; but towards the end of December 1887, when Shaw was thirty-one he records that 'Mrs B. gave me back my letters'. He told Hesketh Pearson that Mrs Besant had drawn up a private marriage contract (since she was not divorced from her first husband), which struck Shaw as so preposterous that he told her 'this is worse than all the vows of all the churches on earth. I had rather be legally married to you ten times over'. This is presumably what led to the return of the letters. Mrs Patterson came upon Shaw's letters to Mrs Besant, and there was a violent explosion. These periodic quarrels—which led Shaw to describe Jenny Patterson as 'that tempestuous petticoat'—were so wearing to his nerves that he told her on one occasion that the affair must become Platonic. She called on him in a highly emotional state, and 'much pathetic kissing and petting after which she went away comparatively happy'. On another occasion: 'J.P. here made it hard to work . . . played Haydn to steady my nerves', 'J.P. came, raged, wept, flung a book at my head etc.' And after one visit to her he concludes the diary entry with the single word 'Revulsion'. Yet there seems to be evidence that Mrs Patterson was not entirely faithful either. One day Shaw records finding another man with her who was 'bent on seduction and we tried which should outstay the other. Eventually he had to go for a train'. When, in his thirty-second year, he writes a commentary on the events of the previous year, he recorded feeling disgusted 'with the trifling of the last 2 years with women'.

The disgust was only temporary; he was enjoying these romantic relationships too much to want to give them up. From a fairly early stage he had believed himself 'irresistible to women' —according to Alice Lockett. His experiences now seemed to confirm this. Edith Nesbit pursued him openly, and wrote sonnets to him. She was imperious and somewhat neurotic, as one can gather from her portrait as Mrs Maddick; on one occasion she persuaded Shaw to walk all the way back to Blackheath with her, then kept him talking until the last train had gone, so he had to walk back home again, arriving at 3.30. She finally became so persistent that Shaw finally had to throw her out of the house, alleging that she would 'compromise herself'. Mrs Nesbit noted in her diary, of another socialist comrade: 'Miss H—— pretends to hate him but my own impression is that she is head-over-ears in love with him.' A fellow socialist named Grace Black accused him in a letter of being too intellectual and not sufficiently interested in human nature; in his reply Shaw accused her of being in love with him, which she immediately acknowledged: 'I guessed you would think I was in love with you. So I am, but that has nothing to do with my letter. . . .' Even when Shaw was twenty-eight, one of his correspondents, Katie Samuel, was confessing that Shaw was 'affecting her peace of mind'; now there were any number of young ladies, whose names appear spasmodically in his correspondence and diaries: Grace Spooner, Bertha Newcombe, Grace Gilchrist; even Karl Marx's daughter Eleanor (who later committed suicide) seems to have been infatuated with Shaw at one stage.

And Shaw remained a philanderer; his feeling about it all is made quite clear in the play of that title. Perhaps because his mother remained basically the feminine archetype that appealed

D

to him, his attitude towards younger women remained unprotective and uninvolved. *The Philanderer* (1893) is one of his few wholly unsuccessful plays, and this is because it is so lacking in artistic detachment; it is a self-congratulatory piece of autobiography, with the hero, like Trefusis of *An Unsocial Socialist*, explaining periodically that women bore him, and then hurrying to another assignation. And it contains one scene that is directly auto-biographical: when Julia Craven bursts in on Charteris during a *tête à tête* with Grace Tranfield. Julia Craven was Mrs Patterson; Grace Tranfield, the actress Florence Farr; and the scene—which took place on 4th February 1893—was recorded in his diary: 'In the evening I went to see F E. [Florence Farr Emery]; and JP burst in on us very late in the evening. There was a most shocking scene; JP being violent and using atrocious language. At last I sent F E. out of the room, having to restrain JP by force from attacking her. . . . Did not get to bed until 4.' It was the end of his relation with Mrs. Patterson, after eight years of ups and downs.

In 1883, when he was reading Marx in the Museum reading room, Shaw made the acquaintance of a tall, restrained Scot of his own age, William Archer. Archer had been brought up in a gloomy sect called the Walkerites, and as soon as he learned to think for himself he became an atheist. In London he began to write for the secularist press, translated Ibsen, and eventually became the leading drama critic of the day. When editor of the *St James Gazette* rejected Shaw as a reviewer because of the death-bed scene in *An Unsocial Socialist*, Archer found Shaw work with the *Pall Mall Gazette* at two guineas a thousand words; in his twenty-ninth year, he made £117 os 3d by his pen. It was just as well that he began earning at last; his father died in the April of 1885. Shaw did not go to Dublin for the funeral; and the strange emotional detachment of the Shaws is revealed in the fact that even Lucy, who was in Dublin at the time, did not bother to attend the funeral.

Archer also obtained work for Shaw as music critic for *The Dramatic Review* and the *Magazine of Music*. In 1886 Archer was offered the job of art critic to *The World*, and Shaw persuaded him to accept the job, promising to go with him around the galleries and keep him awake. In due course Archer sent Shaw half his cheque for an article; Shaw returned it, pointing out: 'No man has a right of property in the ideas of which he is a mouthpiece. . . . If I am to be paid for what I suggested to you, the painters must clearly be paid for what they suggested to me.' Archer then persuaded the editor Edmund Yates to give Shaw the job as art critic, which was worth about £40 a year. Shaw was making money—at least enough to live on; but his name remained completely unknown to the general public. By the end of 1887, eleven years after his arrival in London, Shaw had seen three of his four novels appear serially; a fourth was yet to appear in *Our Corner*, and *Cashel Byron's Profession* had been issued in a small edition of 1,000 copies, printed from the plates of the magazine serial. All the same, his introduction to the serialised version of *Love Among the Artists* has the typical Shavian jauntiness:

'There is an end to all things, even to stocks of unpublished manuscript. It may be a relief to you to know that when this *Love Among the Artists* shall have run its course, you need apprehend no more furbished-up early attempts at fiction from me. I have written five novels in my life; and of these there will remain unpublished only the first—a very remarkable work, I assure you, but hardly one which I should be well advised in letting loose while my livelihood depends on my credit as a literary craftsman.'

It might be worth while at this point to give consideration to this trick of Shaw's—self-praise accompanied by the implication that he is only joking. 'With the single exception of myself, none of us can be described as perfect.' Or the opening of his article 'How Frank Ought to have Done It' (from *Sixteen Self Sketches*):

'Before attempting to add Bernard Shaw to my collection of Contemporary Portraits, I find it necessary to secure myself in advance by the fullest admission of his extraordinary virtues. Without any cavilling over trifles I declare at once that Shaw is the just man made perfect. I admit that in all his controversies, with me or anyone else, Shaw is, always has been, and always will be, right. I perceive that the common habit of abusing him is an ignorant and silly habit, and that the pretence of not taking him seriously is the ridiculous cover for an ignominious retreat from an encounter with him. If there is any other admission I can make, any other testimonial I can give, I am ready to give it and apologise for having omitted it. If it will help matters to say that Shaw is the greatest man that has ever lived, I shall not hesitate for a moment. All the cases against him break down when they are probed to the bottom. All his prophecies come true. All his fantastic creations come to life within a generation. I have an uneasy sense that even now I am not doing him justice. . . .'

Humour, yes; but to accept it simply as humour leaves something unsaid. The key sentence is: 'I perceive that the common habit of abusing him is an ignorant and silly habit, and that the pretence of not taking him seriously the cover for an ignominious retreat. . . .', etc. For this remained a lifelong problem of Shaw's. In the early Fabian days Edith Nesbit wrote in a letter: 'Everyone rather affects to despise him. "Oh, it's only Shaw" . . .' Wells always used this technique in arguments with Shaw, accusing him on one occasion of practising 'the woman's privilege of wanton incoherent assertion'. 'The torrent of fanciful misrepresentation and shrewd insinuation flows; one shrugs one's shoulders.' And Wells considered that he was being fair and perceptive when he wrote: 'You have every element of greatness except a certain independence of your own intellectual excitability'— i.e. except an ability to be intellectually responsible and self-critical.

Shaw's use of wit and mockery had this disadvantage: that anyone who disagreed with him could dismiss him as a trifler: 'Oh, it's only Shaw.' In argument he always remained detached and balanced. Chesterton once remarked: 'It's your intellectual magnanimity that destroys me. If only you were a nasty fellow who lost his temper.' But Chesterton was one of the few who never had recourse to this device of accusing Shaw of 'wanton incoherent assertion'. Wells or Belloc would imply that he never lost his temper because he was never sufficiently serious about anything to get angry.

The point to be grasped is that these humorous assertions of his greatness are Shaw's *substitute* for losing his temper, and in a sense they reveal a loss of temper. Nietzsche in his autobiography has chapters entitled 'Why I am so wise', 'Why I am so clever', 'Why I write such excellent books'. This is obviously not humour, but a sort of gesture of defiance, a counterbalance to his sense of being ignored and dismissed. And to a lesser extent Shaw had the same trouble. For a later edition of *The Intelligent Woman's Guide* Shaw wrote a four-page pamphlet called 'First Aid for Critics', which was pasted into the front of the book, and which revealed how far this refusal to take him seriously was getting on his nerves. 'The reviews mean little, because reviewers are not paid enough to read more than the chapter headings of a long book. . . . A reviewer has to think of his wife and family as well as of the author he reviews; and when I read criticisms clumsily refuting fallacies which my book refutes with sound science and some elegance, or patronisingly calling my attention to considerations which I have insisted on in chapter after chapter, I bear no malice, but, as an old hand, estimate the price of the review and the burdens of the reviewer, and, muttering "Two guineas: three children", or "Fifteen shillings: several children: husband an unappreciated artist". . . . I drop the press cutting into the waste paper basket.' By the time Shaw wrote this, the 'dismissal method' was being used against him with increasing frequency; Eliot, for example, calling him 'dramatically precocious and poetically less than immature'. At one time and another Shaw has probably provoked more ill-natured criticism than any other major writer. His debater's rule of never showing himself to be ruffled forbade him to lose his temper; instead, the irritating grin became broader, and the assertions of his genius more outrageous, with the consequence that Eric Bentley noted: 'There is one critic who has probably been more damaging than all the rest: Shaw himself.'

The real turning point in Shaw's career came when he was thirty-two, after he had been supporting himself as a journalist for four years. In 1888 *The Star* was founded by T. P. O'Connor (known as Tay Pay), whose mind, according to Shaw, 'never advanced

beyond the year 1865, although his Fenian sympathies and his
hearty detestation of the English nation disguised that defect
from him'. Tay Pay was induced to invite Shaw to join the
political staff of *The Star*, but when he read Shaw's first article
he told him that it would be 500 years before such radical stuff
could be acceptable as political journalism. Unwilling to sack a
fellow Irishman, he suggested that Shaw should write a column
on music, his only stipulation being: 'Write about anything but
Bach in B minor.' Typically, Shaw's opening review began:

'The number of empty seats at the performance of Bach's Mass
in B Minor at St James's Hall on Saturday did little credit to the
artistic culture of which the West End is supposed to be the
universal centre. . . .'

Shaw signed the reviews 'Corno di Bassetto', meaning a basset
horn; it appealed to his sense of humour to use a pen name that
people might mistake for an Italian title. It may seem strange that
a man so determined to advertise himself should use a pen name
at all, but this is to forget Shaw's basic shyness. He could write
jauntily about the merits of his novels in *Our Corner* because he
knew it was only being read by a handful of socialist comrades,
and he could lay down the law in *The Hornet* because it was being
published under Lee's name. In writing letters to newspapers he
seemed to take a pleasure in pseudonyms in these early days—on
one occasion 'G.B.S. Larking'—and a large amount of his early
journalistic work is anonymous. The mask seemed to give him a
feeling of freedom:

'On Monday the editor of *The Star* summoned me to a private
conference. "The fact is, my dear Corno," he said, throwing
himself back in his chair and arranging his moustache with the
diamond which sparkles at the end of his pen-handle, "I don't
believe that music in London is confined to St James's Hall,
Covent Garden and the Albert Hall. People must sing and
play elsewhere. . . ." '

This is a prelude to a description of a concert in his best vein
of fantasy:

'A little later the train was rushing through the strangest
places: Shoreditch, of which I had read in historical novels; Old
Ford, which I had supposed to be a character in one of Shakespeare's plays; Homerton, which is associated in my mind with

pigeons; and Haggerston, a name perfectly new to me. When I got into the concert-room I was perfectly dazzled by the appearance of the orchestra. Nearly all the desks for the second violins were occupied by ladies: beautiful young ladies. Personal beauty is not a strong point of West End orchestras, and I thought the change an immense improvement until the performance began, when the fair fiddlers rambled from bar to bar with a sweet indecision that had a charm of its own, but was not exactly what Purcell and Handel meant.' The description ends: 'I am, on the whole, surprised and delighted with the East End, and shall soon venture there without my revolver.'

The essence of this kind of easy improvisation is that it is related by the man the editor addresses as 'My dear Corno', not by the socialist George Bernard Shaw, who occasionally sends chairmen to sleep with the seriousness of his lectures. When, eventually, these two personalities fused, it was not always to the advantage of the serious half.

When he was thirty-two, the fusion was still some years away—about six, to be precise. 'G.B.S.' did not appear until the mid-1890s, when Shaw became a drama critic. As a music critic he is not at his best, for his sympathies are narrow. Quite simply, he was a Wagnerian, and saw everything from the point of view of his love of Wagner. Anything dramatic appealed to him: Handel, Beethoven, Berlioz, Mascagni, Bizet, Verdi. His fine essay on Beethoven (written for the *Radio Times* in 1927) begins: 'A hundred years ago a crusty old bachelor of fifty-seven, so deaf that he could not hear his own music played by a full orchestra, yet still able to hear thunder, shook his fist at the roaring heavens for the last time, and died as he had lived, challenging God and defying the universe.' And this is the kind of thing that interested Shaw in music. So it would be pointless to expect him to exercise 'negative capability' in judging non-dramatic composers: Schumann, Brahms, Mendelssohn, even Mozart. This means that there are some rather curious judgements. 'Die Zauberflöte [does] not belong to the group of works which constitute Mozart's consummate achievement—Don Juan, Le Nozze di Figaro. . . .' 'Schubert's symphonies seem mere debauches of exquisite musical thoughtlessness.' He prophesied that critics of the future will think of Wagner 'greater than Beethoven by as much as Mozart was greater than Haydn'. But it is Brahms who comes in for the hardest knocks. 'Brahms's music is at bottom only a prodigiously elaborated compound of incoherent reminiscences, and it is quite possible for a young lady with one of those wonderful "techniques" . . . to struggle with his music for an hour at a stretch without giving such an insight to her higher powers as [in] half a dozen bars of a sonata by Mozart.' Of the Clarinet Quintet, now generally regarded as perhaps Brahms's finest piece of chamber music: 'I shall not attempt to describe this latest exploit by the Leviathan Maunderer. It surpassed my utmost expectations . . . Brahms enormous gift of music is paralleled by nothing on earth but Mr Gladstone's power of words: it is a verbosity which outfaces its own commonplaceness by dint of sheer magnitude.' Brahms's *Requiem* comes in for some of the most violent attacks, of which this is a sample: 'What those qualities [of the Requiem] are could have been guessed by a deaf man from the mountainous tedium of the unfortunate audience, who yet listened with a perverse belief that Brahms is a great composer. . . .' It is 'an attempt to pass off the forms of music for music itself'. Dvorak, being a disciple of Brahms, comes in for the same sort of attack: 'Dvorak's Requiem bored Birmingham so desperately that it was unanimously voted a work of extraordinary depth and impressiveness.' His Dumky Trio is 'mere rhapsody, . . . pretty enough, but not getting much higher'. The Symphony in G (No. 8) is 'excellent promenade music', 'very nearly up to the level of a Rossini overture'. As can be seen from these extracts, Shaw cannot be excused on the grounds that he was attacking some of the bad works of these composers; he unerringly chose the best to dismiss as trivial or boring. 'Why [is] Mendelssohn's quartet in E flat major to be thrust into our ears at the point of the analytical programme as one of "the happiest productions of the composer's genius".' Mendelssohn was admittedly no great composer, but the E flat major quartet *is* one of his 'happiest productions', and Shaw only had to listen to it to find this out. But he was too concerned to attack the view that Mendelssohn was 'a master yielding to none in the highest qualifications that warrant the name'—a description he felt was deserved only by Wagner—to relax and listen.

His praise is as erratic and unexpected as the blame. A

symphony by Goetz—a rather fine minor composer who died young—has 'the charm of Schubert without his brainlessness, the refinement and inspirations of Mendelssohn without his limitation and timid gentility, Schumann's sense of harmonic expression without his laboriousness . . .', and it places Goetz 'securely above all other German composers of the last hundred years save only Mozart and Beethoven, Weber and Wagner'. The Good Friday Music—which even a devout Wagnerian would admit to falling below the Master's best work—is an experience whose 'enchantments . . . pass all sane word-painting'. He compares it to the Elysian Fields music of Gluck's *Orfeo*: 'Listening to the strains of the Elysian fields the other night, I could not help feeling that music had strayed far away from them, and only regained them the other day when Wagner wrote the Good Friday music in Parsifal. No musical experience between these two havens of rest seems better than either. The Zauberflöte and the Ninth Symphony have a discomforting consciousness of virtue, an uphill effort of aspiration, about them. . . .'

In a later note to *London Music*, added in 1936, Shaw admitted that 'the above hasty (not to say silly) description of Brahms's music will, I hope, be a warning to critics who know too much', and finishes: 'I apologise.' For anyone who loves music every other page of Shaw's music criticism requires a similar apology. He was a bad music critic because he was possessed by ideas that prevented him from listening to the music. On the other hand, he was now 'tuning the Shavian note to some sort of harmony', and learning to express himself on paper with the same authority and confidence as on the lecture platform:

'Something had better be done about this Royal Italian Opera. I have heard Gounod's Faust not less than ninety times within the last ten or fifteen years.' 'I may add, by the bye, that the opera I left for the Symphony was Don Giovanni, as conducted by Signor Randegger. My compliments to that gentleman, with my heartfelt assurance that a more scandalously slovenly, slapdash and unintelligent performance of the orchestral part of a great work was probably never heard in a leading . . . opera house.'

The aim was to establish a personality with his audience, a personality of authority. Shaw had certainly not seen ninety performances of *Faust* in fifteen years (to begin with, he was only seventeen fifteen years earlier). But it was not deliberate falsification either. He was not particularly serious about music criticism; but he was very serious about getting an audience to listen to him. And there was no reason why not. He had a great deal to say, and almost no one who was interested in hearing it. He was thirty-two when he began to write a regular music column; he was nearly forty when he gave it up for drama criticism; and he could still not be considered 'successful' in the sense of having reached the British public. If he was not allowed to write on matters that interested him—politics and social reform—at least he could make the best of music criticism by making it a platform for his own views, and for the presentation of the G.B.S. personality:

'I am, I suppose, in the west country, by which I mean generally any place for which you start from Paddington. To be precise, I am nowhere in particular, though there are certain ascertained localities within easy reach of me. For instance, if I were to lie down and let myself roll over the dip at the foot of the lawn, I should go down like an avalanche into the valley of the Wye. I could walk to Monmouth in half an hour or so. At the end of the avenue there is a paper nailed to a tree with a stencilled announcement that The Penalt Musical Society will give a concert last Friday week (I was at it, as shall presently appear); and it may be, therefore, that I am in the parish of Penalt, if there is such a place. . . .'

This was written when he was thirty-eight, after five years as a music critic. Apart from having developed this casual ease of manner, he had not developed as a critic. He still praised Wagner immoderately as the saviour of music and attacked Brahms as a fraud. He still lacked sympathy for English music—which in those days was represented chiefly by Parry, Stanford and Sir Arthur Sullivan—all far better composers than Shaw would allow. Elgar was luckily unknown at this time; he later became a friend of Shaw's, and Shaw paid lip service to his genius; but in the 1890s he would certainly have hated Elgar's melancholy and classicism as much as he hated Brahms's. What Shaw would have said about Delius, Warlock and Vaughan Williams if they had been composing in the nineties hardly bears thinking about. Luckily, he was about to give up music criticism in favour of his true profession—the drama.

Absurdly enough, the man who was responsible for turning Shaw into a drama critic and playwright denied to the end of his days that Shaw had any dramatic talent. When Shaw met him in 1883, William Archer had already written a study of Henry Irving, and had read the plays of Ibsen in Norwegian as they appeared. (As a child, Archer had often visited an uncle who lived in Norway.) When he came to London—the year after Shaw—Archer brought with him a translation of Ibsen's *Pillars of Society*, which failed to arouse the enthusiasm of any of the publishers who read it. By 1883, when Shaw met Archer, Ibsen had written the major dramas of his middle period—*A Doll's House*, *Ghosts* and *An Enemy of the People*, and Archer read them as soon as they were published. Shaw might have come across Ibsen elsewhere even if he had never met Archer, for Ibsen's real 'discoverer', as far as England was concerned, was Edmund Gosse; but through his meeting with Archer, Shaw came into intimate contact with Ibsen's work and ideas at a time when it was almost unknown in England. ('Henry Gibson,' enquired one editor, 'Who's he?') Archer himself, meeting Ibsen in 1887, was struck by the similarity between the personalities of Ibsen and Shaw—he described Ibsen as 'a paradoxist . . . who goes about picking holes in every "well known fact"'.

Oddly enough, Shaw went out of his way to deny Ibsen's crucial influence on his work, declaring that he had written his first play in 1885 'before I knew of Ibsen's existence'. This simply cannot be true, since his first play, *Widowers' Houses*, was started as a collaboration with Archer, whom he had known for two years. It is not necessary to take the extreme view of H. G. Farmer, Lucy Shaw's biographer, that Shaw was completely without conscience when it was a question of creating the 'Shaw legend'. In the year Ibsen wrote *A Doll's House*, Shaw was writing *The Irrational Knot* which has basically the same theme. There was no influence, as far as *ideas* were concerned; Shaw was already a revolutionary. But the facts speak for themselves. Archer was trying to sell his translation of *Pillars of Society* when he met Shaw, and it had received a matinée performance as far back as 1880, three years before Shaw met Archer. It is inconceivable that Shaw did not read it soon after their meeting, for they immediately became close friends. *Pillars of Society* is a bitter denunciation of the bourgeoisie that might have been written as a Marxian tract. For a man who had just discovered Karl Marx, and who had spent five years of his life writing unwieldy novels, the economy and force of Ibsen's dramatic method *must* have been a revelation, for there was nothing like it in England. Shaw's first play is another Marxian tract on slum landlordism. Understandably, Shaw had no desire to be 'typed' as an Ibsen disciple, and made light of Ibsen's influence. It was true; he was not an Ibsen disciple. But it was Ibsen who turned him into a dramatist instead of a novelist, and his refusal to acknowledge the debt lends colour to H. G. Farmer's accusations.

Ibsen was—naturally—much in vogue among the Fabians; Eleanor Marx-Aveling translated *The Lady from the Sea*. And in 1890 Shaw delivered a course of lectures on Ibsen to the Fabian summer school, which was duly published in 1891 as *The Quintessence of Ibsenism* by Walter Scott, who had already issued the *Fabian Essays in Socialism* the year before. It is one of Shaw's best books. This must be immediately qualified by saying that it is a completely misleading account of Ibsen. It fails as criticism for the same reason the music reviews fail: Shaw is too concerned to express his own ideas to care about expressing other people's. Ibsen's art is closely akin to music—to romantic music, with its mixture of poetry and melancholy. This was understood by another great romantic, Thomas Mann, when he compared Ibsen to Wagner: 'How much they are alike in their tremendous self-sufficiency, in the three-dimensional rotundity and consummateness of the life-work of both; social revolutionary in youth, in age paling into the ritual and mythical. *When We Dead Awaken*, the awesome whispered confession of the production-man bemoaning his late, too late declaration of love of life—and *Parsifal*, that oratorio of redemption: how prone I am to think of the two together, to feel them as one, these two farewell mystery plays, last words before the eternal silence.'* This catches the essence of Ibsen's work with complete accuracy; it is something you would not even guess from reading Shaw on Ibsen. He concludes his account of *When We Dead Awaken*: 'And that is the end . . . of the plays of Henrik Ibsen. The end, too, let us hope, of the idols, domestic, religious and political, in whose

* Sufferings and Greatness of Richard Wagner, *Essays of Three Decades*.

name we have been twaddled into misery and confusion and hypocrisy unspeakable.' According to Shaw, Ibsen's purpose was simply to attack bourgeois idealism and bourgeois hypocrisy, and all the plays are made to fit this bed of Procrustes; in the case of some of the poetic dramas—*Brand*, *Peer Gynt* and *Emperor and Galilean*—it actually inverts Ibsen's meaning: *Brand* is made into an attack on the 'idealism' of a religious crank when it is actually a poem that glorifies heroic individualism and 'out-siderism'.

Shaw supports his own interpretation by placing the emphasis on such plays as *Ghosts* and *An Enemy of the People*—the latter being an Arthur Miller-ish play about a lonely individualist persecuted by a corrupt society. But Ibsen was not an objective social critic; his work is as basically personal as Strindberg's; he saw himself as the lonely individual persecuted by society, as he later saw himself—in *When We Dead Awaken*—as the sculptor who has wasted his life on art instead of living it. He was a poet, and his plays are fragments of autobiography. Shaw, on the other hand, had just survived a long and painful 'awkward age', and had found a measure of freedom and strength in devoting himself to a cause outside himself; he had had enough of contemplating his own personality, and was busy trying to create a new one. He was a sincere socialist; but socialism was also a way of impos-ing his talent on his age. Contemporaries with less talent were already famous,* while he was still a journalist. It was a time for establishing himself as a social reformer and a revolutionary thinker; he was being determinedly objective, and he preferred to interpret Ibsen and Wagner as being equally objective. And so in *The Quintessence of Ibsenism* and *The Perfect Wagnerite*, the two greatest romantics of the late nineteenth century are cast in the role of social reformers preaching the doctrines of Karl Marx. Both are interesting books, but neither can be recommended as an introduction to Wagner or Ibsen.

---

* Rider Haggard—who was exactly the same age as Shaw—was the literary sensation of the mid-eighties, with *King Solomon's Mines* and *She*. Kipling achieved fame in the late eighties with *Plain Tales from the Hills* and *Soldiers Three*. Conan Doyle became a celebrity in 1891 with *The Adventures of Sherlock Holmes*.

In 1895, in his fortieth year, Shaw became drama critic for the *Saturday Review*, edited by Frank Harris, for which he received £6 a week, and during the next three and a half years he gradually became known as the best drama critic in London. But by this time he was already an experienced dramatist.

In 1884 Archer had suggested to Shaw that they collaborate on a play to be called *Rhinegold*, 'I learned from himself', wrote Archer, 'that he was the author of several unpublished master-pieces of fiction. Construction, he owned with engaging modesty, was not his strong point, but his dialogue was incomparable. . . . With a modesty in no way inferior to Mr Shaw's, I had realised I could not write dialogue a bit; but I still considered myself a born constructor. So I proposed . . . a collaboration.' Even in Archer's version the play was to be about a slum landlord and his daughter; the hero would fall in love with the daughter, and end by throwing her father's tainted treasure into the Rhine, metaphorically speaking. Shaw finally read Archer the first two acts of the play in October 1887—not in 1885, as Shaw later declared. In fact, the collaboration stood no chance of success, because Archer's attitude to women was chivalrous and romantic, while Shaw's was perverse and realistic. As we have already seen, Shaw was only capable of creating two types of woman. Blanche Sartorius in *Rhinegold* was a combination of these two: a liar, a flirt and a bully. Archer was revolted by her, and Shaw dropped the two acts into a drawer. In 1891 a Dutchman called J. T. Grein started the Independent Theatre, and launched it with Ibsen's *Ghosts*, which brought violent denunciations from everyone. Grein followed up the sensation with productions of Browning, Strindberg (*The Father*) and Zola. But apart from Browning there seemed to be no English playwrights producing intellectual drama. Grein applied to Shaw, who took his *Rhinegold* out of a drawer, completed it, and called it *Widowers' Houses*. The first two acts had followed Archer's plot faithfully. A young doctor with aristocratic connections falls in love with a girl he meets on a Rhine steamer, and in the first act he proposes and is accepted. In the second act he calls on her in London, and discovers that her father, a self-made man, is actually a slum landlord. He and the girl quarrel and he goes off. Clearly the possibilities for a third act were limited; the lovers had to come together again, and

Shaw simply had to devise a reason. He did this; Grein accepted
the play, and it received a single performance on December 9th,
1892, with Florence Farr playing Blanche. It could not be described as a success. Half the audience booed; the other half—the
socialists—applauded. The reviews were mostly bad, and the
play was published the following year in the Independent Theatre
Series with a preface by Shaw. This was hardly a success, but it
helped to increase Shaw's reputation, which was at last beginning
to snowball.

From the description of the plot, it might be inferred that
Widowers' Houses is simply a workmanlike problem-play. But the
reader who turns to it after reading the novels is in for a shock.
It fully justifies Eric Bentley's assertion that Shaw was primarily
an artist. As soon as he begins to create dramatic dialogue, he is
able to command a kind of magic. Whatever his faults as a novelist
and critic, his plays have a curious inner perfection of form that
approaches music. The propagandist of the *Fabian Essays* and
The Quintessence of Ibsenism disappears; another Shaw takes over,
the Shaw of the pre-Socialist days who served his apprenticeship
writing novels. This Shaw is not an exhibitionist or a controver-
sialist. He is a psychologist who has something in common with
D. H. Lawrence: that is to say, he is intensely aware of the fine
threads of response that stretch between human beings. When
Trench asks Sartorius for his daughter's hand, the stage instructions read: SARTORIUS: (*condescending to Trench's humility from the
mere instinct to seize an advantage, and yet deferring to Lady Roxdale's
relative*). This is not put in to help the actors; no actor could
convey it to an audience. It is put in because when Shaw wrote it,
he was actually present at the discussion between Trench and
Sartorius, and was aware of all the fluctuations of their feelings
towards one another. It is this ability to enter completely into a
situation, to *be* each of the characters in turn, that makes Shaw a
great dramatist. An ordinarily competent dramatist tries to imagine what his characters would say in a given situation. A major
dramatist enters into the situation and *becomes* the characters,
with the consequence that the dialogue has continual flashes of
authenticity which produce the 'shock of recognition'. Shakespeare possesses this power, as Shaw pointed out in an early
review of *Richard III*. Shaw retained it until the last two decades

of his life (and even then, it reappeared in flashes). His plays actually gain by being read rather than seen on the stage because the situations are so vividly created that they only lose subtlety when they are created by actors and actresses. As soon as he begins to create a situation, Shaw is a Pied Piper who draws the reader after him.

When we compare *Widowers' Houses* with any of the novels, one thing stands out: the tightness and economy of the structure. This is nothing to do with the shortness of a play compared to a novel: it is simply that Shaw moves with perfect ease and precision in the drama. He once claimed that he had no idea of how a play would develop when he began to write it. But the impressive thing about his best plays is the feeling of complete inevitability about the development. (I have noticed this when teaching the plays to American students; I would try to give a short sample of the dialogue and the salient points in the development of each play. But plunging into the middle of an act, it was difficult to find a place to start—because each sentence developed so naturally from the previous one—and just as difficult to find a place to stop; there was a close-knit texture that made selection difficult.)

Within the first ten minutes of *Widowers' Houses* one encounters the basic dramatic trick that was to serve Shaw all his life. It might be described as the 'clash of egos', but it would be even more appropriate to describe it as the 'clash of egoists'. He creates tension by introducing two strong—or at least self-opinionated —characters, and then bringing them into conflict. Most dramatists have recourse to this device at some time. But take any play by Ibsen or Chehov or Strindberg—or even Shakespeare—at random, and the chances are that it opens with people whose characters make no immediate impact—Nora decorating the Christmas tree for Helmer, Theseus and Hippolyta discussing their marriage, a valet and a cook talking about Miss Julie. Shaw likes to open with a flourish: 'No eggs! No eggs! Thousand thunders, man, what do you mean by no eggs?' The opening of *St Joan* is one of the most familiar examples of this method—with the establishing of Baudricourt's character as a noisy bully, and then the immediate clash with Joan—but the same formula appears in play after play. It would be a pardonable exaggeration to say that Shaw's plays are a dramatisation of Nietzsche's Will to Power. This would be to misplace the emphasis. Shaw's plays are not basically about the struggle for power or the clash of wills; it is only a device he uses to keep the audience interested. It was a trick he had picked up as a novelist—his first use of it being in the scene between Conolly and Marion's father in *The Irrational Knot*.

And now, in the opening scene of *Widowers' Houses*, he employs it with a sureness of touch that goes beyond anything in the novels. In the short conversation between Trench and Cokane, Cokane is established as a snobbish and self-assertive busybody. Sartorius comes on with his daughter, and proceeds to bully the waiter and snub Cokane—who offers him their table. Then Cokane asks Trench—loud enough to be overheard: 'By the way, Harry, I have often meant to ask you: is Lady Roxdale your mother's sister or your father's?' and Sartorius pricks up his ears. A few moments later, Sartorius and Cokane have introduced themselves, and Trench and Blanche Sartorius try to conceal the fact that they already know one another. It has all taken less than ten minutes.

The scene that follows—in which Trench proposes to Blanche —embodies that Shavian idea that woman is always the pursuer. Trench is nervous and obviously cannot bring himself to say the words.

TRENCH (*stammering*) I only thought—(*He stops and looks at her piteously. She hesitates a moment, and then puts her hand into his with calculated impulsiveness. He snatches her into his arms with a cry of relief*) Dear Blanche! I thought I never should have said it. I believe I should have stood stuttering here all day if you hadn't helped me out with it.

BLANCHE (*Indignantly trying to break loose from him*) I didn't help you out with it.

This is the kind of scene that made Stevenson protest to Archer: 'My God, what women!' But it is very plain that this kind of woman makes better dramatic material than the 'sentimental heroine' that Archer sketched in his outline of *Rhinegold*. The sentimental heroine may be ideal for the novel, but on stage, she seems colourless. Thea Elvsted is the real heroine of *Hedda Gabler*, but she is a nonentity beside Hedda. Portia is more memorable than Ophelia or Desdemona; Shaw's preference for self-assertive women weakened the novels, but it strengthens the plays. The scene in which Blanche beats her maid drew protesting cries from the critics, but there can be no doubt about the dramatic impact of the scene in which it occurs.

It is in the third act that it suddenly becomes clear how far Shaw has progressed since the days of *An Unsocial Socialist* and the *Unfinished Novel*. In *An Unsocial Socialist* the Marxian speeches were of doubtful relevance; in *Widowers' Houses* they are inseparable from the drama; they *are* the drama. Lickcheese, a rent-collector whom Sartorius had dismissed in the previous act for being too lenient with his slum tenants, now returns as a prosperous slum landlord, to warn Sartorius that the London County Council intend to build a new street across his property; if he puts it into good repair, he can get larger compensation. Trench, Blanche's ex-suitor—who has broken with her on account of her father's 'tainted wealth'—has to be called into the conference as the mortgagee of the property. He puts the matter pungently:

'Well, it appears that the dirtier a place is, the more rent you get, and the decenter it is, the more compensation you get. So we're to give up dirt and go in for decency.'

Lickcheese does not disagree; he dots the i's and crosses the t's.

'You see, it's like this, Dr Trench. There's no doubt that the Vestries has legal power to play old Harry with slum properties, and spoil the houseknacking game if they please. That didn't matter in the good old times, because the Vestries used to be ourselves. Nobody ever knew a word about the election; and we used to get ten of us into a room and elect one another, and do what we liked. But that cock won't fight any longer; and to put it short, the game is up for men in the position of you and Mr Sartorius. My advice to you is, take the present chance of getting out of it. Spend a little money on the block at the Cribbs Market end: enough to make it look like a model dwelling, you know: and let the other block to me on fair terms for a depot for the North Thames Iced Mutton Company. Theyll be knocked down inside of two year to make room for the new north and south main thoroughfare; and you'll be compensated to the tune of double the present valuation, with the cost of improvements thrown in. Leave things as they are, and you stand a good chance of being fined, or condemned, or pulled down before long. Now's your time.'

This is good Fabianism; it is also good drama. In the *Back to Methuselah* preface, Shaw once again left the road wide open for detractors when he wrote: 'In my own activities as a playwright . . . I tried slum-landlordism, doctrinaire Free Love (pseudo-Ibsenism), prostitution, militarism, marriage, history, current politics, natural Christianity, national and individual character, paradoxes of conventional society, husband-hunting, questions of conscience, professional delusions and impostures, all worked into a series of comedies of manners in the classic fashion.' This is again an instance of Shaw being his own most hostile critic. In the book already referred to, Raymond Williams explains that Shaw is not a true artist because his method amounts to 'the injection of seriousness in [to] the drama'; and then, referring to the statement quoted above, says 'there are few serious works of literature that are so lacking in complexity that they can be labelled in this way'. Mr Williams is naive. The most perfunctory reading of *Widowers' Houses* shows that it is not a conventional play 'injected' with a theme about slum-landlordism. The implication of Raymond Williams's remarks—and here he typifies the majority of critics hostile to Shaw—is that Shaw sat down one day and said: 'What shall I write about—ah yes, I'll dramatise a Fabian tract,' and the time after that: 'Let's try doctrinaire Free Love (pseudo-Ibsenism) this time.' That the labels were added *after* the plays were written becomes clear when one tries to identify the plays in Shaw's list of subjects. Prostitution is obviously *Mrs Warren's Profession*; militarism refers to *Arms and the Man*. Husband-hunting may be identified, with some hesitation, as *Man and Superman*. But what does 'current politics' refer to? Shaw wrote no such play before *Back to Methuselah*. Or 'paradoxes of conventional society'? As to *John Bull's Other Island*, it might conceivably be described as a play about personal and national character, but a dozen other descriptions would be just as appropriate. The labels—which Shaw invented for the *Methuselah* preface—do not fit the plays. And they do not fit because the plays are too complex to be labelled in this way. To call *Caesar and Cleopatra* a play 'about' history is as inappropriate as calling *Hamlet* a play about spiritualism.

A final point to note about *Widowers' Houses*: for all its social preoccupations, it is no more realistic than a Dickens novel. This is not simply because of the Dickens influence in Sartorius and Lickcheese; it applies to all Shaw's plays. This point should be so obvious as to be hardly worth mentioning; but for some reason, it is not. Fifty years ago it led critics to accuse Shaw of being unable to create real people, of making all his characters mouthpieces for his own ideas. This is clearly untrue; to begin with, only a small percentage of Shaw's characters express ideas; and of these, a great many express ideas that are certainly not Shaw's—the Inquisitor in *St Joan* or the Devil in *Man and Superman*, for example. What the criticism really meant was that Shaw characters *are* 'characters', as distinct from real people as Dickens characters or Gogol characters. In this, his aims as a dramatist are completely different from those of Ibsen or Chehov. A character in Shaw does not behave 'realistically', but he usually behaves convincingly, because the creative vitality of the play keeps it all on the same level. Take the reconciliation scene from the end of *Widowers' Houses*:

'*Trench, left alone, looks round carefully and listens a moment . . . Then he goes on tiptoe to the piano and leans upon it with folded arms, gazing at Blanche's portrait. Blanche herself appears presently at the study door. When she sees how he is occupied, she closes it softly and steals over to him, watching him intently. He rises from his leaning attitude and takes the portrait from the easel, and is about to kiss it when, taking a second look round to reassure himself that nobody is watching him, he finds Blanche close upon him. He drops the portrait and stares at her without the least presence of mind.* BLANCHE (*Shrewishly*). Well? So you have come back here? You have had the meanness to come into this house again? (*He flushes and retreats a step. She follows him up remorselessly*). What a poor spirited creature you must be! Why don't you go? (*Red and wincing, he starts huffily to get his hat from the table; but when he turns to the door with it she deliberately stands in his way; so that he has to stop*). I dont want you to stay. (*For a moment they stand face to face, quite close to one another, she provocative, taunting, half-defying, half-inviting him to advance, in a flush of undisguised animal excitement. It suddenly flashes on him that all this ferocity is erotic: that she is making love to him. His eye lights up: a cunning expression comes into the corners of his mouth: with a heavy assumption of indifference he walks straight back to his chair and plants himself in it with his arms folded. She comes down the room after him).* But I forgot: you have found that there is some money to be made here. Lickcheese told you. You, who were so disinterested, so independent, that you could not accept anything from my father. *(At the end of every sentence she waits to see what execution she has done).* I suppose you will try to persuade me that you have come down here on a great philanthropic enterprise—to befriend the poor by having those houses rebuilt, eh? *(Trench maintains his attitude and makes no sign).* Yes: when my father makes you do it. And when Lickcheese has discovered some way of making it profitable. Oh, I know papa; and I know you. And for the sake of that, you come back here—into the house where you were refused—ordered out. *(Trench's face darkens: her eyes gleam as she sees it).* Aha! you remember that. You know it's true: you cant deny it. *(She sits down and softens her tone a little as she affects to pity him).* Well, let me tell you that you cut a poor figure, a very poor figure, Harry. *(At the word Harry he relaxes the fold of his arms; and a faint grin of anticipated victory appears on his face).* And you, too, a gentleman! so highly connected! with such distinguished relations! so particular as to where your money comes from! I wonder at you. I really wonder at you. I should have thought that if your fine family gave you nothing else, it might at least have given you some sense of personal dignity. Perhaps you think you look dignified at present, eh? *(No reply).* Well, I can assure you that you dont: you look most ridiculous—as foolish as a man could look—you dont know what to say; and you dont know what to do. But after all, I dont see what anyone could say in defense of such conduct. *(He looks straight in front of him, and purses up his lips as if whistling. This annoys her; and she becomes affectedly polite).* I am afraid I am in your way, Dr Trench. *(She rises).* I shall not intrude on you any longer. You seem so perfectly at home that I need make no apology for leaving you to yourself. *(She makes a feint of going to the door; but he does not budge; and she returns and comes behind his chair).* Harry. *(He does not turn. She comes a step nearer).* Harry: I want you to answer me a question. *(Earnestly, stooping over him).* Look me in the face. *(No reply).* Do you hear? (*Seizing his cheeks and twisting his head round*). Look—me in—the—face. (*He shuts his eyes tight and grins. She suddenly kneels down beside him with her breast against his shoulder*). Harry: what were you doing with my photograph just now, when you thought you were alone? (*He opens his eyes: they are full of delight. She flings her arms round him, and crushes him in an ecstatic embrace as she adds, with furious tenderness*). How dare you touch anything belonging to me?

(*The study door opens and voices are heard*). TRENCH: I hear someone coming.

(*She regains her chair with a bound and pushes it back as far as possible. Cokane, Lickcheese and Sartorius come back from the study. . . .*)'

No man would behave like that, and it is doubtful whether a woman would. But Shaw men and women behave like it, and it convinces.

One has also to take into account that Shaw knows perfectly well this is not a happy ending. Trench has landed himself with a virago, and in a few years' time, when the physical attraction has subsided, she will be telling him he cuts a poor figure and meaning it. The whole scene is written with malice intent; it is the final twist of the screw in this drama of social corruption. Shaw is mocking the audience that likes happy endings. G. K. Chesterton caught the point in his book on Shaw:

'I hear many people complain that Bernard Shaw mystifies them. I cannot imagine what they mean; it seems to me that he deliberately insults them. His language, especially on moral questions, is generally as straight and solid as that of a bargee and far less ornate and symbolic than that of a hansom-cabman. The prosperous English Philistine complains that Mr Shaw is making a fool of him. Whereas Mr Shaw is not in the least making a fool of him, Mr Shaw is, with laborious lucidity, calling him a fool. G.B.S. calls a landlord a thief; and the landlord, instead of denying or resenting it, says "Ah, that fellow hides his meaning so cleverly that one can never make out what he means. . . .".'

All of which should underline my point that the only thing Shaw 'injected' into the drama was a seriousness that it had not had before, and that it has not had since.

5 PUBLIC SHAW

On November 13th, 1887 columns of working men decided to march on Trafalgar Square to vindicate their right of public meeting. Morris marched at the head of one column, with Shaw and Annie Besant somewhere farther back. R. B. Cunningham Graham, the travel writer, headed another with the labour leader John Burns. Before Shaw's column reached the square they were dispersed by police with batons. Graham was so badly beaten up by the police that he spent his six weeks in jail in the prison hospital. Three men were killed that day, and many men and women badly injured. Police brutality was extreme; Graham records that he saw policemen beating children as well as women. One woman asked a police sergeant if he had seen her child; he called her a 'damned whore' and knocked her down. Windows and roof-tops were crowded with well-dressed men and women who cheered every time the police knocked someone down. Sentences passed on those who were arrested were savage.

Shaw was asked by a workman: 'What shall we do? Give us a lead.' Shaw said: 'Nothing. Let every man get to the square as best he can.' Later, when someone asked Cunningham Graham, 'Who is Bernard Shaw', he replied gravely: 'He was the first man to run away from the square on Bloody Sunday.' But what Shaw actually displayed throughout that crisis was not cowardice but realism. Public opinion was revolted by the police brutality. A few days later Annie Besant addressed an enthusiastic meeting and advised a return to the square the following Sunday and a more determined resistance to the police and troops. It was left to Shaw and a fellow Fabian, G. W. Foote, to cool down the enthusiasm by pointing out that sticks and stones were of no use against a modern machine gun.

Shaw was thirty-one at the time, and his part in Bloody Sunday was somehow typical of this new decade of his life. The ten years between his twentieth and thirtieth birthdays had been a period of inner-development, of self-discovery through writing. Now it was the time for the creation of a public *persona*. He had come a long way from his self-portrait as 'the hermit of Islington' in *Immaturity*. For what he was now going in for was political plotting with the intention of gaining real political power, or at least, influence. Instead of trying to organise the workers, like Hyndman, or teaching them to make tables, like Morris, the Fabians devised a process of infiltration. Fabians were urged to join the liberal or radical associations in their districts—or, if necessary, the conservative associations: anything to get on to committees and gain voting power. They were urged to try to get themselves sent as delegates to the central liberal and radical unions—the Metropolitan Radical Federation, for example. 'On these bodies we made speeches and moved resolutions, or better still got the Parliamentary candidate for the constituency to move them, and secured reports and encouraging little articles for him in the *Star*. We permeated the party organisations and pulled all the wires we could lay our hands on with our utmost adroitness and energy; and we succeeded so far that in 1889 we gained the solid advantage of a progressive majority, full of ideas that would never have come into their heads had not the Fabians put them there.'*

In 1890 an event of enormous importance for the British Socialist movement had occurred. A well-brought-up young lady with intellectual inclinations noted in her diary: 'Sidney Webb, the socialist, dined here. . . . A remarkable little man with a huge head and tiny body, a breadth of forehead quite sufficient to account for the encyclopedic character of his knowledge. A Jewish nose, prominent eyes and mouth, black hair, somewhat unkempt, spectacles and a most bourgeois black coat shiny with use. But I like the man. There is a directness of speech, an open-mindedness, an imaginative warm-heartedness which will carry

* Shaw quoted by Beatrice Webb, *My Apprenticeship*, p. 451.

him far.' Her name was Beatrice Potter, and two years later she and Webb were married. She treated Webb as a kind of husband-baby, and tolerated his philandering friend Shaw solely because Shaw so obviously admired Webb. Beatrice wrote in her diary: 'We are both of us second-rate minds, but we are curiously combined.' Her tolerance of Shaw may also have been due to an instinctive recognition that he was the only one of the Fabians who was a first-rate mind.

The Webbs had just enough money between them to be genteelly independent; Sidney left his job in the Colonial Office, and they set up house at 41 Grosvenor Road, and started a *salon* in the French style, at which Members of Parliament could meet leading Radicals, and unknown young writers could talk to the wives of dull rich men. (One of these writers was H. G. Wells who later drew a scathing portrait of the Webb ménage in *The New Machiavelli*; but back in 1892 Wells was still an unknown young schoolteacher suffering from tuberculosis.) When Sidney Olivier—also in the Colonial Office—was appointed Governor of Jamaica, Beatrice took his place as one of the four leading Fabians (the other being Graham Wallas). It is somehow typical of the Fabians that one of them should become Governor of Jamaica. As to Webb himself, he differed completely from that other radical of genius, Karl Marx, in being completely unquarrelsome; he always preferred to gain a point by diplomacy and Machiavellianism. Bertrand Russell—who met Shaw and Webb in 1896—records: 'Sidney had no hesitation in using wiles which some would think unscrupulous. He told me, for example, that when he wished to carry some point through a committee where the majority thought otherwise, he would draw up a resolution in which the contentious point occurred twice. He would have a long debate about its first occurrence and at last give way graciously. Nine times out of ten, so he concluded, no one would notice that the same point occurred later in the same resolution.'*

It was working with people like Webb—second-rate minds, but determined to get things done—that developed Shaw's indispensable practical side, and overcame the shyness that was still a basic constituent of his nature. (Russell observed of Shaw:

* *Portraits from Memory*, p. 102.

'Even at this time (1896) he was still shy. Indeed, I think that his wit, like that of many famous humourists, was developed as a defense against expected hostile ridicule.') Shaw and Webb were allies, fellow-conspirators who treated politics as a game. In 1891 they pulled off the *tour de force* of foisting a 'progressive' programme on the Liberal Party and getting it endorsed (reluctantly) by Gladstone; they did this by drawing up a huge sheaf of resolutions for the 1891 election programme, which Shaw read through at a public meeting, deliberately skipping most of them. A Liberal M.P., Mr Beale, dutifully seconded. Then Shaw passed on to *The Star* the text of a brilliant speech which Mr Beale was supposed to have made. The next morning the National Liberal Club was enraged to discover that Mr Beale had foisted a socialist programme on them. Beale, faced with the prospect of explaining that he had been a pawn of the Fabians, preferred to stick by his guns and announce that the Liberals had to move with the times. And Shaw and Webb chortled and slapped one another on the back. To the end of his life Shaw admired politicians who knew what they wanted and were prepared to brush aside democratic procedures to get it. This attitude was based upon a certain cynicism about the actual working of democracy. Boanerges, the Labour leader, explains it to King Magnus in *The Apple Cart*: 'I talk democracy to these men and women. I tell them that they have the vote, and that theirs is the kingdom and the power and the glory. I say to them, "You are supreme: exercise your power." They say, "That's right: tell us what to do"; and I tell them. I say, "Exercise your vote intelligently by voting for me." And they do. That's democracy, and a splendid thing it is too for putting the right men in the right place.' And Magnus says admiringly: 'Magnificent! I have never heard it better described.'

This practical phase of Shaw's life came to a climax in 1897 when he was elected to the St Pancras Vestry, and proved so efficient that he was placed on half a dozen committees, including electricity and housing, and occasionally had to attend to disagreeable tasks such as examining tuberculous cattle. He thoroughly enjoyed this drudgery and spent six years at it, until he was voted off the County Council in 1903.

Meanwhile, Shaw developed that trouble-making trait of his

character which is already present in that early letter that begins: 'I told (Lucy) all! All! ALL!' His shyness caused him to feel something like a horror of conventional tact and good manners. He writes in a letter to Archer in April 1890:

'I was prevented from coming to tea by the plight of my drunkard [Pakenham Beatty, who was just recovering from delirium tremens], who, still in a state of horror, was surrounded by his whispering relatives, who were assembled as if for a funeral. I dispersed them with roars of laughter and inquiries after pink snakes etc, an exhibition of bad taste which at last converted the poor devil's wandering apprehensive look into a settled grin.'

Shaw's response to 'difficult' situations was the healthy one of dispersing them by making them more difficult. Russell remarked that some German delegates to the International Socialist Congress of 1896 'regarded Shaw as an incarnation of Satan, because he could not resist the pleasure of fanning the flames whenever there was a dispute'. Pearson wrote of the early Fabians that 'it took them some time to get used to Shaw, whose method of settling any friction that arose was to betray the confidences of all the parties to it openly in a wildly exaggerated form, the effect of which was that the grievance was forgotten in the general reprobation and denial of Shaw's revelations'. Shy or not, Shaw had his own methods of getting himself noticed and remembered. And this method—of carefully calculated tactlessness—was also applied to his criticism in the fields of music and drama. When Henry Irving—then plain Mr Irving—lectured at the Royal Institution and pleaded for acting to be classified as a fine art, Shaw dotted the i's and crossed the t's by heading his review: 'Why not Sir Henry Irving?' pointing out that what Irving was really saying was that if writers and musicians can be given knighthoods, why shouldn't actors? For Shaw, the situation was only made more amusing by the fact that he was hoping that Irving would produce his play *The Man of Destiny*. (Inevitably, Irving didn't.)

To outsiders, then, it must have seemed quite clear that Shaw was interested chiefly in self-advertisement. He admitted as much in his music criticisms: 'I yield to no man in the ingenuity and persistence with which I seize every opportunity of puffing myself and my affairs. . . . Any sort of notoriety will serve my turn equally.' 'It has taken me twenty years of studied self-restraint aided by the natural decay of my faculties, to make myself dull enough to be accepted as a serious person by the British public; and I am not sure that I am not still regarded as a suspicious character in some quarters.' He seemed to make fun of his interest in notoriety; but the interest was unmistakably there. He was clearly determined to be a public figure; and when, thirty years later, he signed a book to T. E. Lawrence 'To Private Shaw from Public Shaw', it must have seemed to many of his old friends that he had been all too disastrously successful.

This is, of course, the central question of Shaw's career, the heart of the 'case against Shaw'. It is certainly true that Shaw went on 'puffing himself and his affairs' until it became a tiresome mannerism. In *Brave New World* Huxley's Director of Hatcheries speaks of the discovery of sleep-teaching due to a lecture by 'that curious old writer George Bernard Shaw, who was speaking, according to a well-authenticated tradition, about his own genius'. This was published in 1932, and Shaw had been lecturing about his own genius for about forty years by that time.

But it would be a mistake to give too much weight to this kind of criticism; to do so would be to miss the most important point about Shaw: that the mannerisms covered a romantic idealism as fanatical as Shelley's. This is also the key to Shaw's admiration of Morris: that Morris saw no reason why society should not be run by poets instead of businessmen and professional politicians. Shaw understood the complexity of the problem better than Morris, and he defined it in his analysis of Wagner's *Ring* in 1898. Alberic the Dwarf represents the men who care only for money and power. 'If there were no higher power in the world to work against Alberic, the end of it would be utter destruction. Such a force there is, however, and it is called Godhead. The mysterious thing we call life organises itself into all living shapes . . . rising to the human marvel in cunning dwarfs and in laborious muscular giants. . . . And these higher powers are called into existence by the same self-organisation of life still more wonderfully into rare persons who may by comparison be called gods, creatures capable of thought, *whose aims extend far beyond the satisfaction of their bodily appetites and personal affections*, since they perceive that it is only by the establishment of a social order founded on common

bonds of moral faith that the world can rise from mere savagery':
[my italics]. In the *Ring*, according to Shaw, Wotan is the symbol
of Godhead, of the 'poet, with his vision of what life might be'.
And his problem is how to set up Godhead in a world of stupid
giants and grasping dwarfs. 'Godhead, face to face with Stupidity,
must compromise. Unable to enforce on the world the pure law
of thought, it must resort to a mechanical law of commandments
to be enforced by brute punishments. . . . Thus Godhead's resort
to law costs it half its integrity—as if a spiritual king, to gain
temporal power, had plucked out one of his eyes.' Which is why,
according to Shaw, Wagner's Wotan has only one eye—having
given the other in exchange for Freia, who represents the forces
of the law.

As an interpretation of Wagner this may or may not be accurate;
but it is a precise statement of the problem that preoccupied
Shaw from the beginning to the end of his life. The poet shrinks
from the everyday business of the world because he finds it
crude and repetitive; he feels most at home when contemplating
distant horizons; the world produces a kind of claustrophobia.
He is inclined to turn away and let the world go hang; but this
is really to choose sterility and death, for man is not yet capable
of sustaining a purely mental intensity. This is the lesson that is
driven home again and again by the romantics of the nineteenth
century and by Yeats's 'tragic generation' of the 1890s. Shaw was
a romantic who had no intention of being a member of any
tragic generation. He preferred the Wotan compromise to the
ineffectuality of the aesthetics. The first necessity was a public
persona, the ability to challenge practical men on their own level:
in short, camouflage. We know how successful he was in this.
But the Shaw *persona* was created to be the servant of an intran-
sigent aesthetic idealism. He wrote in the Morris preface: 'Now
though nobody gave me credit for it in those days (very few do
even now) I had a keen sense of beauty, not at all blunted by the
extent to which my poverty had obliged me to starve it.' This
sense of beauty had been strong since the day the family moved
into Torca Cottage overlooking Killiney Bay and the Dublin
mountains, and it was the real driving force behind his socialism;
like Ellie Dunn, he understood that the soul 'eats music and pictures and books and mountains and lakes and beautiful things to

wear and nice people to be with. In this country you cant have
them without lots of money: that is why our souls are so horribly
starved'. 'To me, living in a world of poor and unhappy people
is like living in hell', he wrote in a letter.* Yeats and his 'tragic
generation' turned away from the 'hell' with a shudder. Shaw
deliberately made the more difficult choice.

But it must be emphasised this choice was not merely a personal
matter that concerned no one but Shaw. He lived at the end of a
century when more than 50 per cent of the major poets and artists
had died tragically, and would continue to do so for a long time
to come. He was convinced that the poets had to be persuaded
not to turn away from the problem, but to accept that they, and
only they, could solve it satisfactorily. He saw it not merely as
a question of making a world fit for poets to live in—for poets
can make the choice that Shaw himself made—but of making a
world fit for children to grow up in:

'First, then, I lay it down as a prime condition of sane society,
obvious as such to anyone but an idiot, that in any decent community, children should find in every part of their native country,
food, clothing, lodging, instruction, and parental kindness for the
asking. For the matter of that, so should adults; but the two cases
differ in that as these commodities do not grow on the bushes,
the adults cannot have them unless they organise and provide
the supply, whereas the children must have them as if by magic,
with nothing to do but rub the lamp.'†

At the time Shaw was preaching to audiences of workmen on
street corners, Yeats was writing poems with such lines as:

'The wrong of unshapely things is a wrong too great
    to be told;
I hunger to build them anew and sit on a green knoll
    apart.'

Shaw felt exactly the same, but saw that rebuilding the world
and sitting on a green knoll apart are incompatible activities. At
the same time, he was aware that there is a strong Hamlet-
tendency in most poets that would make a simple invitation to
become socialists the worst possible approach. A remark about

* And repeated it in *Buoyant Billions* (1947).
† Children and Game, Preface to *Misalliance*.

Hamlet written in 1897 reveals his awareness of the problem: 'He is a man in whom the common personal passions are so superseded by wider and rarer interests, and so discouraged by a degree of critical self-consciousness which makes the practical efficiency of the instinctive man on the lower plane impossible to him, that he finds the duties dictated by conventional revenge and ambition as disagreeable a burden as commerce to a poet.' And this is why the most important single theme in all his work, from *The Perfect Wagnerite* to *Buoyant Billions* (in which he invents the term 'world-betterer' for the Wotan-types) is that of the relation of the poet or mystic to a society run by 'practical' men. And the argument is invariably presented from the point of view of the poet, never of the practical men. The practical men may be well-meaning enough, like Broadbent in *John Bull's Other Island* or Morell in *Candida*, but in the last analysis, they are inadequate. *It is the poets themselves who have to face the task of changing society.* It was a revolutionary thesis—nothing less than a flat contradiction of the basic assumption of romanticism: that the 'world' and the poet are irreconcilably at odds, because he wants something out of 'life' that life cannot give, pure contemplation of truth and beauty. Socrates first stated this idea clearly when he said that his death should be a consummation, since the philosopher spends his life trying to separate the body and the spirit. It is a Buddhistic position, from which life is regarded as basically evil or tragic, and it can be found in all the great romantics, from Shelley to Wagner. Blake contradicted it; so did Goethe and Nietzsche; but the spirit of the age was against them. And it was against Shaw. As far as his most important contribution was concerned, literature continued as if he had never existed; the tradition of romantic pessimism and world-rejection continued in Proust and Kafka and Eliot and Greene—in fact, in every writer who has exerted any influence on the twentieth century.

Edmund Wilson, one of Shaw's most sympathetic critics, has suggested that 'egoism like Shaw's was a disability like any disability—which you had to carry with you all your life. When he was young, it had been amusing, he had carried it off with panache; but it had become disagreeable with his later years, and one saw then that it was compulsive, incurable'.*

There is a fair amount of truth in this; but it oversimplifies. It was not a matter of an amusing mannerism that became a habit, but an altogether more complex business. Shaw was a romantic idealist who was determined to live for his ideals and not to die for them; like Wagner, he wanted to make sure that he was heard loud and clear. He achieved the paradoxical result of being accepted by the Philistines and rejected by the poets and idealists of whom he regarded himself the spokesman. Eric Bentley pointed out that Shaw died a disappointed man, a man who once said: 'I have solved every important problem of our time, and people still go on propounding them as if they were unsolved.' He had certainly solved *the* most important problem of his time, the romantic problem that lies across the path of Western civilisation like a great fallen tree. And because of the manner in which he chose to call attention to the problem—in plays like *Candida, Major Barbara, John Bull's Other Island, Heartbreak House*—no one paid any attention to what he was saying. Critics wrote theses about Proust, Joyce, Kafka, Eliot, who treated the same problem and left it unsolved; Shaw was ignored. It must have been a disconcerting sensation, like shouting at the top of your voice and no sound coming out. There was a certain irony in the situation: supreme success leading to complete failure in the most important sphere of all. The 'compulsive egoism' of the later years becomes understandable. It was a way of keeping the flags flying. Wells, who was in much the same situation, chose the other alternative: angry prophecies of doom and defeat. Both had to learn the unpleasant lesson that in England nothing fails like success. Carlyle had commented on this same English characteristic when he wrote: 'If Jesus were to come today, people would not even crucify him. They would ask him to dinner, and hear what he had to say, and make fun of it.'

But it would be several years before Shaw made this discovery. In the 1890s it was still a long way off. There seemed no reason why he should not unite the roles of revolutionary and philosopher. On the one hand, he could write about his dramatic criticisms: 'I must warn the reader that what he is about to study

* *The Bit Between My Teeth*, p. 48.

is not a series of judgements aiming at impartiality, but a siege laid to the theatre of the nineteenth century by an author who had to cut his own way into it at the point of the pen and throw some of its defenders in the moat.' But this was only the public aspect of the fight. 'Meanwhile I placidly wrote plays, but was confirmed in my peculiar doctrine that a point will be reached in human mental development when the pleasure taken in brain work by St Thomas Aquinas and the Webbs (and saints and philosophers generally) will intensify to a chronic ecstasy surpassing that now induced momentarily by the sexual orgasm. . . .'* *This* was the really revolutionary part of Shaw's philosophy. He was telling the exact truth when he wrote (in *The Intelligent Woman's Guide*): 'I am myself by profession what is called an original thinker, my business being . . . to draft new creeds and codes.' What he was saying was something so revolutionary that there was no one alive in his own time who was ready for it; even as I write this, twenty years after his death, there is still no sign that anyone has fully grasped its significance.

Let us return to 1892, the year of the production of *Widowers' Houses*. Shaw was still working as a music critic, writing now under the initials G.B.S. The current love affair was with Florence Farr, who played Blanche in *Widowers' Houses*. The Webbs had just married and started their *salon*; they had spent their honeymoon in Ireland investigating trade societies, beginning as they meant to continue. ('Marriage is a waste-paper basket of the emotions,' said Webb, and Beatrice agreed with him.) Shaw and Webb continued to work and plot together. And Shaw, surprisingly enough, made no attempt to follow up *Widowers' Houses*. Perhaps he was too busy. Or, more probably, he simply had no ideas. It was the violent scene between Jenny Patterson and Florence Farr in February 1893 that seems to have started him off on *The Philanderer*—a play he later came to heartily dislike. As has already been noted, this play is a retrogressive step in Shaw's career as a dramatist, and it received no performance until 1901. The reason for its failure is easy to define; it lacked the seriousness that Shaw was bringing to his work as a Fabian. But this could not be said of the next subject that engaged his atten-

* *New York Times* book review, November 18th, 1945. Quoted Henderson, p. 336.

E

tion. Sometime in 1893, the actress Janet Achurch—of whom Shaw became extremely fond—suggested Maupassant's *Yvette*, an absurd story about the virtuous daughter of a courtesan, as the subject for a play. Shaw commented: 'Oh, I'll work out the truth about that mother one day.' Beatrice Webb had also suggested that he should write about a 'real modern lady of the governing class'. In Maupassant's story, Yvette is the innocent heroine who decides to commit suicide rather than become a kept woman, although she ends by deciding for life and love after all. (Maupassant, of course, had a masculine aggressive attitude towards women that meant that he took a certain pleasure in showing the girl's ultimate surrender.) The mere outline of the story was probably enough to make Shaw toy with the idea of turning her into a Shavian heroine with a mind of her own. The result, *Mrs Warren's Profession* is perhaps the best of Shaw's early plays. Maupassant's Yvette becomes Vivie Warren, a typical Shaw heroine—common-sensible, unsentimental and businesslike, with a handshake that makes men wince and a taste for cigars. The aristocratic courtesan becomes the dynamic Mrs Warren, 'vulgar but . . . a genial and fairly presentable old blackguard of a woman'. And the major scene of the play is—inevitably—a clash of wills between the two. Mrs Warren begins by trying to assert her authority with her daughter. Vivie, well able to take care of herself, retaliates by bullying her mother to the point of tears:

VIVIE: Are you my mother? . . . Then where are our relatives? my father? our family friends? You claim the rights of a mother: the right to call me fool and child; to speak to me as no woman in authority over me at college dare speak to me; to dictate my way of life; and to force on me the acquaintance of a brute whom anyone can see to be the most vicious sort of London man about town. Before I give myself the trouble to resist such claims, I may as well find out whether they have any real existence.

This provokes Mrs Warren to give an account of how she became a brothel madame, and the situation between them is reversed; it is now Vivie who is shaken and humbled. And Shaw drives home the economic and moral lesson at the end of the scene:

VIVIE (*more and more deeply moved*) Mother; suppose we were both as poor as you were in those wretched old days, are you quite sure you wouldnt advise me to try the Waterloo bar or marry a labourer, or even go into a factory?

MRS WARREN (*indignantly*) Of course not. What sort of a mother do you take me for? How could you keep your self respect in such starvation and slavery?

Comic relief, which *Widowers' Houses* and *The Philanderer* lacked, is provided by the Reverend Samuel Gardner and his rakish son Frank.

REV S. I have not seen [Miss Warren] in church since she came.

FRANK. Of course not: she's a third wrangler. Ever so intellectual. Took a higher degree than you did; so why should she go to hear you preach?

REV S. Dont be disrespectful, sir.

FRANK. Oh, it dont matter: nobody hears us. Come in . . . I want to introduce you to her. Do you remember the advice you gave me last July, gov'nor?

REV S. (*Severely*) Yes. I advised you to conquer your idleness and flippancy, and to work your way into an honorable profession and live on it and not upon me.

FRANK. No: thats what you thought of afterwards. What you actually said was that since I had neither brains nor money, I'd better turn my good looks to account by marrying somebody with both. Well, look here. Miss Warren has brains: you cant deny that.

REV S. Brains are not everything.

FRANK. No, of course not: theres the money——

REV S. (*Interrupting him austerely*) I was not thinking of money, sir. I was speaking of higher things. Social position, for instance.

FRANK. I dont care a rap about social position.

REV S. But I do, sir.

FRANK. Well, nobody wants you to marry her.

Archer read it and pronounced it a masterpiece, Grein did not agree, so the idea of a production by the Independent Theatre was shelved. The Lord Chamberlain read it and refused to issue a licence. Six years after it was written, the newly formed Stage Society—a theatre club—agreed to produce it, only to find that owners of theatres, music halls and hotel ballrooms were afraid to risk crossing the Lord Chamberlain. Several galleries and theatres agreed to allow the club to present the play, and then backed out. It was finally performed on January 5th, 1902, eight years after it was written. It was a discouraging beginning for a man who intended to lay siege to the theatre.

The Philanderer fared no better. The actor Richard Mansfield considered it for American presentation in 1895, then changed his mind. It had to wait until 1905 for its first production. So far he had written three plays and had only one single performance. And music criticism was becoming an exhausting chore. In the preface to *Plays Unpleasant* (1898) he comments: 'In my weekly columns, which I once filled full from a magic well that never ran dry or lost its sparkle provided I pumped hard enough, I began to repeat myself; to fall into a style which, to my great peril, was recognised as at least partly serious; to find the pump tiring me and the water lower in the well.' But at least the writing of *Mrs Warren's Profession* seems to have proved to him that he was really a playwright, for he immediately went on to the writing of a new play without pausing for breath. This was *Arms and the Man*, and, dramatically speaking, it was Shaw's breakthrough.

Shaw later implied that *Arms and the Man* was written as a matter of habit. 'You cannot write three plays and then stop.' What actually happened was that Florence Farr's friend, Annie Horniman, decided to finance a season of plays at the Avenue Theatre, Charing Cross, and their first play, *A Comedy of Sighs*, by John Todhunter—a friend of Yeats's father—was a flop. Florence Farr rushed to Shaw to ask if they could replace it with *Widowers' Houses*. Shaw saw his opportunity, declared that he would prefer to write them a new play, and turned out *Arms and the Man* at top speed. He was still scribbling the last act—on the tops of buses—when the first was in rehearsal. It was produced on April 21st, 1894, and was a decisive success, running for nearly three months, and making Shaw £90. (It lost Miss Horniman £4,000.) As a result of this, Shaw told his old Dublin friend McNulty in early July: 'I have taken the very serious step of cutting off my income by privately arranging to drop the World business [music criticism] at the end of the season; and now, if I cannot make something out of the theatre, I am a ruined man; for I have not £20 saved; and Lucy and Kate Gurly (my mother's half-sister) are now members of the family. I am about to begin the world at last.' He started another play—*Candida*—which was finished before the end of the year.

The story of the first night of *Arms and the Man* is told by W. B. Yeats in his *Autobiographies*. (Yeats's *Land of Heart's Desire* was also produced that season at the Avenue Theatre.)

'On the first night the whole pit and gallery, except certain members of the Fabian Society, started to laugh at the author and then, discovering that they themselves were being laughed at, sat there not converted—their hatred was too bitter for that—but dumbfounded, while the rest of the house cheered and laughed. In the silence that greeted the author after the cry for a speech one man did indeed get his courage and boo loudly. "I assure the gentleman in the gallery," was Shaw's answer, "that he and I are of exactly the same opinion, but what can we do against a whole house who are of the contrary opinion?" And from that moment, Bernard Shaw became the most formidable man in modern letters, and even the most drunken of medical students knew it.'*

What was it that made *Arms and the Man* so successful when *Mrs Warren's Profession*—a far better play—could not even find a theatre? The answer is not, as Yeats thought, its anti-romanticism, but its romanticism. Bluntschli, the Swiss mercenary soldier who breaks into Rainas's bedroom in the opening scene of the play, is the typical Shaw hero, whom we already know from the novels. He is basically of the same type as Conolly of *The Irrational Knot* and Dr Kincaid of the *Unfinished Novel*. But whereas the commonsense realism of Conolly and Kincaid restricted their field of action, Bluntschli's has the opposite effect, and makes him the ideal foil for the romantic idealists of the Petkoff household. The novels were serious, and their characters drawn with realism. But *Widowers' Houses* had taught Shaw that Dickensian caricatures are more effective on the stage. Now he combined all the lessons he had learned so far. He had simply added one more twist to the romantic play, created another kind of romantic hero, and then surrounded him with amusing carica-

* Yeats, *The Trembling of the Veil,* Book IV, 'The Tragic Generation'. Henderson's version of Shaw's line is less ponderous: 'My dear fellow, I quite agree with you; but what are we two against so many?'

tures. The old trick of the clash of egos is again turned to good account—this time it is Bluntschli versus Sergius, Raina's fiancé and a hero of the Bulgarian army. But it is worth noting that Sergius is not a caricature, even though his romantic militarism is shown to be absurd beside Bluntschli's realistic eye-to-business. For the sake of dramatic tension, he has to be a worthy antagonist; therefore he is given a degree of intelligence and wry self-consciousness. But it should be noted that Bluntschli can also beat Sergius on his own ground of masculine accomplishment; when Sergius challenges him to a duel, Bluntschli accepts casually and when Raina tries to intervene, tells her: 'No harm will be done: I've often acted as sword instructor. He wont be able to touch me; and I'll not hurt him.'

It was the superficial anti-romanticism of the plays that led Shaw's critics to accuse him of poking fun at his audience, of changing his position so that no one was quite sure where he stood. Bluntschli is a realist; he also admits to being a hopeless romantic. Sergius is a romantic militarist; but he is also aware that he is a fraud. Raina is a sentimental girl; she is also a liar; when Bluntschli accuses her of being a liar, she tries outraged innocence, and then suddenly laughs and admits it. It seems to be Shaw's aim to make sure that no one in the play behaves as they are expected to. In *Heartbreak House* Mangan complains: 'The very burglars cant behave naturally in this house.'

The moment one recognises that a Shaw play is as fundamentally romantic as *The Prisoner of Zenda* or *King Solomon's Mines*, the apparent complexity vanishes. If Bluntschli is not as obviously heroic as Rudolph Rassendyl or Allan Quatermain, this is only because he is more intelligent and self-critical than they are. As Bluntschli marches off at the end of *Arms and the Man*, Sergius says: 'What a man! Is he a man?'—the conventional hero acknowledging the supremacy of the new Shavian hero. In the ordinary romantic novel, the hero's virtues are emphasised by contrasting him with less virtuous and heroic characters. In a Shaw play the hero's intelligence and realism are emphasised by contrasting him with less intelligent and realistic characters. The only rule for the creation of these characters is that they should *not* do the kind of things that their counterparts in the romantic novel would do. Romantic women are honest and demure; Shaw women are dishonest and flirtatious. Romantic servants are faithful, respectful and not particularly intelligent; Shaw servants are contentious, disrespectful, and usually more intelligent than their masters. The Shaw drama is ultimately the drama of the intelligent man in the world of the less intelligent, and every detail in the play is engineered to bring out the contrast.

This is why *Arms and the Man* was an immediate success. It appealed to the romanticism of the audience while flattering its intelligence. The real reason that *Widowers' Houses* and *Mrs Warren's Profession* struck people as 'unpleasant' was that they were not constructed according to this basic Shaw formula; they have no hero and no happy ending. (*The Philanderer* had a hero and is not really an 'unpleasant' play; to include it among the *Unpleasant Plays* was an act of camouflage in keeping with its last sentence: 'Never make a hero of a philanderer'—when that is precisely what Shaw had done.)

And now Shaw had found his formula he stuck to it. The first thing that strikes one as one looks down the table of contents in Shaw's *Complete Plays* is that the best plays are the ones that stick to this formula: *Candida, The Devil's Disciple, Man and Superman, John Bull's Other Island, Major Barbara, The Apple Cart, In Good King Charles's Golden Days*. Plays without a Shaw hero may reach a high level of stagecraft or interest—*Getting Married, Misalliance, Androcles and the Lion*, even *Back to Methuselah*—but they are clearly in a lower bracket of artistic effectiveness. *Pygmalion* is perhaps his frankest use of romanticism-disguised-as-anti-romanticism, and it is significant that its successful musical version simply gave it the expected romantic ending.

It might be assumed that Shaw now had London before him; that managers would ask him for plays; that other theatres would ask to read the plays he had written so far. Nothing of the sort happened. It would be ten years more before he received anything but token success in England. The actor Richard Mansfield took *Arms and the Man* to New York in September 1894, but it ran for only sixteen performances. Shaw used his too-abundant leisure in the latter half of 1894 lecturing for the Fabians, reading

Buckle's *History of Civilisation*, and writing another play, *Candida*. Fortunately, salvation appeared before he reached the point of bankruptcy in the person of Frank Harris, who had just bought a moribund paper called *The Saturday Review*. Harris, now known chiefly as the author of *My Life and Loves*, was one of the more remarkable personalities in the London of the 1880s and 1890s. A short, surly-looking man with a barrel chest and handlebar moustache, he had been a cowboy, a lawyer and one of the builders of Brooklyn Bridge. Pearson (who knew him well) describes him as looking like a bruiser and a racing tout. He spoke in a deep voice that could be heard streets away, and his conversation was Rabelaisian. In the 1880s he had made a success of editing the *Evening News* by specialising in sport, crime and sex, and printing the scabrous details of fashionable divorce cases. Harris was an indefatigable amorist, a liar of remarkable inventiveness (as any reader of *My Life and Loves* soon discovers), and he later became a confidence man and a blackmailer. The amusing thing was that he liked to think of himself as a philosopher and classical scholar, whose interest in Jesus sprang from his own Christ-like character. He must have struck Shaw as a living proof of his theory that real people are full of self-contradictions.

It was Harris who now offered Shaw the job of drama critic on the *Saturday Review*. Shaw hesitated, then accepted. It was not a fateful decision. Although his three years as a drama critic would bring him a certain notoriety and introduce him to a great many actors and actresses, they made no real difference to his career, except to provide a source of income. Dr Johnson once defined criticism as 'a study at which men grow important and formidable at very small expense'. Shaw's period as a drama critic certainly made him important and formidable in the world of the theatre, and the expense to himself—in terms of creativity—was not great. He was not a good drama critic, any more than he was a good music critic, because he was chiefly interested in expressing his own views. Predictably, he attacked the censor, praised Ibsen, and attacked whatever he thought trivial or sentimental. Since there were even less good dramatists around in the nineties than good composers, a great deal of Shaw's criticism sounds negative. There are a number of occasions when this negative approach was justified, as in the article on *Cymbeline*:

'It is for the most part stagey trash of the lowest melodramatic order, in parts abominably written, throughout intellectually vulgar, and, judged in point of thought by modern intellectual standards, vulgar, foolish, offensive, indecent and exasperating beyond all tolerance. There are times when one asks despairingly why our stage should ever have been cursed with this 'immortal' pilferer of other men's stories and ideas, with his monstrous rhetorical fustian, his unbearable platitudes, his pretentious reduction of the subtlest problems of life to commonplaces against which a Polytechnic debating club would revolt, his incredible unsuggestiveness, his sententious combination of ready reflection with complete intellectual sterility, and his consequent incapacity for getting out of the depth of even the most ignorant audience, except when he solemnly says something so transcendentally platitudinous that his more humble-minded hearers cannot bring themselves to believe that so great a man really meant to talk to them like their grandmothers. With the single exception of Homer there is no eminent writer, not even Sir Walter Scott, whom I can despise so entirely as I despise Shakespear when I measure my mind against his. The intensity of my impatience with him occasionally reaches such a pitch, that it would positively be a relief to me to dig him up and throw stones at him, knowing as I do how incapable he and his worshippers are of understanding any less obvious form of indignity. To read Cymbeline and to think of Goethe, of Wagner, of Ibsen, is, for me, to imperil the habit of studied moderation of statement which years of public responsibility as a journalist have made almost second nature to me.'

This kind of thing is certainly worth saying, and it needs saying today as much as it did seventy years ago. It is certainly not to deny that Shakespeare was a playwright of genius, any more, I imagine, than Shaw would have denied that Homer was a poet and Scott a novelist of genius. The key phrase of the above paragraph is: 'his sententious combination of ready reflection with complete intellectual sterility'. Shaw also saw Shakespeare's virtues for he goes on: 'But I am bound to add that I pity the man who cannot enjoy Shakespear. His gift of telling a story (provided someone else told it to him first); his enormous power over language, as conspicuous in his senseless and silly abuse of it as in his miracles of expression; his humour; his sense of idiosyncratic character; and his prodigious fund of that vital energy which is . . . the true differentiating property behind the faculties . . . of the man of genius enable him to entertain us so effectively that the imaginary scenes and people he has created become more real to us than our actual life.' But behind this creative vitality there is, as Shaw recognised, an intellectual sterility that is half disguised by the vaguely philosophical character of much of his dialogue. Shaw's central characters are all of a higher degree of intelligence than the average; with the exception of Hamlet, none of Shakespeare's central characters can be described as intelligent. This hardly matters; it applies to most great writers, including Shaw's own favourite, Dickens. Why, then, bother to draw attention to Shakespeare's intellectual sterility, since he never professed to be an original thinker? The answer is obvious: because Shaw *was* an original thinker, who still had all his important work before him, and he was wasting his time reviewing amusing absurdities like *Cymbeline* instead of getting on with his own work. An artist's deficiencies are seldom really important in assessing his stature. Nietzsche described the music of Brahms as 'the melancholy of impotence', and he was right; Hugo Wolf pointed out the negative emotion underlying most of Brahms's music; he was also right. It makes no difference to Brahms's greatness, which is a question of purely musical stature. On the other hand, it is important to the understanding of Nietzsche or Wolf to understand why they disliked Brahms; and it is important to the understanding of Shaw to understand why he attacked Shakespeare. His objection, expressed in the preface to the *Plays for Puritans*, is that Shakespeare understood human weakness without understanding human strength. 'Shakespear's Anthony and Cleopatra must needs be as intolerable to the true puritan as it is distressing to the ordinary healthy citizen, because, after giving a faithful picture of the soldier broken down by debauchery, and the typical wanton in whose arms such men perish, Shakespear finally strains all his huge command of rhetoric and stage pathos to give a theatrical sublimity to the wretched end of the business, and to persuade the foolish spectators that the world was well lost by the twain. . . . Out, out, brief candle! cries Shakespear, in his tragedy of the literary man as murderer and witch-consulter. Surely the time is past for patience with writers who, having to choose between giving up life in despair and discarding the trumpery moral kitchen scales in which they try to weigh the universe, surreptitiously stick to the scales, and spend the rest of the lives they pretend to despise in breaking men's spirits.' This is no longer a tongue-in-cheek attack on 'bardolators' but a serious statement of the basic insight that made Shaw an original thinker.

All this would hardly be worth saying, except that Shaw's attitude to Shakespeare has aroused so much misunderstanding. Hesketh Pearson devotes a particularly silly chapter of his book to attacking Shaw and defending Shakespeare, and it completely misses the point. It is in a fundamental sense impossible to attack or defend Shakespeare. He is there; and he has been there too long to be made unfashionable by an attack. And a defence is irrelevant unless it counters the *reasons* behind an attack. Shaw's reason was that he was concerned with the intelligent and creative aspect of human nature, with what he called, in one of his criticisms, the 'classical'. 'What I mean by classical is that he can present a dramatic hero as a man whose passions are those which have produced the philosophy, the poetry, the art and the statecraft of the world, and not merely those which have produced its weddings, coroner's inquests and executions.' By this standard Shakespeare seldom rises to the level of the classical, no matter how great he may be on a purely creative level.

Shaw's drama criticisms made him feared in the theatre, but certainly not liked. Henry Irving, whom Shaw attacked repeatedly for his alterations to the Shakespearian text, remarked: 'I should be delighted to pay his funeral expenses at any time.' Beerbohm Tree told Pearson: 'The First-night nervousness was bad enough, but the night before his criticism appeared was worse.' Ellen Terry's comment was: 'He's a darling, and knew how to say nasty things so nicely.' (Shaw never attacked her.) Mrs Patrick Campbell said: 'We pretended he was not serious, but our fingers trembled as we turned to his articles. A good riddance; but *how* we shall miss what he might have said about the others.'

Some managers attempted to bribe Shaw by agreeing to present one of his plays at some vague date in the future, and offering an 'advance' on royalties. This is what Irving did, the play in question being *The Man of Destiny*, a one-act study of Napoleon. Shaw declined to be bribed, and his plays remained unperformed in London's larger theatres.

Plays now followed one another with hardly a pause in between: *Candida* in 1894, then *The Man of Destiny*, *You Never Can Tell* in 1895, *The Devil's Disciple* in 1896. Shaw once said that he would give up playwriting if he couldn't produce at least six plays before the age of forty; he managed nearly eight. But nothing much seemed to happen to them. *Candida* was accepted by Richard Mansfield but abandoned as impossible in rehearsal. He also rejected *The Man of Destiny*, which Shaw wrote specially for him. *You Never Can Tell*, deliberately written as an attempt at a 'popular' play for the West End, only achieved an unprofitable Stage Society performance. It was all rather discouraging, and Shaw's health began to run down. There was a return of the headaches and neuralgia of his younger days. He had a tooth pulled out, but the trouble turned out not to be toothache but nerve pains. Bertrand Russell almost put an end to Shaw's career; they were out bicycling when on holiday with the Webbs, and Russell, with the vagueness of a philosopher, stopped his bicycle suddenly halfway down a hill to look at a signpost turning the bicycle sideways across the road. Shaw hurtled down the hill and into the bicycle. Shaw luckily escaped with a few bruises, and, according to Russell, kept overtaking the slow train by which Russell had to journey back to London (his bicycle being smashed) and jeering whenever he saw Russell at a station. A year later Shaw came off the bicycle again, trying to avoid a woman, and landed on his cheek, which needed several stitches. Finally, a shoe that was laced too tightly caused an abscess in his left foot, and there was a complete breakdown in health that brought drama criticism to an end.

Fortunately, the drama criticism had become unnecessary as a source of income. In October 1897 Shaw had his first financial windfall. *The Devil's Disciple* was presented in New York by Mansfield, and was enormously successful. It netted £25,000, of which Shaw received 10 per cent. Thus at the time of his accident in mid-1898 Shaw was no longer living by hand-to-mouth journalism.

It was at this point that the eternal philanderer decided to get married. His choice was an Irishwoman, Charlotte Payne-Townshend, whom he had met at the Webbs in 1896—when Shaw was forty, Charlotte 39. She was rich enough to have given Sidney Webb a thousand pounds to start the London School of Economics, and to take a flat above it at £300 a year; but she was not a 'millionairess', as Shaw described her in a letter to Ellen Terry.*

The reasons behind Shaw's marriage have never been fully understood, because no biographer has faced squarely that what Shaw wanted was a mother figure. In a letter to Ellen Terry in July 1897 he says: 'I will put an end to it all by marrying. Do you know a reasonably healthy woman of about sixty, accustomed to plain vegetarian cooking, and able to read and write enough to forward letters when her husband is away, but otherwise uneducated? Must be plain featured . . .' Charlotte Payne-Townshend was plain-featured; in fact, she resembled Shaw's mother temperamentally as well as physically. Her mother had been a virago who made her father thoroughly unhappy, so she had a horror of the idea of marriage and children. Sexually, she was cold. This suited Shaw perfectly. 'I found sex hopeless as a basis for permanent relations and never dreamt of marriage in connection with it', he wrote in another letter. Shaw was naturally ascetic; beautiful women were creatures who could touch his imagination; but they were not intended for domesticity. The consequence was that his sexual relations tended to be flirtations. Beatrice Webb understood him when she wrote: 'It is not the end [of lovemaking] he cares for. It is the *process*. His sensuality has all drifted into sexual vanity—delight in being the candle to the moths.' And elsewhere, with even more penetration: 'he is kindly, and has a cat-like preference for those persons to whom he is accustomed'. Shaw was now in his forties, and he had spent his whole life living with his family; domesticity was his way of life. But his mother and

* She had about £4,000 a year.

sister did not prevent him from having love affairs; this was the main disadvantage of the idea of marriage. 'The greatest sacrifice in marriage is the sacrifice of the adventurous attitude towards life: the being settled', he wrote in the preface to *Androcles and the Lion*. 'Those who are born tired may crave for settlement; but to fresher and stronger spirits it is a form of suicide.' On the other hand, his mother would not live for ever; she was approaching seventy; it was time he set up an establishment of his own. The only other choice on the horizon was Bertha Newcombe, a painter, to whom Shaw's friends conspired to marry him. Their 'affair' had been drifting on for five years. She was also plain and ladylike, but had a streak of possessiveness that alarmed Shaw: or, to put it another way, she could not be described as motherly.

A letter to Ellen Terry in November 1896 explains Shaw's choice of Charlotte as well as anything can:

'The truth is she is a clever woman. She knows the value of her unencumbered independence, having suffered a good deal from family bonds and conventionality before the death of her mother and the marriage of her sister set her free. The idea of tying herself up again by a marriage before she knows anything—before she has exploited her freedom and money power to the utmost—seems to her intellect to be unbearably foolish. Her theory is that she wont do it. She picked up a broken heart somewhere a few years ago, and made the most of it* (she is very sentimental) until she happened to read "The Quintessence of Ibsenism", in which she found, as she thought, gospel, salvation, freedom, emancipation, self-respect & so on. Later on she met the author, who is, as you know, able to make himself tolerable as a correspondent. He is also a bearable companion on bicycle rides, especially in a country house where there is nobody else to pair with. She got fond of me and did not coquet or pretend that she wasnt. I got fond of her because she was a comfort to me down there.'

So from an early stage Charlotte made no secret of having succumbed to the Shaw charm. 'All this winter they have been lovers—of a philandering and harmless kind', Beatrice recorded. Shaw got accustomed to her and fond of her; many of his letters

* This infatuation was with Axel Munthe, later the author of *The Story of San Michele*.

to her are simply chatty accounts of his doings that might have been written to Ellen Terry or anyone else he thoroughly liked. He missed her when she went off on a world tour with the Webbs; and when she returned from Rome because she heard he was ill, he was touched. And his condition of physical feebleness was now so extreme that he obviously needed someone to nurse him. He had been getting increasingly exhausted for months working on the vestry. 'Oh Ellen, I am the world's pack-horse; and it beats my lean ribs unmercifully.' It was not improbable that he might even become a permanent invalid if the foot got worse. So, with misgiving, he proposed to Miss Payne-Townshend; he was at the end of his resources. 'The thing being cleared . . . of all such illusions as love interest, happiness interest, and all the rest of the vulgarities of marriage, I changed right about face on the subject and hopped down to the Registrar, who married me to her on one leg.' The Registrar apparently started to marry her to Wallas, their best man, who was better dressed than Shaw.

Perhaps the oddest thing of all is that Shaw, who had been enjoying love affairs now for over a decade, accepted the notion that the marriage should be sexless. This, at least, has been asserted by most of Shaw's biographers. Janet Dunbar, the biographer of Mrs Shaw, is inclined to question the idea. 'It is probable that after Shaw was well again they enjoyed as normal and intimate a life as other married couples do; but they were not young.' This is hardly accurate; they were in their early forties, at which age the sexual powers of most civilised men and women are unimpaired. One of Charlotte's friends later asserted that she died 'a vestal virgin'; but since Charlotte was far too reticent to speak to even her most intimate friends of her sexual life, this has to be regarded as unproved. Nevertheless, it must be acknowledged that *if* sex played an unimportant part in their marriage this would have been consistent with Shaw's general attitude to marriage and to Charlotte. 'Healthy marriages are partnerships of companionable and affectionate friendship', he wrote in the preface to *Getting Married*; '. . . cases of chronic lifelong love, whether sentimental or sensual, ought to be sent to the doctor, if not the executioner'. The marriage of the Bishop and his wife in that play—and of King Magnus and his queen in *The Apple Cart*—illustrates Shaw's view of the nature of marriage. That it was, in the last analysis, a second best, seems to be proved by his remark to Hesketh Pearson in 1944, after the death of Charlotte: 'If you had had forty years of love and devotion such as I have had, you would know what freedom meant, and I am enjoying this here for the first time.'

6 BEYOND THE GOSPEL OF EFFICIENCY

With his days of journalistic drudgery behind him, a play that had earned £25,000, and a rich wife to share his future, Shaw's 'long apprenticeship' was finally and decisively over. But as far as the commercial theatre was concerned there was still a long way to go. When he finished *Candida* towards the end of 1894 he was aware that it was the closest he had come to creating a box-office success, and events proved him right. He assured Mansfield that the play 'is the most fascinating work in the world. . . . By the way, there's probably money in the piece', and told Janet Achurch that he anticipated a first-night success. Richard Mansfield allowed himself to be persuaded, put the play into rehearsal, and then dropped it. '. . . your play of Candida is lacking in all the essential qualities. The stage is not for sermons—*Not my stage* . . . Candida is charming—it is more than charming—it is delightful . . . but—pardon me—it is *not* a play. . . .' He explained that he wanted to act, 'and hugging my ankles for three mortal hours won't satisfy me in this regard'. The actor-manager George Alexander had already declined it. Janet Achurch finally gave it a few performances in the provinces, with a moderate degree of success, but it had to wait nine years before Arnold Daly tried out a matinée performance in New York, and startled everybody by making the play the hit of the season. In England *Candida* eventually achieved six performances in 1904—ten years after it was written—and two revivals in the following year. Mansfield refused to admit he was wrong even after Daly's success, and commented: 'Fads will have their day.'

We have already discussed the importance of the poet and the mystic in Shaw's scheme of things, and his heterodox theory that poets should be the architects of society. Eugene Marchbanks is the first of a long line of 'outsider' figures in Shaw's plays. (Owen Jack in *Love Among the Artists* is the only one in the novels.) For this reason, and for several others that will emerge, *Candida* deserves closer analysis.

Shaw calls *Candida* 'a mystery'—perhaps meaning to hint at an identification of its heroine with the Virgin Mary—but on the surface, the play seems straightforward enough. The eighteen-year-old poet falls in love with Candida, the wife of the Reverend James Morell, a socialist clergyman (based on Stuart Headlam). Morell agrees to allow Candida to choose between them; she chooses her husband, and the poet walks out into the night. The last line of the play reads: 'But they do not know the secret in the poet's heart.'

'The secret' was explained by Shaw in a letter to James Huneker in 1904:

'Dont ask me conundrums about that very immoral female Candida. Observe the entry of W. Burgess [Candida's father]: "Youre the lady as hused to typewrite for him." "No." "Naaow: she was young-er." And therefore Candida sacked her. Prossy is a very highly selected person indeed, devoted to Morell to the extent of helping in the kitchen, but to him the merest pet rabbit, unable to get the slightest hold on him. Candida is as unscrupulous as Siegfried: Morell himself sees that "no law will bind her". She seduces Eugene just exactly as far as it is worth her while to seduce him. She is a woman without "character" in the conventional sense. Without brains and strength of mind she would be a wretched slattern and voluptuary. She is straight for natural reasons, not for conventional ethical ones. Nothing can be more coldbloodedly reasonable than her farewell to Eugene: "All very well, my lad; but I dont quite see myself at fifty with a husband of thirty-five." It is just this freedom from emotional slop that makes her so completely mistress of the situation.

'Then consider the poet. She makes a man of him finally by showing him his own strength—that David must do without Uriah's wife. And then she pitches in her picture of the home, the onions, and the tradesmen, and the cosseting of the big baby

Morell. The New York *hausfrau* thinks it a little paradise, but the poet rises up and says: "Out, then, into the night with me"— Tristan's holy night. If this greasy fool's paradise is happiness, then I give it to you with both hands, "life is nobler than that". That is the "poet's secret". The young things out in front weep to see the poor boy going out lonely and broken hearted in the cold night, to save the proprieties of New York Puritanism: but he is really a god going back to his heaven, proud, unspeakably contemptuous of the "happiness" he envied in the days of his blindness, clearly seeing that he has higher business on hand than Candida. She has a little quaint intuition of the completeness of his cure; she says "he has learnt to do without happiness".

'As I should certainly be lynched by the infuriated Candidamaniacs if this view of the case were made known, I confide it to your discretion . . . I tell it to you because it is an interesting sample of the way in which a scene, which should be conceived and written only by transcending the ordinary notion of the relation between the persons, nevertheless stirs the ordinary emotions to a very high degree, all the more because the language of the poet, to those who have not the clue to it, is mysterious and bewildering and therefore worshipful. I divined it myself before I found out the whole truth about it.'*

There are a few points worth comment before we pass on. This observation that a scene that should transcend the ordinary emotions *can* move them deeply is one of Shaw's most important discoveries, and is the answer to the unperceptive comment that his characters are merely dramatised ideas. When he writes according to this principle, as in the third act of *Man and Superman* or the last act of *Back to Methuselah*, the result is the total engagement of the reader's emotions as well as intellect; when he tries to 'write down' to his audience, as in some of the other *Methuselah* plays, the result is artistic failure.

The other point to note here is that Shaw believes that if the poet is a sufficiently good poet, he automatically possesses the strength and detachment to transcend these minor emotional shocks. It is not coldness or logic that allows him to walk off unscathed, but the faculty that *makes* him a poet. The minor

* Quoted by Arthur H. Nethercot, *Men and Supermen,* p. 15, Harvard 1954.

romantic allows himself to die of disappointment, as Ernest Dowson died when the girl he was in love with married a waiter. The major romantic shrugs it off and becomes stronger through it; he may even create literature out of it, as Goethe created *Werther* out of a Candida-type situation.

But Shaw's account of the play in his letter to Huneker is misleadingly straightforward. Significantly Morell himself is not analysed. But it is Morell's relation to Eugene that constitutes the major problem of this play. There is an ambiguity that arises out of the nature of the two egos that are made to 'clash' in *Candida*. In most Shaw plays, the clash is between intelligence and stupidity, the higher evolutionary types and the lower. It is easy to see exactly where Shaw's sympathies lie in the conflict between Vivie Warren and her mother, between Bluntschli and Sergius. Here the situation is more complicated. The Reverend James Morell holds all Shaw's own political beliefs, and he is using his talent for platform oratory to make them reach the widest possible audience. In the opening scene of the play, when Morell tells his father in law to 'give me a good scoundrelly reason for wanting to be friends with me', he emerges as the typical Shaw hero, as disconcertingly realistic as Conolly or Bluntschli. And then Candida returns from a journey with Eugene, and Eugene takes the first opportunity to tell Morell he is in love with Candida. At first Morell is kindly and patronising, and tells Eugene he is making a fool of himself:

MARCHBANKS. Oh, do you think I dont know all that? Do you think that the things people make fools of themselves about are any less real and true than the things they behave sensibly about? (*Morell's gaze wavers for the first time. He forgets to warm his hands, and stands listening, startled and thoughtful.*) They are more true: they are the only things that are true. You are very calm and sensible and moderate with me because you can see I'm a fool about your wife; just as no doubt that old man who was here just now is very wise over your Socialism, because he sees that you are a fool about it. (*Morell's perplexity deepens markedly. Eugene follows up his advantage, plying him fiercely with questions.*) Does that prove you wrong? Does your complacent superiority to me prove that *I* am wrong?

In the long speeches by Morell that follow, Shaw notes the

'great artistic beauty of delivery' in the stage instructions; but what Morell says is sound and reasonable. Eugene's reaction is violent:

MARCHBANKS (*Looking round wildly*). Is it like this for her here always? A woman with a great soul, craving for reality, truth, freedom; and being fed on metaphors, sermons, stale perorations, mere rhetoric. Do you think a woman's soul can live on your talent for preaching?

Morell protests reasonably that his talent is like Eugene's, 'the gift of finding words for divine truth', and Eugene retorts: 'It's the gift of the gab, nothing more and nothing less.' And it is at this point that the reader begins to suspect that Shaw's sympathies are closer to Morell than to Eugene. It brings to mind the end of *Man and Superman*:

ANN (*Looking at him with fond pride and caressing his arm*). Never mind her, dear. Go on talking.

TANNER. Talking!

Universal laughter.

Or Lady Britomart Undershaft:

LADY BRITOMART. Stop making speeches, Andrew. This is not the place for them.

UNDERSHAFT (*punctured*). My dear: I have no other means of conveying my ideas.

LADY BRITOMART: Your ideas are nonsense.

Shaw himself had a great deal of experience of hit-and-run critics who dismissed him without staying to argue the point—as do most writers of ideas; he must have been aware that Eugene's strength in argument is the strength of a kind of stupidity; he can shake Morell's confidence because his intense personal preoccupation allows him to be shatteringly unfair, while Morell's fair-mindedness prevents him from resorting to the same tactics. Besides, Morell has befriended Eugene when he found him on the Embankment; he responds by trying to steal Morell's wife: Shaw's views on such matters were fairly strong. Lastly, we know Shaw's opinion of romantic poets who wanted to 'sit on a green knoll apart' and complain about the world instead of trying to change it. In a music criticism of 1880 he wrote: 'At [twenty] fairyland is not forgotten. The impulse to hear "the horns of elfland" is genuine and spontaneous. At twenty-six

fairyland is gone; one is stronger, more dexterous, more bumptious.' Morell has outgrown the horns of elfland; Eugene hasn't.
Morell recognises Eugene's worth: 'for dont think, my boy, that
I cannot see in you . . . promise of higher powers than I can ever
pretend to'; Eugene fails to recognise Morell's. When all this is
taken into account, it becomes hard not to believe that the
meaning of the play is the exact reverse of what appears on the
surface, and that the 'secret in the poet's heart' is Eugene's
sudden recognition of his own selfishness and immaturity. Shaw's
account in the letter to Huneker makes it hard to see what he was
getting at. It seems to be a reversal of position, of the kind that
made critics think that Ibsen intended *The Wild Duck* as a satire
on his own earlier plays. Shaw was certainly capable of such
apparent self-contradictions, as when he made the king in *The
Apple Cart* defeat his socialist cabinet.

But the explanation of the ambiguities of *Candida* is probably
more simple. It has been the general view of Shaw's critics that
the poet was based on the young Shelley; what is far more probable is that Marchbanks was drawn from W. B. Yeats.

Shaw had known Yeats since 1888; Yeats, who was then
twenty-three, wrote in a letter: 'Last night at Morris's I met
Bernard Shaw, who is certainly very witty. But, like most people
who have wit rather than humour, his mind is somewhat wanting
in depth.' The priggishness of the characterisation cannot be set
down to Yeats's age; he repeated it periodically throughout his
life. '[Shaw] is a logician, and a logician is a fool when life, which
is a thing of emotion, is in question; it is as if a watch were to
try to understand a bullock.' This was written to Lady Gregory
in 1910. To the end of his life Yeats believed Shaw to be a
'watch'—that is, a man who is constitutionally unable to grasp
the nature of poetry because of a brilliant *but mechanical* intellect.
Eliot and Pound adopted the view without notable modifications,
and it is still widely accepted today. In his autobiography, written
in 1922, Yeats says:

'. . . I listened to *Arms and the Man* with admiration and
hatred. It seemed to me inorganic, logical, straightness, and not
the crooked road of life, yet I stood aghast before its energy. . . .
He was right to claim Samuel Butler for his master, for Butler
was the first Englishman to make the discovery, that it is possible

to write with great effect without music, without style, either good or bad, to eliminate from the mind all emotional implications and to prefer plain water to every vintage. . . . Presently I had a nightmare that I was haunted by a sewing machine, that clicked and shone, but the incredible thing was that the machine smiled, smiled perpetually.' Yeats was making the usual mistake of the shy, sensitive man—of supposing that an apparently self-confident person could never have been shy or sensitive. At thirty-seven, Shaw's period of immaturity was over; at twenty-eight, Yeats was still in the midst of his. Even so, he found Shaw difficult to summarise: '. . . when Wilde said: "Mr Bernard Shaw has no enemies but is intensely disliked by all his friends", I knew it to be a phrase I should never forget, and felt revenged upon a notorious hater of romance, whose generosity and courage I could not fathom.' If he had recognised that Shaw was as uncompromisingly romantic as himself it might have made the generosity and courage easier to fathom. But there were various reasons why Yeats should feel defensive. In the passage describing the opening of *Arms and the Man* he avoids mentioning the reason that the audience was mocking and hostile; it was because his own fairy play *The Land of Heart's Desire* had been used as a curtain-raiser.* The play is about a girl who is stolen by the fairies, and Yeats's comment on the programme: 'The characters are supposed to speak in Gaelic', may also have excited a certain amount of derision. That an audience that was unsympathetic to his own play should be impressed by Shaw must have struck Yeats as a further proof that Shaw was really 'one of them'. He admitted to admiring Shaw: 'He could hit my enemies, and the enemies of all I loved, as I could never hit'; but his attitude remained ambiguous: 'We all hated him with the left side of our heads while admiring him immensely with the right side.' And the situation was aggravated by Shaw's relation with Florence Farr. Yeats had been attracted by her,† and wanted her as a collaborator in his plays since 1890. From 1891 until 1896 she was involved in a love affair with Shaw. It was not until after this was over that she finally became the active collaborator that Yeats hoped for, reading his poetry aloud in a deliberately sing-song manner

* Joseph Hone: *W. B. Yeats,* p. 107.
† 'He was accounted in love with her by his sisters', J. Hone, p. 74.

known as 'cantillating', and acting in his plays.* Shaw had some scathing comments to make on cantillating, although he basically agreed with Yeats's theory that poetry should be made to sound like poetry, and not like prose.

Shaw had seen a great deal of Yeats at William Morris's in the early nineties, but it was not until 1894 that they shared a theatre and leading lady. It was immediately after this that Shaw wrote *Candida*, as if to demonstrate to Yeats that he understood as much about poets, and their desire to hear 'the horns of elfland' as Yeats himself. There are occasions when Eugene's speeches sound like a parody of Yeats; for example, when Candida asks Eugene to buy her a scrubbing brush:

MARCHBANKS (*softly and musically, but sadly and laughingly*). No, not a scrubbing brush, but a boat; a tiny shallop to sail away in, washed by the rain, and dried by the sun; where the south dusts the beautiful green and purple carpets. . . .

This raises the suspicion that Shaw had seen Yeats's poem *The Cloths of Heaven* in manuscript; in fact, Eugene's general manner of rhapsodising is reminiscent of many of the poems Yeats wrote between 1890 and 1900.

If Yeats saw *Candida*—and there is no evidence that he did—it failed to convince him that Shaw understood poets. In 1900 he was writing to Lady Gregory:

'I saw Shaw today . . . He came to the "Three Kings" on Saturday. I replied to a speech of his and pleased the Fellowship very much by proving that Shaw's point of view belonged to a bygone generation—to the scientific epoch—and was now "reactionary". He had never been called a reactionary before.'

Shaw must have found it equally odd to be called a relic of the scientific epoch, since his suspicion of science was exactly what made Wells classify him as a poet. 'Science is always wrong; it never solves a problem without raising ten more.' But then, Yeats found even Tennyson's *In Memoriam* 'too scientific'. His

---

* C. G. Du Cann says misleadingly in *The Loves of Bernard Shaw* that 'She left Shaw for the poet . . . Yeats', and quotes Shaw as saying: 'Yeats was such a handsome man that I knew I hadn't an earthly.' Shaw's *Collected Letters* make it clear that it was Shaw who broke off the affair (Vol. 1. pp. 676–8), and that the Yeats collaboration began after this.

view of Shaw remained unchanged into old age; at sixty-five, he found *The Apple Cart* 'theatrical in the worst sense of the word . . . and the theme was just rich enough to show the superficiality of the treatment'. Yeats was nothing if not consistent; although his last poem, *Under Ben Bulben*, reveals that he now held a view of art as an instrument of evolution that is strictly Shavian.

The two greatest writers of their time never established a *rapport*; but Shaw understood Yeats better than Yeats understood Shaw.

Candida is a kind of milestone in Shaw's development. It makes one aware how far he had travelled since *An Unsocial Socialist* a decade earlier. Trefusis has a sense of purpose, but it is merely social purpose, a passion for social justice. It is a long way from this to Eugene's 'life is nobler than that'. The social reformer has become a secondary character in *Candida*. Even the sexual relation has become a secondary matter: 'he is really a god going back to his heaven, proud, unspeakably contemptuous of the "happiness" he envied in the days of his blindness, clearly seeing that he has higher business on hand than Candida'. What has happened to Shaw since *An Unsocial Socialist* is that he has gained a clear intuition of the 'higher business' than Candida or socialism or the conflict of religion and science. Perhaps the most interesting chapter of Percy Smith's *Unrepentant Pilgrim* is Chapter 6, 'Evolution of a Believer', which traces Shaw's development from the callow atheism of the Moody and Sankey letter to the religious conviction that made him declare in 1896: 'I am a resolute Protestant; I believe in the Holy Catholic Church; in the Holy Trinity of Father, Son (or Mother, Daughter) and Spirit; in the Communion of Saints, the Life to Come, the Immaculate Conception and the everyday reality of Godhead and the Kingdom of Heaven.'* The tone of the passage is reminiscent of William Blake—and it is interesting to recall that Shaw later declared Irving Fiske's essay 'Bernard Shaw and William Blake'

* 'On Going to Church', *The Savoy*, January 1896.

to be 'the best thing ever written about me'.* There was no sudden conversion to this religious view of himself and his purpose, as he explains in a letter to Bland of 1884: 'The coming into clearer light of this consciousness has not occurred to me as a crisis. It has been gradual.' And this is true; there is no point in his work at which one can see the change beginning. The negative element in Shaw's 'religion' was always present, from the asceticism of Robert Smith to the basic distrust of sex in Sidney Trefusis. His account of Ibsen's *Brand* in 1890 seems to indicate that he was still unable to fathom the religious passion. And there is nothing in *The Philanderer, Mrs Warren's Profession, Arms and the Man*, to indicate a change of heart. Even after writing the long letter to Bland in which he describes this new consciousness of purpose, he was writing to Henry Arthur Jones: 'My passion, like that of all artists, is for efficiency, which means intensity of life. . . .' But he failed as a novelist because the mere passion for efficiency is not enough to create a hero, any more than it makes a real heroine of Vivie Warren. All this indicates why *Candida* was a turning point in Shaw's creative life. For the first time he sees beyond the gospel of efficiency, and begins to understand his real business as a playwright: the imaginative projection of the 'higher evolutionary types'.

And it is by this purpose that Shaw must ultimately be judged. This is the ground on which he stakes his claim to greatness: that more than any of his predecessors, he is concerned to *show* what he means by the 'higher evolutionary type'. The surprising thing about the major writers of the nineteenth century is that so few of them took up the challenge of trying to present human greatness. Goethe himself was great, but his Faust and Wilhelm Meister are not. Ibsen's attitude towards greatness is always ambiguous; Brand is destroyed by the evolutionary impulse that makes him reject 'common humanity'. Tolstoy's heroes—Peter Bezukhov and Constantin Levin—hardly rise above the level of well-meaning fools. Only Wagner and Nietzsche took up the

---

* Originally 'Bernard Shaw's debt to William Blake'—Shavian tract No. 2 (1951)—this is, in fact, one of the few pieces about Shaw that recognises from the beginning his total *seriousness* as a social and religious thinker. It has been reprinted in the *Twentieth Century Views* volume on Shaw edited by R. J. Kaufmann (Prentice-Hall Inc, New Jersey 1965).

challenge; but Siegfried and Zarathustra are types rather than persons. Dostoevsky's novels are also concerned with this struggle of the religious or evolutionary impulse in man; but, like the others, he preferred to present it in tragic terms. Shaw wanted to present it positively, *since he did not believe that being obsessed by the evolutionary impulse is a tragic destiny*. Like William Morris, Shaw saw no reason why visionaries should not attempt to change the world to try to make it more like their visions. This was his central subject. Tolstoy was a determinist about history; he believed that individual men have very little to do with the march of world events. Shaw took the opposite view: that history is the expression of some 'force' expressing itself through individuals, and that consequently the most fascinating subject for the dramatist—or novelist—is the conflict between this higher power and the forces of reaction and stagnation. This is why, from the beginning, his drama is the drama of the clash between creativity and strong-minded conventionality. It might be said that he is obsessed with strong-minded disagreeable people; the novels and plays are full of them, from Mrs Froster in *Immaturity* to the Duke of York (the future James II) in *Good King Charles*. These disagreeable people are nearly always bullies, and it is perhaps the central feature of Shaw's drama that the browbeaters can always be browbeaten by an intelligent man who knows his own mind:

MORELL (*with weary calm*). I dont believe you.

BURGESS (*rising threateningly*). Dont say that to me again, James Mavor Morell.

MORELL (*unmoved*). I'll say it just as often as may be necessary to convince you that its true. I dont believe you.

BURGESS (*collapsing into an abyss of wounded feeling*). Oh, well, if youre determined to be hunfriendly, I spose I'd better go.

It is this trick that makes Shaw such a good dramatist. It is almost a kind of wish-fulfilment: Shaw's heroes never think of all the clever things they might have said *after* an argument; they think of them and say them at the time. His plays show the intelligent, sensitive characters completely dominating the sort of people who normally get the best of it in real life. In this he differs not only from his master Dickens—who treats Mrs Clennam and Mrs Gargery as necessary evils—but from most of the major writers of the twentieth century, who have continued to show the intelligent and sensitive man trapped in his inability to act.

Yeats's objection to Shaw was that his plays are 'inorganic and logical', implying that they are *too* successful in what they are trying to do, and that what they are trying to do is not really worth doing. Once one understands what Shaw was really trying to do, it can be seen that they are anything but inorganic and logical; they are fumbling, unsuccessful attempts to create a new kind of hero and to solve an immense problem: the problem of how the evolutionary force, acting through individuals—and therefore acting blindly and instinctively, hindered by ignorance and personal motivations—can avoid tragedy and waste. History is full of martyrs, but martyrdom is an expensive way of propagating an idea. Can the vehicles of the evolutionary force learn to avoid the pitfalls and make full use of their powers? This is the problem of which Shaw became conscious after *Candida*. This is why the ending of *Candida*—with the poet walking out, unscathed, into 'Tristan's holy night'—marks an epoch in Shaw's development.

That Shaw was only half-conscious of his basic aims is shown by comparing *Candida* with the two plays that followed it, *The Man of Destiny* (1895) and *You Never Can Tell* (1896–7). Both are light and amusing; both are dramatically successful—*You Never Can Tell* is Shaw's most popular play with audiences—and both are completely unimportant. Shaw apparently decided that Napoleon would be a suitable part for Richard Mansfield—who had already made a success as Napoleon in another play—and that he could make Napoleon one of his 'higher evolutionary types'. In fact, Shaw has no sympathy with military men, and the play never comes to life. It was intended to be light, and it ends by being trivial. It was the kind of thing that seemed to justify Yeats's most destructive criticisms. This is even more true of *You Never Can Tell*, which is as consciously 'light' as *The Philanderer*, but lacks even an interesting central character. Valentine, the hero, is not unlike Frank Gardner, the exuberant rake of *Mrs Warren's Profession*. He falls in love with the daughter of a dedicated feminist who has brought up her children to be sceptical and precocious. The comedy consists in his gradual breaking-down of the cold and proud Gloria until she ends by proposing to him. Shaw is never at his best in love scenes; Walkley put it neatly when he said that Shaw's view of love is not 'the exchange of two fantasies', as in Chamfort, but 'the exchange of two explanations'. This follows naturally from Shaw's view that love is unimportant compared to religion; but it is one of the least successful aspects of the Shavian drama. It was basically the same problem that he had encountered in the novels: that if the hero is to be strong and self-controlled, then he cannot fall in love, or at least, cannot be made to undergo the violent fluctuations of emotion that make Othello and Des Grieux interesting to us. It is not that Shaw is incapable of making love convincing; we are perfectly ready to believe that Cusins is in love with Major Barbara, that Sir Colenso Ridgeon is in love with Jennifer Dubedat, that the Captain in *Androcles* is in love with Lavinia. Shaw knows as much about love as any romantic novelist, and the male-female relation plays an important part in most of his plays. But since the definition of a Shaw hero is a man who has 'higher business on hand' than worshipping a woman, it follows that Shaw can hardly be concerned to show people falling in and out of love, and that when he does so for the sake of the drama, he approaches the whole business rather flippantly. Bluntschli has to marry Raina to wind up the play, but his proposal, like the rest of his character, has to be as efficient as clockwork. If people actually fall in love in a Shaw play, they have to be minor characters; in that case, the lovemaking is conducted on a brisk, matter-of-fact level. In *The Village Wooing* the characters are not even given names:

A. (*the man*). Are you married?

z. (*the woman*). No. Why? Have you any intentions?

A. Dont be in a hurry. Weve known each other less than ten minutes.

z. How much better do you think you will know me when we have talked for twenty years?

A. That is profoundly true. Still, I must think it over.

z. Nobody would ever marry if they thought it over.

This was admittedly written when Shaw was seventy-five; but it is not very different from the 'wooing' in *Arms and the Man* or

Man and Superman. When Shaw's sympathies are not engaged, he still writes amusingly; but it is Yeats's sewing machine.

But the year 1896—the year of *The Devil's Disciple*—marks the beginning of Shaw's great creative period, which lasted exactly a decade. Almost every play he wrote in this period—with the exception of a few minor works—is a masterpiece. It is also the period of his best critical book *The Perfect Wagnerite* (1898).

The immediate success of *The Devil's Disciple* is understandable. It is the first play in which all the Shavian principles are exemplified—that is to say, in which he pulls out all the stops. It is set in New England at the time of the American revolution. At the beginning of the play we are introduced to Mrs Dudgeon— sour, shrewish and puritanical (Shaw admitted his debt to Dickens' Mrs Clennam), and then to the minister Anthony Anderson, another healthy, muscular Christian like Morell. The family gather for the reading of a will. When the atmosphere of chilly, narrow-minded puritanism has been sufficiently established, the 'devil's disciple', Dick Dudgeon, comes in. The 'clash of egos' is instantaneous and satisfactory.

MRS DUDGEON (*rising and confronting him*). Silence your blasphemous tongue. I will bear no more of this. Leave my house.

RICHARD. How do you know its your house until the will is read? (*They look at one another for a moment with intense hatred; and then she sinks, checkmated, into her chair.*)

Inevitably, the will reveals that Dick is now master of the house. And after Dick has shocked all his respectable relatives with a speech in which he explains that he used to pray secretly to the devil—'he comforted me, and saved me from having my spirit broken in this house of children's tears'—she goes out, green with malice, shouting: 'My curse on you! My dying curse!' Dick's comment is: 'It will bring me luck.'

In the second act, Dick calls on the minister and his pretty wife Judith—who loathes Dick—and stays to tea while Anderson goes off to administer comfort to Mrs Dudgeon, who is dying. The British soldiers arrive and mistake Dick for Anderson—he is in his shirtsleeves—and arrest him. They intend to hang someone as an example. Dick tells Judith Anderson to find her husband and get him out of harm's way. She kisses him before they take him away, and faints. And in the scene that follows, when

Anderson returns, we can gauge Shaw's skill as a dramatist. What would happen in real life, of course, is that Judith would say: 'They came to arrest you and arrested Dick by mistake'—but that would destroy all the suspense. And so for another quarter of an hour, Anderson has to go on believing that it was Dick the soldiers came for, while the tension mounts; when finally she understands what has happened, his true character emerges; he becomes the man of action, and leaps on his horse. Any normal husband would, of course, explain what he intends to do, but that would again spoil the suspense, so Anderson rides off and leaves Judith believing that he has simply deserted Dick.

The third act is—as it should be—the best in the play. Judith visits him in prison, tells him of her husband's flight, and begs him to save himself. He tells her that his death won't break her heart, and Judith, placing her hands on his shoulders, whispers: 'How do you know?' And it is at this point that Dick makes the speech that is the point of the play:

'What I did last night, I did in cold blood, caring not half so much for your husband, or for you, as I do for myself. I had no motive and no interest: all I can tell you is that when it came to the point whether I would take my neck out of a noose and put another man's into it, I could not do it. I dont know why . . . but I could not and cannot.'

The trial scene that follows is another excellent example of the drama of the clash of egos—in this case, Dick and General Burgoyne. The latter is cultured, intelligent, with a vein of self-mockery.

RICHARD. I think you might have the decency to treat me as a prisoner of war, and shoot me like a man instead of hanging me like a dog.

BURGOYNE (*sympathetically*). Now there, Mr Anderson, you talk like a civilian, if you will excuse my saying so. Have you any idea of the average marksmanship of the army of His Majesty King George the Third? If we make you up a firing party, what will happen? Half of them will miss you: the rest will make a mess of the business and leave you to the provo-marshall's pistol. Whereas we can hang you in a perfectly workmanlike and agreeable way. (*Kindly*) Let me persuade you to be hanged, Mr Anderson?

In the final scene on the gallows Anderson gallops up at the last minute with a safe-conduct. It is not quite clear why this should prevent them from hanging Dick—they know by this time that he is not Anderson—but this hardly matters. Anderson explains that he has found his true profession in his hour of trial; he is a soldier at heart, not a clergyman. Whereas, quite clearly, Dick is a clergyman at heart. . . . The play ends with Dick being carried off in triumph on the shoulders of the townspeople, after promising Judith—who is ashamed of doubting her husband— that he will never tell Anderson what happened in prison.

It is in a play like this that one can see the advantage of Shaw's 'anti-romanticism'. If it had been presented 'straight', without the ironic overtones, Shaw would have been classified with Marie Corelli and Mrs Henry Wood. As it is, he gets the best of both worlds. The audience can revel in the romantic situations while convincing themselves that the pleasure is intellectual; they are involved while apparently uninvolved. It had never been done before. Earlier dramatists tried to involve the audience in the play as if it were reality; but Shaw—as Brecht recognised—knew that 'the mere reproduction of reality does not give the impression of truth'. It was also Brecht who observed: 'Probably every single feature of all Shaw's characters can be attributed to his delight in dislocating our stock associations.'* That is to say, Shaw invented the 'alienation effect' which became the centre of the Brechtian drama.

Inevitably, some early interpreters missed the point. Murray Carson, who played Dick in the first commercial performance in England, was convinced by a critic that Dick must be secretly in love with Judith to risk his life for her husband, 'and that his explicit denial of his passion was the splendid mendacity of a gentleman whose respect for a married woman . . . sealed his passion-palpitating lips. From the moment that this fatally plausible explanation was launched, my play became my critic's play, not mine. Thenceforth, Dick Dudgeon every night confirmed the critic by surreptitiously imprinting a heart-broken kiss on a stray lock of her hair whilst he uttered the barren denial'. Shaw tried to destroy the ground for this interpretation in the stage instructions of the printed version: '[Judith] is pretty and proper and

---

* 'Three Cheers for Shaw', *Berliner Börsen-Courier*, July 25th, 1926. Reprinted in *Brecht on Theatre*, Methuen, London 1964.

ladylike, and has been admired and petted into an opinion of herself sufficiently favourable to give her a self-assurance which serves her instead of strength.' All the same, it was not entirely the obtuseness of the critic and the actor that produced the misinterpretation. Again, the technical expertise of the play conceals its flaws as an exposition of ideas. Shaw once remarked of *Hamlet*: 'Had Shakespear plumbed his play to the bottom he would hardly have allowed Hamlet to send Rosencrantz and Guildenstern to their death. . . .'* And if Shaw had plumbed *The Devil's Disciple* to its bottom he would have found some more effective way of conveying Dick's 'natural Christianity' than the purely negative one of allowing himself to be arrested in another man's place. 'What happened to Hamlet', says Shaw, 'was what had happened fifteen hundred years before to Jesus. Born into the vindictive morality of Moses he has evolved into the Christian perception of the futility and wickedness of revenge and punishment, founded on the simple fact that two blacks do not make a white. But he is not philosopher enough to comprehend this as well as apprehend it.'† When Shaw placed Dick Dudgeon in a similar situation, he was also not philosopher enough to comprehend it as well as apprehend it, although he advanced his theory of Hamlet as a 'higher evolutionary type' in his review of 2nd October 1897, not long after the play was finished. Dick represents this instinctive 'higher morality', and Anderson— although a minister—represents the old morality of murder and militarism; unfortunately, none of this is explicit.

It is worth pausing, at this point, to consider the implications of Shaw's theory of 'higher evolutionary types'. Since the theory is the core of Shaw's work, it is necessarily the core of a book such as this.

Shaw writes badly about love because he is not concerned with the so-called 'natural urges' which are the stock in trade of most dramatists. What interests him are the apparently illogical impulses that move men to creativity or religion.

* Postscript, *Back to Methuselah*, World Classic edition, 1944.
† Ibid.

F

Now in this respect, he could hardly have been born at a worse time. In the second half of the nineteenth century people were getting tired of Victorian high-mindedness as exemplified by Matthew Arnold and Ruskin. At the time when Shaw was writing his early plays Freud was developing a theory of human nature that was the perfect antidote to 'high-mindedness', in that it found the true source of human behaviour in the 'lower impulses' of the subconscious mind. Psycho-analysis emphasised the violent and irrational side of human nature. Religion was an illusion; sex was the real driving impulse behind creativity. And later on, when sex seemed inadequate to explain man's destructiveness, Freud posited another basic drive: *thanatos*, the 'death wish'.

What Shaw was asserting was diametrically opposed to this. According to Shaw, man possesses 'higher impulses' that are just as instinctive as his lower impulses. Freud was a reductionist; he reduced the higher to the lower; Shaw was an evolutionist who saw the lower as a distorted version of the higher. Anderson's militarism is not an expression of a death-wish or frustrated sex-drives; it is just a cruder version of the evolutionary impulse that makes Dick risk his life.

Freud's emergence paralleled Shaw's, and his influence on the 'advanced' thought of his time was incomparably greater than Shaw's, since Freud was a 'scientist' and Shaw a mere playwright. Besides, it must be borne in mind that Shaw achieved fame as an iconoclast, an enemy of convention and hypocrisy, an advocate of social reform—and not as a philosopher with a theory of evolution. His contradiction of Freud—and of scientific 'reductionism' in general—carried no weight. It was more exciting to be told that Florence Nightingale suffered from repressed sexuality than that she was driven by an evolutionary impulse that transcended the sexual urge.

This should not be construed as a dismissal of Freud. His achievement in liberating the age from Victorian rationalism was greater than Shaw's, for it carried more weight. He emphasised that human behaviour is determined by vast forces that lie below the level of everyday consciousness, and this in itself was one of the greatest revolutions in modern thought; it completely altered the concept of human personality so that it came to include the 'depths'. And this was as much 'revolution' as his age could absorb. What Shaw did was to take *two steps* beyond Victorian rationalism, and to insist that the 'depths' contained positive and creative forces. Even if this had been fully understood in the first two decades of this century, it would have sounded like an attempt to let in religion and superstition through the back door. (In fact, this is exactly what Wells *did* accuse Shaw of.)

Half a century later Shaw's views are being more and more widely accepted by scientists and psychologists.* For example, Abraham Maslow, the 'existential psychologist' and President of the American Psychological Association, writes:

'[Existential psychology] draws some of the truly revolutionary consequences of the discovery that human nature has been sold short, that man has a higher nature which is just as "instinctoid" as his lower nature, and that this higher nature includes the needs for meaningful work, for responsibility, for creativeness, for being fair and just, for doing what is worthwhile and preferring to do it well.'† We are back with Shaw's definition of the classical as that which has 'produced the philosophy, the art, the poetry and the statecraft of the world, and not merely . . . its weddings, coroner's inquests and executions'. Twenty years after Shaw's death his 'mystical' views are seen to be as scientifically sound as Freud's pessimistic reductionism. It was Shaw's misfortune that he took two steps when the other major thinkers of his time only took one. We are now in a position—but only just in a position—to understand this, and to see why Shaw's comments on the science of his time appeared so anti-scientific to contemporaries like Wells. Shaw wrote: 'Impostor for impostor, I prefer the mystic to the scientist—the man who at least has the decency to call his nonsense a mystery, to him who pretends that it is ascertained, weighed, measured, analysed fact.' Wells wrote in his autobiography: 'To [Shaw], I guess, I have always appeared heavily and sometimes formidably facty and close-set; to me, his judgements, arrived at by feeling and expression, have always had a flimsiness. I want to get hold of Fact, strip her of her inessentials, and, if she behaves badly, put

* A theme I touch on in the Postscript to this volume.
† Preface to *Eupsychean Management*, Japanese edition (1967).

her in stays and irons; but Shaw dances round her and weaves a wilful veil of confident assurances about her as her true present-ment' (p. 540). In retrospect it can be seen that Wells missed the point. His attempt to grapple with Fact at close quarters only meant that he failed to see overall meanings. Shaw was in the position of the hero of Wells's *Country of the Blind*, who could see too far, and was consequently regarded as a madman.

What we can also see in retrospect is that the misunderstandings were partly Shaw's own fault. As late as 1926—when Shaw's reputation was already in eclipse—Brecht defended his method of self-advertisement, saying: 'Shaw's . . . doctrine is that if one is to express oneself freely . . . one has first of all to overcome a certain inborn fear: of being conceited.' There is some truth in this; but in reading Shaw's preface to *The Devil's Disciple* it is impossible not to feel that he was overdoing it.

'But the stage tricks of *The Devil's Disciple* are not, like some of those of *Arms and the Man*, the forgotten ones of the sixties, but the hackneyed ones of our own times. Why, then, were they not recognised? Partly, no doubt, because of my trumpet and cartwheel declamation. The critics were the victims of the long course of hypnotic suggestion by which G.B.S. the journalist manufactured an unconventional reputation for Bernard Shaw the author. In England as elsewhere the spontaneous recognition of really original work begins with a mere handful of people, and propagates itself so slowly that it has become a commonplace to say that genius, demanding bread, is given a stone after its possessor's death. The remedy for this is sedulous advertisement. Accordingly, I have advertised myself so well that I find myself, whilst still in middle life, almost as legendary a person as the Flying Dutchman. Critics, like other people, see what they look for, not what is actually before them. In my plays they look for my legendary qualities, and find originality and brilliancy in my most hackneyed claptraps. . . . Not, of course . . . the really able critics—for example, you, my friend, now reading this sentence. The illusion that makes *you* think me so original is far subtler than that. . . .'

This is frank enough. Shaw believed that self-advertisement would ensure that he did not starve. But when he wrote this preface he was already married to his 'green-eyed millionairess' and had made £3,000 on *The Devil's Disciple*. This no doubt explains the new level of effrontery. For it must be borne in mind that Shaw was *not* as 'legendary as the Flying Dutchman' in 1898. He had a small reputation as a music critic and drama critic, and he had written half a dozen plays, not one of which had been commercially successful in England. He is simply trying again the trick he used in the preface to *Love Among the Artists* in *Our Corner*. It is essentially a confidence trick, since it involves representing himself as far more important and substantial than he really is, in the hope of being accepted at his own valuation. It may have served his purpose, but as far as the English were concerned, it overserved it. James Agate remarked: 'The English instinctively admire any man who has no talent and is modest about it.' Conversely, no amount of talent can reconcile them to what looks like conceit.

If the financial security of marriage led to a new degree of self-assertion, it also gave him the relaxation he needed to produce a masterpiece, *Caesar and Cleopatra*. He spent his honeymoon at Haslemere writing *The Perfect Wagnerite*. He was just beginning to recuperate from the abscessed foot when he made a foolhardy attempt to descend the stairs on crutches. '. . . the crutches got planted behind my centre of gravity and shot me into the air. I snatched at a bannister on the landing above, and caught it in my right hand; but it snapped like an Argoed tree;* & I was precipitated fifty fathoms or thereabouts into the hall, with my left arm doubled up in ruin under me . . .' And then, when he had finally had the arm set: 'a cat, shut up accidentally in the pantry, simulated a burglar so successfully that I sallied out, walking recklessly on the bad foot, at three in the morning, & thereby did myself as much harm as possible'. A few weeks later his health seemed so much improved that he tried to ride a bicycle with one foot, and fell off, spraining his ankle. 'My situation is a solemn one. Life is offered to me on condition of eating beefsteaks. My weeping family crowd around me with

* Argoed was the name of the house in Monmouthshire taken by Sidney and Beatrice Webb.

Bovril and Brand's Essence. But death is better than cannibalism. My will contains directions for my funeral, which will be followed not by mourning coaches, but by herds of oxen, sheep, swine, flocks of poultry, and a small travelling aquarium of live fish, all wearing white scarves in honour of the man who perished rather than eat his fellow-creatures.' The foot kept discharging, although a new house at Hindhead improved his health, and various operations were necessary to remove bits of necrosed bone. Unable to sit still, he sprained the bad foot yet again in the early part of 1899, and still again in April while trying to ride a bicycle.

At least the long period of enforced rest gave him time to 'plumb his play to the depth'; he had decided to write a historical play about Caesar's visit to Egypt. Mommsen's history of Rome suited him better than Plutarch, since Plutarch alleges that Cleopatra had a son by Caesar, and Mommsen fails to mention this. He ended by making fairly equal use of Mommsen and Plutarch, and adding a great deal from his own imagination. He later told Pearson: 'Although I was forty-four or thereabouts when I wrote the play, I now think I was a trifle too young for the job; but it was not bad for a juvenile effort.' This was not modesty; doctors suspected that the basic trouble was tuberculosis; in which case, it might well be his last play. It had to be a major statement.

The healing was extremely slow. On September 2nd, 1899, he was writing to his French translator, Jules Magny, from Ruan Minor in Cornwall:

'I am in retreat at the seaside, preparing for a trip round the Mediterranean, from which I expect to return on the 31st October to work as usual. Most of my ailments are healed; but my foot is still weak in consequence of my having sprained it badly three times by premature attempts to bicycle with it.

'I am sorry I did not know know about Kufferath when I wrote that review for the Chronicle. They would not put in a second article for the sake of a foreign book not newly published; so I am afraid there is nothing to be done now in the way of making it known. I will send it back to you by parcel post as soon as I get it back from Haslemere, where it was accidentally included in a set of books presented by my wife to the local public house! I do not review regularly for any paper; and as my terms are special ones, I cannot volunteer contributions: I only write when I am asked by an editor.'*

It is worth noting that although in *Caesar and Cleopatra* Shaw had at last produced an undisputable masterpiece, nobody was interested, and it had to wait nine years to be produced in England (except for a single copyright performance at Newcastle). Archer's comment about it was '. . . Shaw has invented a new genre in this sort of historical extravaganza, though fortunately no one but he is likely to practise it.' Walkley dismissed it as a 'comic opera'. Even in America—which had responded so well to its immediate predecessor—it only managed to get a single student performance in Chicago in 1901. It even received a production in Germany—by Max Reinhardt in 1906—before it was seen in England.

It is arguable that *Caesar and Cleopatra*, taken all-in-all, is Shaw's greatest play. The reason for this is clear enough: apart from *Heartbreak House* and *As Far as Thought Can Reach*—both written when he was past his peak—it is the only play in which he is completely in earnest. Shaw's chief weakness was his flippancy—exemplified in *You Never Can Tell*, or in the last of the *Plays for Puritans, Captain Brassbound's Conversion*. There was a part of Shaw that was an actor, that revelled in his own person-ality, as can be seen from the extract of the *Devil's Disciple* preface already quoted. This is, of course, an oversimplification. No major writer can be divided in this way into a Jekyll and Hyde, although most of them are capable of producing a potboiler or a piece of journalism. Nevertheless, in Shaw's case, there is more justification than usual, for a large percentage of his plays are simply an exploitation of the Shaw personality and the Shaw tricks. This can certainly not be said of Ibsen or Tolstoy.

Shaw's Caesar, like his Shotover, was a projection of his most serious aspect. There is something almost symphonic about the writing of the beginning of the first act:

* I have included most of this letter, not only because it contains some interesting sidelights on Shaw, but because I came upon it in a rather peculiar way. Taking out a volume of my *Encyclopaedia Britannica*—which I had bought new some years before—one day, I found the letter inside it. I still have no idea of who put it there, or when. It is typewritten on the green-tinted paper that Shaw used to rest his eyes. I have no idea who Kufferath was.

'*The same darkness into which the temple of Ra and the Syrian palace vanished. The same silence. Suspense. Then the blackness and stillness break softly into silver mist and strange airs as the windswept harp of Memnon plays at the dawning of the moon. It rises full over the desert; and a vast horizon comes into relief, broken by a huge shape which soon reveals itself in the spreading radiance as a Sphinx pedestalled on the sands. The light still clears until the upraised eyes of the image are distinguished looking straight forward and upward in infinite fearless vigil, and a mass of colour between its paws defines itself as a heap of red poppies on which a girl lies motionless, her silken vest heaving gently and regularly with the breathing of a dreamless sleeper, and her braided hair glittering in a shaft of moonlight like a bird's wing.*

'*Suddenly there comes from afar a vaguely fearful sound (it might be the bellow of a Minotaur softened by great distance) and Memnon's music stops. Silence: then a few faint high-ringing trumpet notes. Then silence again. Then a man comes from the south with stealing steps, ravished by the mystery of the night, all wonder, and halts, lost in contemplation. . . .*'

In spite of the touch of rhetoric ('infinite fearless vigil') and the Swinburnian echoes ('south with stealing steps') this comes as close to poetry as anything Shaw ever wrote. Shaw was not a poet; his occasional attempts to sound like one are embarrassing. But he was a musician, and much of *Caesar and Cleopatra* has the the feeling of unity of mood of Wagner's *Ring* (since it was written immediately after *The Perfect Wagnerite* one suspects some influence here).

The speech that Caesar makes to the Sphinx is equally fine:

THE MAN. Hail, Sphinx; salutation from Julius Caesar! I have wandered in many lands, seeking the lost regions from which my birth into this world exiled me, and the company of creatures such as I myself. I have found flocks and pastures, men and cities, but no other Caesar, no air native to me, no man kindred to me, none who can do my day's deed and think my night's thought. . . .'

And reading this one becomes very sharply aware of the real 'Shaw problem'. If this speech had been written by Tolstoy or Goethe we would accept it as a poignant expression of the loneliness involved in greatness. Coming from the man who wrote *The Philanderer* and *You Never Can Tell*, it raises doubts. It is not that greatness and a sense of humour are incompatible; there is a great deal of humour in Beethoven's music. But this speech is written by the man who says in his preface:

'Again, they tell me that So-and-so, who does not write prefaces, is no charlatan. Well, I am. I first caught the ear of the British public on a cart in Hyde Park, to the blaring of brass bands, and this not at all as a reluctant sacrifice of my instinct of privacy to political necessity, but because, like all dramatists and mimes of genuine vocation, I am a natural-born mountebank.'

And one becomes aware that Shaw is trying to have it both ways. Humour is a way of refusing to be pinned down, of responding to an attack with 'I was only joking'. The humorist has, in a sense, renounced his right to speak seriously; if he attempts to reclaim it, his admirers may feel he is cheating. This is what happened to Shaw; this is the reason that Walkley called *Caesar and Cleopatra* 'a comic opera' and Archer felt it was merely a historical extravaganza. And to some extent Shaw played up to this idea by deliberately scattering anachronisms throughout the play; the harbour at Alexandria has a steam-winch, and the characters use modern phrases: Egypt for the Egyptians, the New Woman, Disraeli's Peace with Honour, and so on. But since Caesar himself is represented as having a sense of humour, these seem natural enough. What is more serious is that *Caesar and Cleopatra* should be sandwiched between a parody of conventional melodrama (*The Devil's Disciple* was originally written for William Terris, a famous actor of melodrama, who was unfortunately murdered by a lunatic before he could produce it), and another of Shaw's deliberate 'tomfooleries', *Captain Brassbound's Conversion*. One begins to understand why Shaw never made the impact he hoped for on his contemporaries.

But once we forget Shaw's 'incorrigible clowning', and concentrate on the play itself, it is difficult to understand how Walkley and Archer could have been so obtuse. What Shaw wanted to do here was to portray a Caesar who has outgrown the military ambitions of his youth and—like Hamlet—the moral codes of his time. It may seem paradoxical that Shaw should choose Caesar, who spent his life engaged in war and political intrigue, to exemplify his concept of the 'higher evolutionary type'; but it was essential to Shaw's purpose that his central character should be the 'world-leader' type. A humane philosopher might be more convincing than a humane dictator; but then it was Shaw's central belief that the 'higher evolutionary types' should be world leaders. Throughout his life he showed a tolerance for men-in-power that led some of his later critics to accuse him of fascism. He never subscribed to the anarchist belief that power corrupts; at least, his feeling was that whether it corrupts or not, man has to learn to handle it. He admired men who were not afraid to seek power, because it seemed natural to him that any intelligent man should want power to reorganise the world. This was why he tried—unsuccessfully—to make a hero out of Napoleon; but there the facts of history were against him. The facts as interpreted by Mommsen were less intractable. 'The old divine theory worked', says King Magnus, 'because there is a divine spark in us all; and the stupidest or worst monarch or minister, if not wholly god, is a bit of a god—an attempt at a god—however little the bit and unsuccessful the attempt.' And a monarch or a minister, no matter how bad, is at least a man who deals with facts—with political, social and biological facts. And having started life as a shrinking, subjective person, Shaw attached great importance to the discipline of grappling with fact. It was this aspect of him that made him so repellant to Yeats, Eliot and other neo-romantics, and so attractive to Brecht.

Shaw's Caesar, then, is a new step in his development, beyond the unsocial socialist and the unworldly poet and the devil's disciple who is a natural Christian. He is Shaw's first—and perhaps most successful—attempt to portray the visionary-turned-world betterer.

During the long period of his illness Shaw admitted to Beatrice Webb that 'somebody before the operation suggested the possibility of my dying under the anaesthetic, and I found that the prospect was not in the least disagreeable to me—rather too tempting to be dwelt on, if anything'. The statement is surprisingly 'romantic' for Shaw, who normally had no patience with Wagnerian death worship. But then, his Caesar is also a romantic character. Driven from country to country by his search for 'the lost regions from which my birth into this world exiled me', he is actually closer to Yeats than to Mommsen or Plutarch. The play owes its power to this romantic—almost morbid—impulse that drives it. C. B. Purdom has pointed out that Caesar's long speeches are really operatic arias. The whole quality of the play is close to music.

The romantic impulse carried over into the title of his next play, *The Witch of the Atlas*. But by this time—the second part of 1899—he was almost recovered from the illness. Shelley's ethereal witch became another healthy, common-sensible Shavian heroine —Lady Cicely Waynflete. It was a bad idea of Shaw's to try to follow up his portrait of a hero who is 'a little bit of a god' with a heroine who is supposed to be a little bit of a goddess. Shaw did not believe in goddesses, and his attempts to put them on the stage are never convincing. Lady Cicely flatters, cajoles, mothers and bullies all the men in the play. There is something oddly disagreeable about this attempt of Shaw's to force her on his audience as the sort of person they ought to admire; one wonders whether *he* really admired such a type, or whether he was simply trying to create a part for Ellen Terry (who in the event rejected it). He called the play 'a religious tract'—presumably because Captain Brassbound, the 'hero', finds himself at the last moment unable to kill a man for revenge. In fact, *Captain Brassbound's Conversion* (as it was finally called) is neither a good tract nor a good play. It is an example of how far Shaw could misunderstand his own genius when the daemon of paradox and self-advertisement was upon him.

Perhaps Shaw recognised this; it was two years before he began another play—*Man and Superman*—and four before he finished it. By then the new century had arrived—a century in which Shaw was to become the most famous writer of his time.

7 WORLD CELEBRITY

The year 1900 found Shaw back in robust health again, with the additional satisfaction of having proved that a man can recuperate as well on nuts and lettuce as on meat. He had every reason to feel satisfied with life. He had moved into Charlotte's flat at 10 Adelphi Terrace—behind the Strand, overlooking the river and the Embankment Gardens. Charlotte had settled an annuity of £600 on his mother (whom she nevertheless disliked). The strenuous days of theatre criticism were behind him, and his activities as a Fabian and St Pancras vestryman could be just as exacting as he wanted them to be. Beatrice Webb was not entirely happy about his playwriting activities; she had noted in her journal of the previous year: 'He still writes, but his work seems to be getting unreal: he leads a hothouse life. . . .' She was not entirely happy about Shaw's marriage either, for Charlotte obviously enjoyed being a married woman, and—intentionally or otherwise —made the Webbs feel intruders when they came to stay. Charlotte was also slightly less co-operative than she had been about money for the London School of Economics:

'If you want University Endowments from me you should not have married me to an anarchist. I have consulted G.B.S. as to whether I should send you a thousand pounds. He tells me that if I do so it will please you and Beatrice . . . besides providing outdoor relief for a certain number of stuttering nincompoops who are too feeble to earn their livings in the professions. On the other hand, he declares, it will extend the present machinery for perverting and repressing research. . . . On the whole, he cannot

conceive any method by which £1,000 can be made to produce
more widespread social mischief. . . . He suggests that if you were
to produce Candida with that £1,000, you would not only do
some real good to Society but possibly get your money back with
100 per cent to have over for the School.' The upshot was not an
outright refusal, but a cautious and conditional promise: 'I am
not so light hearted about giving money away as I was . . . You
yourself refused to guarantee the National Provincial Bank for
more than twenty years, and we have now reached a time of life
at which we realise what a very short time twenty years is.'

Shaw's literary career seemed to be progressing satisfactorily,
but at no great speed. 'I was rated in the theatrical world of
London as an absurd pamphleteer, who had been allowed to
display his ignorance of the rudiments of stage technique and his
hopeless incapacity for representing human nature. . . .' Ellen
Terry's flat refusal of *Captain Brassbound's Conversion* was a
disappointment and a considerable setback, and since no one else
seemed very interested in producing Shaw plays, this aspect of his
career seemed to be marking time, and he concentrated on Fabian
essays. There was even some thought of going into Parliament.

One result of the sudden release from the strain of daily
journalism was that he ceased to enjoy meeting strangers; Charlotte noted on several occasions that he found people tiring. This
almost lost him one of the most valuable contacts of his life.
One day towards the end of 1900,* a young German playwright,
Siegfried Trebitsch, knocked on the door of their flat with a letter
of introduction from Archer. He wanted to translate Shaw's
plays into German. Shaw's immediate response was to call
upstairs to his wife: 'Charlotte, here's a young lunatic Archer's
sent me who wont listen to reason. You come and calm him
down,' and to leave the room. Luckily, Mrs Shaw was impressed
by any man who thought her husband a genius, and could see
no harm in trying to get his plays published in Germany; she
persuaded Shaw to come back and talk to Trebitsch. The result
was that Fischer Verlag brought out the plays, and *The Devil's
Disciple* and *Arms and the Man* were performed in Vienna in

* Janet Dunbar gives 1901 as the year; Henderson, 1900. No doubt the
publication of the second volume of Shaw's letters will clear up the confusion.

1903 and 1904, and two years later had spread as far as Prague and Copenhagen. Europe took Shaw very seriously; the Danish critic George Brandes wrote: 'He has continued to be misunderstood by his countrymen. . . . Off their path, a solitary wanderer, he has gone his own way and succeeded with the chosen few.'

Dramatically speaking, he was at the height of his powers. The complete absence of performance of his plays led him to think in terms of publication in book form. Grant Richards had already published the two volumes of *Plays Pleasant and Unpleasant* with some success and they had also appeared in America; in 1901, the *Three Plays for Puritans* came out. Now he began to think of a play that should occupy a volume to itself, a 'Book of Genesis for the Bible of the Evolutionists'. The result, which was nearly two years in the writing, was *Man and Superman*, 'A Comedy and a Philosophy'. Written at the exact mid-point of Shaw's life, it is his most completely 'Shavian' play. Tolstoy objected that it was frivolous, and to a large extent he was right. It is the last bow of Sidney Trefusis, the unsocial socialist, who now reappears as John Tanner, M.I.R.C.—Member of the Idle Rich Class. The enormous momentum of the play—and it surges on for five hours like a roller coaster—is derived almost entirely from Tanner's speeches. The humour from his constant failure to make himself understood.

ANN. But, Jack, you cannot get through life without considering other people a little.

TANNER. Ay; but what other people? It is this consideration of other people—or rather this cowardly fear of them which we call consideration—that makes us the sentimental slaves we are. To consider you, as you call it, is to substitute your will for my own. How if it be a baser will than mine? Are women taught better than men or worse? Are mobs of voters taught better than statesmen or worse? Worse, of course, in both cases. And then what sort of a world are you going to get, with its public men considering its voting mobs, and its private men considering their wives? What does Church and State mean nowadays? The Woman and the Ratepayer.

ANN [*placidly*]. I'm so glad you understand politics, Jack: it will be most useful to you if you go into parliament. [*He collapses like a pricked bladder.*]

What becomes clear from this play is that Shaw's aim was always to create *the drama of pure intelligence*. *Man and Superman* makes no compromises—unless the sub-plot of the clandestine marriage of Violet and Hector Malone is regarded as a romantic concession; the interest derives solely from the ideas. At every opportunity, Tanner goes off at a tangent:

RAMSDEN [*very deliberately*]. Mr Tanner: you are the most impudent person I have ever met.

TANNER [*seriously*]. I know it, Ramsden. Yet even I cannot wholly conquer shame. We live in an atmosphere of shame. We are ashamed of everything that is real about us; ashamed of ourselves, of our relatives, of our incomes, of our accents, of our opinions, of our experience, just as we are ashamed of our naked skins. Good Lord, my dear Ramsden, we are ashamed to walk, ashamed to ride in an omnibus, ashamed to hire a hansom instead of keeping a carriage, ashamed of keeping one horse instead of two and a groom gardener instead of a coachman and footman. The more things a man is ashamed of, the more respectable he is. Why, youre ashamed to buy my book, ashamed to read it: the only thing youre not ashamed of is to judge me for it without having read it; and even that only means youre ashamed to have heterodox opinions. Look at the effect I produce because my fairy godmother withheld from me this gift of shame. I have every possible virtue that a man can have except——

RAMSDEN. I am glad you think so well of yourself.

TANNER. All you mean by that is that you think I ought to be ashamed of talking about my virtues. You dont mean that I havent got them: you know perfectly well that I am as sober and honest a citizen as yourself, as truthful personally, and much more truthful politically and morally.

This is perhaps the point to make a minor observation about Shaw's punctuation. From a very early stage, he used semicolons where most people would use a comma ('Mr Tanner; you are the most impudent person I have ever met'), and colons where most people would use a semi-colon ('. . . ashamed to read it: the only thing youre not ashamed of . . .'). There is no harm in this; but his other idiosyncrasy, refusal to use apostrophes, leads to difficulties. He can write 'youre' instead of 'you're' without ambiguity; but he cannot write 'were' instead of 'we're', and even 'Im' instead of 'I'm' would look odd; so he is forced to write it out fully, slowing down the flow: 'Good Lord, my dear Ramsden, we are ashamed to walk . . .', 'I am as sober and honest a citizen as yourself . . .' Some of his other innovations are more reasonable. Since 'till' is short for 'until', it is logical to spell it 'til'. The same may be said of the dropping of italics for titles; it is certainly simpler to write Candida instead of *Candida*; 200 years ago all proper names were italicised; in another 200 years, no doubt we shall have adopted Shaw's practice of dispensing with all italics that are not intended for emphasis. His use of 'shew' instead of 'show' is perhaps his most dubious innovation. The point to note is that even in a small matter like punctuation, we encounter the basic Shaw problem: common sense or exhibitionism; realism, or just the desire to be different?

The 'Book of Genesis' part of *Man and Superman* is its third act, a dream sequence that takes place in hell; it is a long discussion—so long that it can be performed as a separate play—on human evolution. The participants are Tanner's ancestor Don Juan, the Devil, the statue of the Commendatore (who dragged Don Juan off to hell in Mozart's opera) and Dona Ana de Ulloa—Ann Whitefield in a previous incarnation. Shaw's hell is not an unpleasant place, except to a man driven by the evolutionary appetite; on the contrary, it is the home of pleasure and seekers after pleasure, that is to say, of people whose evolutionary appetite is so feeble that they have nothing to think about but themselves. Dona Ana—the Commendatore's daughter—has just died, and finds Don Juan sitting alone in empty space, brooding bitterly on the dreariness of eternal pleasure. Later, the Devil and the Commendatore arrive, and Juan tries to explain to Ana why he finds hell so sickening: for a man with a sense of purpose, hell is to be condemned to inactivity. This leads him to expound his evolutionary doctrine, which is the reverse of Darwin's Natural Selection by chance. For Shaw, life is a purposive force that is attempting to invade the realm of matter. Above all else, it is a drive for organisation, that began with unicellular organisms and then learned to organise itself into more complex units. Its

problem is the conquest of matter. To do this, it needs to understand the laws of matter; and this, in turn, requires consciousness
and reason. '. . . to Life, the force behind the Man, intellect is a
necessity, because without it he blunders into death. Just as Life,
after ages of struggle, evolved that wonderful bodily organ the
eye, so that the living organism could see where it was going and
what was coming to help or threaten it, and thus avoid a thousand
dangers that formerly slew it, so it is evolving today a mind's eye
that shall see, not the physical world, but the purpose of Life
and thereby enable the individual to work for that purpose instead
of thwarting and baffling it by setting up shortsighted personal
aims as at present.'

This is as clear as it could be and it should stand at the head
of Shaw's works as his ultimate justification. Life aims at intellect
as its most important objective. Walt Whitman or D. H. Lawrence
would reject such a view with a shudder, declaring that intellect
is only man's top layer, and that to attach too much importance
to it is to detract from man as a whole, as a total being. But this
is to miss the point. Shaw would agree that man must evolve as
a whole, emotionally, intuitively, as well as intellectually. But
what is necessary at this point in evolution is a sense of conscious
purpose. In the past, religion has been the expression of man's
evolutionary drive, and through the organisation of the Church
it became a living force in society. 'That [Natural Selection]
accounts for nothing in any religious sense is of course true; for
it leaves untouched the whole sphere of will, purpose, design,
intention, even consciousness; and a religion is nothing but a
common view of the nature of will, the purpose of life, the
design of organism, and the intention of evolution. Such a
common view has been gradually detaching itself from the welter
of negation provoked by the extremely debased forms of religion
that have masqueraded as Christianity in England during the
period of petty commercialism from which we are emerging.'*
Shaw was being too optimistic in believing that a new religion was
detaching itself from the 'welter of negation' caused by the
church's loss of credit; but he grasped clearly the historical
nature of the problem that had destroyed so many of the romantics. A society without a religion is like a ship without a steersman;

---

* Foreword to the popular sixpenny edition of *Man and Superman*, 1911.

it is at the mercy of chance and its own worst elements. Moreover, in such a society, even the men who possess evolutionary purpose are hindered and frustrated, since there is no natural place for them except as entertainers. In a theocratic society, the church offers a natural refuge to artists, philosophers and musicians as well as to men of religious vocation; in a materialistic society, large numbers of them are rendered sterile, not only because there is no place for them, but because they possess no conscious purpose to replace the discredited religion. Shaw had experienced the problem at first hand, over twenty years, struggling to find a place in a society with no particular place for genius. The novels had been a long, immense false start; even Fabianism had been a second-best, an outlet for the frustrated energies of idealism; for, as Beatrice Webb noticed, that kind of work requires a second-rate mind. Even playwriting failed to provide the necessary outlet for his creativity until he stumbled upon his true theme: the evolutionary impulse and its workings. What made Shaw the greatest playwright of his time was the total commitment to a purpose; he felt himself to be an instrument of the evolutionary force as a saint feels himself the servant of God. His own development would certainly have been smoother if he had not been obliged to find out every step of the way for himself. It followed clearly that his own business was to mark out the way clearly for those who would come after him. Admittedly, he could only write the first book of the Bible; this would be no substitute for a church. It still meant that every man of genius would have to stand alone, without support—which meant that an entirely new level of strength would be necessary for these outsiders in the future. But strength arises out of a sense of purpose; and purpose can be seen by the light of the intellect. Hence the need for the 'mind's eye that shall see . . . the purpose of Life'. And the first step was to state all this as clearly as possible. *Don Juan in Hell* is exactly what Shaw called it; the Book of Genesis of the Bible of Evolutionism.

It is interesting to look back over the route Shaw had travelled to reach this point. First there was Smith, the 'hermit' of *Immaturity*, the man who merely feels 'separate' from society. Then comes the man of purpose: the engineer of *The Irrational Knot* and the composer of *Love Among the Artists*. The poet in *Candida* marks a new level of intensity of evolutionary purpose, beyond the socialism of Sidney Trefusis and Morell. But in Dick Dudgeon, the purpose marks time; it merely ensures that in a crisis he cannot save his own skin by betraying another man. In Caesar, it seems to have found an outlet at last; but on closer examination, this proves to be untrue. Caesar does not conquer the world because he is driven by the force behind evolution, but because he is driven by the politics of Rome and his own natural dominance. As to the evolutionary urge, it finds expression in this romantic longing for 'the lost regions', the home of 'some eternal sentinel below, whose post I could never find'. When Rufio warns him that there are too many daggers in Rome, Caesar replies: 'It matters not; I shall finish my life's work on my way back; and then I shall have lived long enough.' This is not far from the death-romanticism of *Tristan and Isolde*.

John Tanner, in *Man and Superman*, is another social reformer like Trefusis; but his ancestor and alter ego, Don Juan, has advanced to a more direct level of evolutionary purpose. '. . . as long as I can conceive something better than myself I cannot be easy unless I am striving to bring it into existence or clearing the way for it. That is the law of my life. That is the working within me of Life's incessant aspiration to higher organisation, wider, deeper, intenser self-consciousness, and clearer self-understanding.' He intends to go to heaven because 'If the play still goes on here and on earth, and all the world is a stage, heaven is at least behind the scenes. But heaven cannot be described by metaphor. Thither I shall go presently because there I hope to escape at last from lies and from the tedious, vulgar pursuit of happiness, to spend my eons in contemplation . . .' Dona Ana asks: 'Is there nothing in heaven but contemplation, Juan?' and he replies: 'In the heaven I seek, no other joy. But there is also the work of helping Life in its struggle upwards. Think of how it wastes and scatters itself in its ignorance and blindness. It needs a brain, this irresistible force, lest in its ignorance it should resist itself.'

I have tried to show that no matter how successful Shaw's plays may appear to be dramatically, they remain oddly fumbling, journeyman works on their most interesting level—the level of the ideas they set out to dramatise. It is as if a philosopher were to write an enormous and erudite work on the meaning of human existence, and end by admitting that he has no idea of the answer. Shaw's plays are all about the same theme: the obscure creative drive of the 'Life Force', and the way that it makes people do things they find difficult to understand in terms of everyday logic. One of the clearest statements of the theme—which also happens to be one of his worst plays—is *The Shewing Up of Blanco Posnet* (1909), set in a highly improbable Wild West and written in an even more improbable Americanese. Blanco is a horse-thief and a self-proclaimed bad man, who gives up his stolen horse to a woman who needs to get her dying child to a doctor. He is caught and put on trial. But just as he 'went soft' and gave his horse to the woman, so the witness against him—a prostitute—goes soft when the moment comes to give evidence. Blanco ends by preaching a sermon:

'. . . I'm a fraud and a failure. I started in to be a bad man like the rest of you. . . . I took the broad path because I thought I was a man and not a snivelling canting turning-the-other-cheek apprentice angel. . . . Why did I go soft. . . .? Why did the Sheriff go soft? Why did Feemy go soft? What's the game that upsets our game? Our game is a rotten game. . . . T'other game may be a silly game; but it aint rotten. . . . When I played it I cursed myself for a fool; but I lost the rotten feel all the same.'

This is among the worst dialogue Shaw ever wrote, but it makes his theme very clear. And having grasped this theme—that the force behind evolution is propelling us in a certain direction—we encounter the obvious question: *Which* direction? What are we supposed to *do*? To say we have to stop playing the 'rotten game' is a beginning, but it is negative. Shaw is also quite clear that sainthood is not the answer. Saints were embodiments of this evolutionary drive in the past, and will no doubt continue to be so; but simple goodness is only the basic condition of evolution. What is necessary at this point is *conscious*, purposive movement instead of the instinctive impulse to goodness; we must develop the 'mind's eye' to see the purpose of evolution.

The 'modern' acts of *Man and Superman* deal once again with the instinctive aspect of the evolutionary drive:

TANNER. I will not marry you. I will not marry you.

ANN. Oh, you will, you will.

TANNER. I tell you, no no, no.

ANN. I tell you, yes, yes, yes.

TANNER. No.

ANN. [*coaxing—imploring—almost exhausted*] Yes. Before it is too late for repentance. Yes.

TANNER [*struck by the echo from the past*] When did all this happen to me before? Are we two dreaming?

ANN. . . . No. We are awake; and you have said no: that is all.

TANNER [*brutally*] Well?

ANN. Well, I made a mistake: you do not love me.

TANNER [*seizing her in his arms*] It is false: I love you. The Life Force enchants me: I have the whole world in my arms when I clasp you. But I am fighting for my freedom. . . .

His ancestor Don Juan had had exactly the same experience:

DON JUAN: Bah! what need I add? Do you not understand that when I stood face to face with Woman, every fibre in my clear critical brain warned me to spare her and save myself. My morals said No. My conscience said No. My chivalry and pity for her said No. My prudent regard for myself said No. . . . And whilst I was in the act of framing my excuse to the lady, Life seized me and threw me into her arms as a sailor throws a scrap of fish into the mouth of a seabird.

This is what fascinates Shaw: this enormous force that ignores our human preferences, our logic and intellect. It fascinates him because to be suddenly gripped by it is to see that human beings are not the accidental products of a mechanical universe—that they are not 'alone'. As social animals, we live in a narrow but apparently logical world with a well-defined identity and position. But man is the satellite of a double star; there is also an inner-world that seems to have a completely different set of laws from the rational universe. And in fact, if we judge this 'rational universe' by its own laws, we see that it is not self-complete and self-explanatory; space must end somewhere, time must have a stop; but the alternative propositions sound equally 'logical': space is infinite; time has neither beginning nor end. The answer to these paradoxes must be that the outer universe is not self-complete; it is only half a universe. The inner world is the other half. But at present we know very little about this inner world.

It is only within the present century that its existence has been clearly recognised by psychology.

What interests Shaw is what happens when the 'second star' begins to exert its gravitational pull on human beings living in their narrow, logical universe. And if his work was to continue to develop beyond *Man and Superman*, it had to attempt to explore this problem more deeply, or at least, to treat new aspects of it. If evolution strives to become conscious, then a whole new dimension of knowledge becomes necessary. At the moment, man is an instinctive creature, almost as passive as a tree. And if we can imagine a tree that wants to evolve into a human being, we can see that it will need to move out of its narrow, passive exist-ence into a completely different *form of life*. And what would the equivalent of this 'evolutionary leap' be for human beings? Obviously, we are narrow, hide-bound, passive; this pattern of passive acceptance has to be somehow broken up. The tree is surrounded by a whole complex, infinite universe of which it is unaware, because it lacks 'senses'. What man reaches towards could almost be defined as some *new sense or faculty*, the capacity to see infinite potential and complexity where at present he sees a world he takes for granted.

What is so remarkable about *Man and Superman* is that in spite of its lightness of touch, and in spite of its uncompromising intellectualism, it remains such a powerful and moving play. The third act—*Don Juan in Hell*—particularly achieves the symphonic quality of *Caesar and Cleopatra*, demonstrating once again that when Shaw was most obsessed by ideas he was at his best as an artist. The opening of the act is one of Shaw's most successful absurdities—the political brigands having a debate on whether anarchists or social democrats have the most personal courage. Tanner and his chauffeur Straker are captured by the brigands and held to ransom. The meeting between Tanner and the president of the brigands is a classic moment:

MENDOZA [*with dignity*] Allow me to introduce myself: I am Mendoza, President of the League of the Sierra! [*Posing loftily*] I am a brigand: I live by robbing the rich.

TANNER [*promptly*] I am a gentleman: I live by robbing the poor. Shake hands.

This brief exchange illustrates another aspect of Shaw that is always a delight: the highly civilised level at which his characters interact. The masters of the world—General Burgoyne, Caesar, Andrew Undershaft, Charles II, King Magnus—are all reasonable and cultured men, who allow their subordinates to say what they like to them. And this is not a failure of realism on Shaw's part, but an important part of his artistic purpose. He believes that it is the artist's business not only to project that which might be, but that which *should* be, since he also believes that works of art can influence the course of evolution.

When the brigands fall asleep, the hell scene begins:

'. . . *the sky seems to steal away out of the universe. Instead of the Sierra there is nothing: omnipresent nothing. No sky, no peaks, no light, no sound, no time nor space, utter void. Then somewhere the beginning of a pallor, and with it a faint throbbing buzz as of a ghostly violoncello palpitating on the same note endlessly. A couple of ghostly violins presently take advantage of this bass . . . and therewith the pallor reveals a man in the void, an incorporated but visible man, seated, absurdly enough, on nothing.*'

This curiously haunting atmosphere persists through two hours of philosophical discussion, until the Devil and the Statue are descending in a kind of lift:

ANA. Stop! [*The trap stops*]

THE DEVIL. You, Señora, cannot come this way. You will have an apotheosis. But you will be at the palace before us.

ANA. That is not what I stopped you for. Tell me: where can I find the Superman?

THE DEVIL. He is not yet created, Señora.

THE STATUE. And never will be, probably. Let us proceed: the red fire will make me sneeze. [*They descend*]

ANA. Not yet created! Then my work is not yet done. [*Crossing herself devoutly*] I believe in the Life to Come. [*Crying to the universe*] A father! a father for the Superman!

[*She vanishes into the void, and again there is nothing; all existence seems suspended infinitely. Then vaguely there is a live human voice crying somewhere. One sees, with a shock, a mountain peak shewing faintly against a lighter background . . .*]

The police have arrived in search of Tanner, and the dream is over. And typically, Tanner refuses to betray the brigands to the police, declaring that they are his escort, and '*Mendoza, with a Mephistophean smile, bows profoundly. An irrepressible grin runs from face to face among the brigands. They touch their hats, except the Anarchist, who defies the State with folded arms'.*

It was typical of Shaw that he was not contented simply to make *Man and Superman* the embodiment of his evolutionism, but that he had to complicate the issue by adding another thesis: that it is woman, not man, who is the pursuer. Furthermore, he used the preface to expound his anti-Freudian doctrine that sex may be superseded by higher appetites: '. . . the world's books get written, its pictures painted, its statues modelled, its symphonies composed, by people who are free from the otherwise universal dominion of the tyranny of sex. Which leads us to the conclusion, astonishing to the vulgar, that art, instead of being before all things the expression of the normal sexual situation, is really the only department in which sex is a superseded and secondary power . . .' In addition to his five-hour play and a thirty-page preface he also wrote a seventy-page *Revolutionist's Handbook and Pocket Companion*, purporting to be the work of John Tanner, which was added as an appendix. Eighteen years later, he observed correctly: 'The effect was so vertiginous, apparently, that nobody noticed the new religion in the centre of the intellectual whirlpool.'

But the real reason that *Man and Superman* failed to make the impact Shaw expected was that it was *a play*. Bergson's *Creative Evolution*, which appeared three years later, influenced the climate of European philosophical thought in spite of the increasing trend of materialism and positivism. There is nothing in Bergson's book that Shaw would have been incapable of writing, and in one important sense, Bergson's theory is cruder than Shaw's, for he over-emphasises the inability of reason to grasp the flowing contours of life, and thus tends towards the anti-intellectualism that D. H. Lawrence later made fashionable. Shaw understood the importance of the intellect in the evolutionary scheme; that it will lead the way to the creation of the 'mind's eye' capable of seeing the purpose of Life. Bergson speaks of the development of 'intuition', 'instinct that has become disinterested and self-conscious', and fails to emphasise the importance of intellect.

It is true that Bergson's fashion as a philosopher waned in less than a decade, and that he was virtually forgotten by 1920; nevertheless, his ideas at least gained a following, and some of his followers were men of his own intellectual stature: William James, T. E. Hulme, Teilhard de Chardin. By comparison, Shaw was without influence; not a single one of his intellectual equals agreed with him. In later years, his fame tended to obscure his lack of real influence; but Shaw was aware of it. He was the world's foremost playwright of ideas, and no one took his ideas seriously.

As far as performances went, 1903 was one of Shaw's worst years since he began writing plays; the only production in England was of a version of *Cashel Byron's Profession* written in blank verse and presented in a single performance that Shaw did not even attend. Charlotte was insisting that they do a great deal of travelling; her idea was to make Shaw rest; she had not yet grasped that Shaw's idea of rest *was* work. In March 1904 Shaw was badly beaten when he stood again for St Pancras in the elections for the London County Council, although he was apparently the only Progressive candidate in London who failed to get in. Beatrice Webb called it a 'humiliating defeat', but it seems possible that Shaw engineered his own defeat by refusing to make any concessions in his election campaign—declaring himself a Freethinker, refusing to dispense bribes, and demanding the nationalisation of alcoholic beverages. In 1902 he promised W. B. Yeats a new play for the Irish Literary Guild at the Abbey Theatre, Dublin—he had sketched out the idea of the contrast of the English and Irish temperaments in a conversation with Yeats as early as 1900. This was no more successful than his last two plays; the Guild declared it 'beyond their resources', meaning presumably that it had too many characters (twelve); the real reason was probably that the Irish peasantry are represented as sluggish, narrow-minded and dishonest. (The reception of Synge's *Playboy* in 1907 certainly justified their caution.)

But the tide *was* turning. There was the Vienna performance of *The Devil's Disciple* which presented Shaw to Europe; it was hardly a great success, but it was a beginning. And then, in December 1903, a young American actor, Arnold Daly, decided to try out a matinée performance of *Candida* in New York; the play he was currently acting in looked like folding, and he urgently needed an alternative. It confounded all Mansfield's predictions by making an immediate success, and after 150 performances in New York, it went on tour and continued its triumphal procession throughout America.

At the Stage Society Shaw had met a young actor, Harley Granville Barker, who had already written *Prunella*, in collaboration with Laurence Housman, and *The Marrying of Ann Leete*, a curious work in which the conclusion anticipates *Lady Chatterley's Lover*. Barker was the only playwright of this period who might have achieved a stature approaching Shaw's; four of his six plays are masterpieces. In 1904 Barker had not yet reached maturity as a playwright; but it was he who decided to follow up the New York success of *Candida* with a few matinées at the Royal Court Theatre in Sloane Square. It received half a dozen performances in April and May 1904, and was successful enough to decide Barker, in partnership with J. E. Vedrenne (the manager of the Court), to present five of Shaw's plays in an 'experimental' season. Hesketh Pearson says without exaggeration that the three-year partnership of Barker and Vedrenne was the most noteworthy episode in English theatrical history since Shakespeare and Burbage ran the Globe. The first real Shaw success at the Court was the rejected Abbey play, *John Bull's Other Island*, in November 1904. The night of November 1st, 1904, was, in fact, the turning point in Shaw's life as a playwright. If the first performance of *Arms and the Man* had made him 'the most formidable man in London', the first performance of *John Bull's Other Island* made him the most famous writer in Europe. What happened was simply that a new public discovered Shaw—the upper-class intelligent public, that had never bothered with Stage Society performances, and that had thought of Shaw as a tiresome radical. The Court changed all that. Quite suddenly it was obvious that a new star had risen in the literary sky. Success was enormous and instantaneous. The Prime Minister, Mr Balfour, went to see it four times, taking various other political celebrities with him. And the ultimate seal of success was set upon the play—and upon Shaw—when in March 1905 King Edward VII commanded a performance of the play, and laughed so heartily that he broke the chair he was sitting on.

There were a great many other plays presented at the Court during the 1904–5 season, including works by Schnitzler, Hauptmann, Maeterlink, Yeats, Euripides and Barker's own *Prunella*; but it was fundamentally a Shaw season. The other four plays by Shaw were *Candida, You Never Can Tell, Man and Superman* and a triviality called *How He Lied to Her Husband*. Of these, *Man and Superman* was by far the most successful, with Granville Barker as Tanner. Later in the year *Man and Superman* was presented in New York by Robert Loraine, and was as immediate and startling a success as *The Devil's Disciple* and *Candida* had been; Loraine even brought the *Don Juan in Hell* act to the Court in 1907 and made a success of it.

Shaw was 'in'. His royalties were enormous. (Loraine made £40,000 out of *Man and Superman* alone,* and went on to produce most of Shaw's other plays.) *Man and Superman* had been published by a new publisher, Constable and Co., having been rejected by John Murray, but in effect Shaw was now his own publisher, since he paid for the printing and superintended every detail of the paper, print and binding. After nearly thirty years of 'literary struggle' Shaw was in the seat of power. Arnold Daly even took the rash step of producing *Mrs Warren's Profession* in America in 1905, first in New Haven—where the theatre's licence was revoked—then in New York—where half the cast was arrested. The scandal only added to the uproar surrounding Europe's newest literary celebrity.

But an ominous note already sounds when we examine the list of plays presented at the Court in 1905. Shaw declared that he had made 'an original play' out of the old materials of the eternal triangle; the result was *How He Lied to Her Husband*. It is the first of many plays that reveal a disturbing lack of self-criticism. Like *You Never Can Tell* and *The Admirable Bashville* it is one of his 'tomfooleries'. But *You Never Can Tell* was written when he was trying to establish himself as a playwright, and *Bashville* was

* Of which Shaw got 10 per cent.

written only to prevent *Cashel Byron's Profession* from being pirated. One might defend *How He Lied to Her Husband* by saying that it was written as a curtain-raiser to *The Man of Destiny*, and that in any case it is not intended to be taken seriously; but this would be to miss the point. If it was a good joke, it would be a good play; but it is a bad joke. The poet assures the betrayed husband that he is not in love with his wife; in fact, he finds her unattractive; the husband is outraged, and is not placated until the poet assures him that he *is* in love with his wife and has asked her to run away with him. At this, the husband is so gratified that he offers to pay for the printing of a volume of love poems written to his wife. What is disturbing about the play is not that it is trivial and absurd, but that it reveals the same kind of failure of artistic judgement as *The Shewing Up of Blanco Posnet*. It is like a successful comedian telling an obviously unfunny joke with the conviction that it will bring the house down. Shaw's success had been built upon a trick that might be called 'deflationary realism'. He shows that the successful soldier is not the heroic militarist but the level-headed mercenary, that the rabble-rousing socialist orator is a pampered baby who is entirely dependent on his wife, that prostitution is economic good-sense for under-privileged women, that the chief business of a conqueror of the world is collecting taxes. His reversal of the normal concepts of heaven and hell in *Man and Superman* is an example of the same trick of paradox. In all these cases Shaw justifies his assertion: 'When a thing is funny, search it for a hidden truth.' But the trick can become mechanical; an absurdity is presented, with the implication: 'I am more serious than you think.' In some cases this is true (as *Blanco Posnet* demonstrates). In others it comes close to being an insult to the intelligence of the audience—as when, at the end of the 'recruiting pamphlet' *O'Flaherty, V.C.* (1915), O'Flaherty declares he is going back to the front because it is more peaceful than home. It is as if Shaw experiences a compulsion to see how far he can go in snapping his fingers at the audience—as when he calls *The Music Cure* (1913) 'A Piece of Utter Nonsense' or *The Fascinating Foundling* (1909) 'A Disgrace to the Author'—making a virtue of a critic's perfectly accurate comment.

It might seem that the simple answer to all this is to fall back

on the notion of Shaw as a dual personality—the serious philosopher and the mountebank G.B.S. But while there is obviously
much truth in this view, we must bear in mind an important
objection: that Shaw's humour was an integral part of his
genius. It is quite impossible to think of *Man and Superman* or
Major Barbara turned into 'straight' discussion plays in the
manner of Granville Barker, because humour lies at the root of
the whole conception. All the characters and situations are
conceived in terms that give rise simultaneously to the humour
and the ideas. No, the truth is that when Shaw thinks in terms of
ideas that are important to him the humour becomes their vehicle.
When he decides to exercise his gift of humour on its own he not
only tends to become trivial but to become subtly objectionable.

I raise the question at this point—when discussing Shaw's
greatest creative period—because I suspect that it was the over-
whelming success that came with the Barker-Vedrenne season that
tilted the balance. At this stage in his career it hardly mattered.
Artistically speaking—the level on which they must ultimately be
judged—*Man and Superman, John Bull's Other Island, Major Barbara*
and even *The Doctor's Dilemma* are the high point of Shaw's
achievement, because they are the embodiment of some of the
most important things he had to say. There is a curious perfection about them; it is hard to imagine a single line in any of them
being changed. But in the period that follows, the inner-pressure
drops, the G.B.S. *persona* becomes more prominent. This is
already apparent in *The Doctor's Dilemma*, which is devoted to
one of Shaw's less serious beliefs, the dishonesty of the medical
profession. And after *The Doctor's Dilemma* Shaw never again
achieves this perfect balance between ideas and humour, the
philosopher and the mountebank. This is not necessarily important in considering his actual achievement, which remains
enormous when all the objections have been given full weight.
But it *does* explain why his influence diminished steadily after
about 1910, why his reputation with the intelligentsia waned as
his fame grew. He wrote in the preface to *Plays Unpleasant*: 'I had
not achieved a success; but I had provoked an uproar; and the
sensation was so agreeable that I resolved to try again.' He went
on trying until, like the boy who shouted 'Wolf' too often, no
one took any notice.

Shaw's enormous success in 1905 was only one of the factors that contributed to the loss of artistic drive. There were many others. To begin with, it was a period of National optimism and high spirits. Britain was prosperous as never before, and no one was particularly worried about the steady build-up of the German navy, since it was a national dogma that Britannia ruled the waves. The rest of Europe might be having its troubles—anarchists exploding bombs in France, workers marching on the Winter Palace in St Petersburg—but England had its parliamentary tradition that kept everything working smoothly. The emergence of Bernard Shaw was an example: a royal command performance of a play by a man who had led the workers on Trafalgar Square less than twenty years before; in Russia he would have been in Siberia. In the 1906 Election, twenty-nine out of fifty Labour candidates were successful, which meant in effect that the Fabians and their allies were now respectable politicians instead of revolutionaries.

There was also a new and extremely active literary generation, of which Shaw was the central figure. Kipling, Conan Doyle and Haggard were still immensely popular, but they were already regarded as a little old-fashioned compared with the rising lights. There was G. K. Chesterton, to whom the adjective 'brilliant' was applied almost as monotonously as to Shaw. *The Napoleon of Notting Hill* (1904) and *The Man Who Was Thursday* (1908) introduced into literature a note of enormous optimism with curiously mystical undertones. Wells had turned from his works of pessimistic science fiction to novels of almost Dickensian humour and to the dreams of *A Modern Utopia* (1905). Chesterton's friend Belloc produced in 1902 that breezy masterpiece *The Path to Rome*. Arnold Bennett's *Old Wives Tale* (1908) seemed to prove that the younger writers could produce novels to rival the great Victorians. John Galsworthy went one better by producing the first volume of the *Forsyte Saga* and his first play *The Silver Box* in the same year (1906). Since the death of Wilde in 1900, J. M. Barrie was regarded as Shaw's most serious rival on the stage, and his *Peter Pan* (1904) certainly achieved a greater popularity than anything Shaw ever wrote. Even that dour man of genius Joseph Conrad unbent to the extent of writing a thoroughly Wellsian novel, *The Secret Agent*, in 1907. Maugham had no less than four plays running in London in the following year. And to prove that the gaiety of the 1890s was not dead, H. H. Munro ('Saki') produced a whole series of stories full of Wildean epigrams between 1902 and 1910. Even English music was flourishing with the emergence of Delius and Elgar.* Altogether, there seemed every reason for believing that England was in the midst of a golden age.

For the most part, Shaw declined to join in the fun. 'When I have met him among my more festive friends', wrote G. K. Chesterton in his *Autobiography*, 'he has always stood up starkly for his negative ideals, sometimes to the point of defiance. . . . It were not wholly wise, perhaps, to tell the whole story of that great supper party in a vast tent in a garden in Westminster; after which eggs were boiled in Sir Herbert Tree's hat (because it was the most chic and shining of the hats of the company); and I remember indulging in a wild fencing match with real swords against a gentleman who was, fortunately, more intoxicated than I. The whole of that great occasion was actually recorded in cold blood, of all places in the world, in a French newspaper. The reason was that a little French journalist, after making a placid and witty speech full of compliments, had then indulged in the treacherous Gallic trick of strict temperance. I remember that his article (which was highly unreliable), began with the words, " 'I denounce Shaw. He is sober.' Who said these words? These were the words of [H.G.] Wells;" and continued in an equally personal vein. But it is really true, and I know that Shaw would think it merely consistent and creditable, that he himself got up and sternly protested and then stalked out of the room, as a seventeenth-century Puritan might have left a tavern full of Cavaliers.'†

But Shaw was not always unbending; Chesterton tells of another occasion when Shaw persuaded him to take part in a

---

* 'Later [Sir Thomas Beecham] gave a brilliant dissertation on the lack of genuine emotion he divined in the plays of George Bernard Shaw. Delius agreed. He had once lunched with Shaw who, discussing his own work, had remarked: "Delius, I am the Richard Strauss of literature." ' (Eric Fenby, *Delius as I Knew Him*, p. 86.) The comparison was hardly likely to endear Shaw to Delius.

† Shaw denied this story.

cowboy film together with Barrie, Archer, Granville Barker and Lord Howard de Walden; they were, in fact, photographed in their cowboy costumes. It was part of the spirit of the period. So were the numerous debates in which Shaw engaged with Chesterton—notable for light-heartedness rather than for the importance of anything that was said.* And so was the amusing but unperceptive book that Chesterton wrote about Shaw in 1909, and which Shaw reviewed in *The Nation* as 'the best work of literary art I have yet provoked'. The introduction to the book is typical and brief:

'Most people either say that they agree with Bernard Shaw or that they do not understand him. I am the only person who understands him, and I do not agree with him.'

His chief complaint against Shaw seemed to be that he was not trivial enough:

'The best way to shorten winter is to prolong Christmas; and the only way to enjoy the sun of April is to be an April Fool. When people asked Bernard Shaw to attend the Stratford Tercentenary, he wrote back with characteristic contempt: "I do not keep my own birthday, and I cannot see why I should keep Shakespeare's." I think that if Mr Shaw had always kept his own birthday he would be better able to understand Shakespeare's birthday—and Shakespeare's poetry.'

In the preface to *Misalliance* (1910) Shaw wrote: '. . . I did not learn my school lessons, having much more important ones in hand, with the result that I have not wasted my life trifling with literary fools in taverns as Johnson did when he should have been shaking England with the thunder of his spirit.' In fact, he wasted far too much time with literary fools between 1905 and the beginning of the war—the years in which he was at the height of his powers. For almost a decade, very little thunder issued from his spirit or his pen.

But it would be a mistake to attribute this entirely to external causes—to success and financial security and the spirit of the period. There is also the fact that in the great trilogy of his maturity—*Man and Superman, John Bull's Other Island* and *Major Barbara*—Shaw had explored almost every aspect of the problem that interested him most—the relation of the 'higher evolutionary

* See Vincent Brome's *Six Studies in Quarrelling*, Cresset, 1958.

type' to modern industrial society. The two later plays are more complex than *Man and Superman*; in fact *Major Barbara* is the most complex and difficult work he ever wrote.

John Bull's Other Island (1904) is, line for line, probably Shaw's funniest play. The Englishman Tom Broadbent and the Irishman Larry Doyle are partners in an engineering business. Doyle, like Shaw, has left Ireland when young and made a success working in double harness with his English partner. His objections to Ireland are the ones that Shaw makes in the *Immaturity* preface:

'Oh, the dreaming! the dreaming! the torturing, heart-scalding never satisfying dreaming, dreaming, dreaming! [*Savagely*] No debauchery that ever coarsened and brutalised an Englishman can take the worth and usefulness out of him like that dreaming. An Irishman's imagination never lets him alone, never convinces him, never satisfies him; but it makes him that he cant face reality nor deal with it nor handle it nor conquer it: he can only sneer at them that do . . . It's all dreaming, all imagination. He cant be religious. The inspired churchman that teaches him the sanctity of life and the importance of conduct is sent away empty; while the poor village priest that gives him a miracle or a sentimental story of a saint, has cathedrals built for him out of the pennies of the poor. He can't be intelligently political: he dreams of what the Shan Van Vocht said in ninetyeight. If you want to interest him in Ireland youve got to call the unfortunate island Kathleen Ni Hoolihan and pretend she's a little old woman. It saves thinking. It saves working. It saves everything except imagination, imagination, imagination: and imagination's such a torture that you cant bear it without whisky. [*With fierce shivering self-contempt*] At last you get that you can bear nothing real at all: youd rather starve than cook a meal; youd rather go shabby and dirty than set your mind to take care of your clothes and wash yourself; you nag and squabble at home because your wife isnt an angel, and she despises you because youre not a hero; and you hate the whole lot round you because theyre only poor slovenly useless devils like yourself. [*Dropping his voice like a man making some shameful confidence*] And all the while there goes on a horrible, senseless, mischievous laughter. When youre young, you exchange drinks with other young men; and you exchange vile stories

G

with them; and as youre too futile to be able to help or cheer them, you chaff and sneer and taunt them for not doing the things you darent do yourself. And all the time you laugh! laugh! laugh! eternal derision, eternal envy, eternal folly, eternal fouling and staining and degrading, until, when you come at last to a country where men take a question seriously and give a serious answer to it, you deride them for having no sense of humour, and plume yourself on your own worthlessness as if it made you better than them.'

The first part of the speech is fairly clearly aimed at Yeats and the Celtic movement (Yeats wrote a play called *Kathleen Ni Houlihan*), and this is made even clearer by some of his other comments: 'If I had gone to the hills nearby to look back upon Dublin and to ponder upon myself, I too might have become a poet like Yeats, Synge and the rest of them. But I prided myself on thinking clearly, and therefore could not stay. Whenever I took a problem or a state of life of which my Irish contemporaries sang sad songs, I always pursued it to its logical conclusion, and then inevitably it resolved itself into a comedy. That is why I did not become an Irish poet . . . I could not stay there dreaming my life away on the Irish hills. . . .'

All this would seem to indicate that Doyle is partly autobiographical, and is intended to be the hero of the play. Before the play finishes, it is clear that this is not so; Peter Keegan, the unfrocked priest and mystical 'Outsider' is its real hero. It is Keegan's theory that this world is hell, and that we have all been sent here as a punishment. For Tom Broadbent this is just another example of Irish cleverness, while for Larry Doyle it is an infuriating example of the romantic woolly-mindedness that he hates.

BROADBENT . . . leaving politics out of the question, I find the world quite good enough for me: rather a jolly place, in fact.

KEEGAN [*looking at him with quiet wonder*] You are satisfied?

BROADBENT. As a reasonable man, yes. I see no evils in the world—except, of course, natural evils—that cannot be remedied by self-government and English institutions. I think so, not because I am an Englishman, but as a matter of common sense.

KEEGAN: You feel at home in the world, then?

BROADBENT. Of course. Dont you?

KEEGAN [*from the very depths of his nature*] No.

Knowing Shaw's doctrine of the importance of facing reality and conquering it, we might suspect that Keegan is intended to be one of his portraits of the world-rejecting artist, like Eugene Marchbanks, or Louis Dubedat in *The Doctor's Dilemma*. But when, in the final scene of the play, Broadbent tells him that 'the world belongs to the efficient', Keegan demonstrates that he can meet him on these grounds too, in one of Shaw's most remarkable examples of 'deflationary realism'.

KEEGAN [*with polished irony*] I stand rebuked, gentlemen. But believe me, I do every justice to the efficiency of you and your syndicate. You are both, I am told, thoroughly efficient civil engineers; and I have no doubt the golf links will be a triumph of your art. Mr Broadbent will get into parliament most efficiently, which is more than St Patrick could do if he were alive now. You may even build the hotel efficiently if you can find enough efficient masons carpenters and plumbers, which I rather doubt. [*Dropping the irony, and beginning to fall into the attitude of the priest rebuking sin*] When the hotel becomes insolvent [*Broadbent takes his cigar out of his mouth, a little taken aback*] your English business habits will secure the thorough efficiency of the liquidation. You will reorganise the scheme efficiently; you will liquidate its second bankruptcy efficiently [*Broadbent and Larry look quickly at one another; for this, unless the priest is an old financial hand, must be inspiration*]; you will get rid of its original shareholders efficiently after efficiently ruining them; and you will finally profit very efficiently by getting the hotel for a few shillings in the pound. [*More and more sternly*] Besides these efficient operations, you will foreclose your mortgages most efficiently [*his rebuking forefinger goes up in spite of himself*]; you will drive Haffigan to America very efficiently; you will find use for Barney Doran's foul mouth and bullying temper by employing him to slave-drive your labourers very efficiently; and [*low and bitter*] when at last this poor desolate countryside becomes a busy mint in which we shall all slave to make money for you, with our Polytechnic to teach us how to do it efficiently, and our library to fuddle the few imaginations your distilleries will spare, and our repaired Round Tower with admission sixpence and penny-in-the-slot mutoscopes to make it interesting, then no doubt your English and American share-

holders will spend all the money we make for them very efficiently in shooting and hunting, in operations for cancer and
appendicitis, in gluttony and gambling; and you will devote what
they save to fresh land development schemes. For four wicked
centuries the world has dreamed this foolish dream of efficiency;
and the end is not yet. But the end will come.

To which Broadbent replies, not in the least put out: 'Too true,
Mr Keegan, only too true. And most eloquently put. It reminds
me of poor Ruskin: a great man, you know. I sympathise. Believe
me, I'm on your side.'

Keegan's speech is a splendid example of Shaw's favourite
dramatic tricks: handing one of his leading characters all the
winning cards. This is, of course, the attraction of all adventure
novels and heroic dramas; but whereas in the heroic drama, we
identify with the hero who is physically invincible, Shaw raises
the whole thing to a higher level, so that we identify with the
man who is intellectually invincible. But once again, it is worth
noting that the formula of a Shaw play is basically the old heroic
formula of *The Three Musketeers* transformed by intelligence. It
is not a very long way from the formula of the Sherlock Holmes
stories.

It can be seen that *John Bull's Other Island* is an oddly complex
play. On one level it is about Shaw himself returning to Ireland,
to 'that hell of littleness'. In the scenes between Larry and his
family and Nora Reilly, the girl who has waited for him in Ross-
cullen, the message comes over unmistakably: that anyone who is
worth anything will leave this kind of thing behind him and seek
out serious work in the real world. It is a flat rejection of Yeats
and Irish sentimental nationalism. (Yeats's comment on the play
was: 'It is fundamentally ugly and shapeless, but it certainly
keeps everybody amused.') And then, before the poets of the
Celtic twilight can accuse him of being a materialist, he indicates
that there *can* be a figure who transcends the romantic poet *and*
the businessman. Keegan ends the play with a credo in which he
describes his notion of heaven: 'It is a country where the State
is the Church and the Church the people: three in one and one in
three. It is a commonwealth in which work is play and play is life:
three in one and one in three. It is a temple in which the priest is
the worshipper and the worshipper the worshipped: three in one

in which all life is human and
and one in three. It is, in short,
omes very close to describing
human race.

hn Bull's Other Island is, then,
is the violent rejection of the
e of the emotion reveals how
tration Shaw experienced in
rejection of the poetry that
tion as simplicity and charm,
talism. (When Larry sings a
land I'll forget her never', and
says: 'Oh, it doesnt mean any-
most English patriotic senti-
of the Englishman comes in
e points out that the realistic
f his feelings as the romantic
where Broadbent proposes to
k, the stage instructions end:
*or of her ignorance of it, that when
es very much as an Irishman does
when he is drunk.'*

On the other hand, the realistic Irishman Larry Doyle is a
dupe of his own gospel of efficiency, as well as being too self-
critical for his own good. After Broadbent's remarks on his
admiration for Ruskin, Keegan says: 'Come, Mr Doyle! is this
English sentiment so much more efficient than our Irish sentiment, after all? Mr Broadbent spends his life inefficiently admiring
the thoughts of great men. . . . We spend our lives efficiently
sneering at him and doing nothing. Which of us has any right to
reproach the other?' In *Time and Western Man*, Wyndham Lewis
pointed out that Joyce's Stephen Dedalus has all the characteristics
of Larry Doyle. The comment is perceptive. This kind of narrow
and fastidious intellectualism tends to be self-defeating, to waste
itself in a capacity for analysis and criticism. It lacks the broader
vision of what has to be done.

Keegan is the 'poet with his vision of what life might be',
yet even Keegan spends his days dreaming at the Round Tower
and clinging to the past. And so when, at the end of the play,

Keegan goes off down the hill, and Larry and Broadbent go to choose a site for the hotel, the whole thing is left curiously unresolved. When Yeats said that Shaw's drama was 'logical straightness, and not the crooked road of life', he could hardly have made a less accurate comment. When Shaw is at his best the effect is of music whose meanings cannot be translated into words.

As if aware of this ambiguity, Shaw makes another attempt to objectify the problem in *Major Barbara*—his most complex attempt yet. And, absurdly enough, he ends by raising twice as many problems.

Even Yeats could not have claimed *Major Barbara* was shapeless; the form has a Jamesian simplicity. Major Barbara Undershaft of the Salvation Army is the daughter of a millionaire armaments manufacturer whom she has not seen since childhood. When Undershaft comes to visit his children he and Barbara exchange invitations: he is to go to her Salvation Army shelter; she is to visit his cannon factory. Barbara warns him:

BARBARA. Take care. It may end in your giving up the cannons for the sake of the Salvation Army.

UNDERSHAFT. Are you sure it will not end in your giving up the Salvation Army for the sake of the cannons?

It sounds an unlikely contingency, but it is precisely what does happen. Why it happens is the subject of the play.

But the real conflict of *Major Barbara* is not between Barbara and her father, but between Undershaft and Barbara's fiancé, Adolphus Cusins. Cusins is a poet and a Greek scholar, based to some extent on Gilbert Murray—the translator of the Euripides plays at the Court.

'*Cusins is a spectacled student, slight, thin haired, and sweet voiced. . . . His sense of humor is intellectual and subtle, and is complicated by an appalling temper. The lifelong struggle of a benevolent temperament and a high conscience against impulses of inhuman ridicule and fierce impatience has set up a chronic strain which has visibly wrecked his constitution. He is a most implacable, determined, tenacious, intolerant person who by mere force of character presents himself as—and indeed actually is—considerate, gentle, explanatory, even mild and apologetic, capable possibly of murder, but not of cruelty or coarseness.*'

Andrew Undershaft has the same latent power:

'*Andrew is, on the surface, a stoutish, easygoing elderly man, with kindly patient manners, and an engaging simplicity of character. But he has a watchful, deliberate, waiting, listening face, and formidable reserves of power, both bodily and mental, in his capacious chest and long head. His gentleness is partly that of a strong man who has learnt by experience that his natural grip hurts ordinary people unless he handles them very carefully, and partly the mellowness of age and success.'*

And having noted these two descriptions it is unnecessary to look further for the reason that *Major Barbara* is one of Shaw's greatest plays. Whenever he creates two characters he obviously admires their interaction is enough to ensure that the play will be a major work. If there is not room for two major characters in a play, then a lesser character will do to create the clash of egos, as in *Man and Superman* or *Caesar and Cleopatra*. (A disrespectful subordinate, like Rufio in the latter, is one of Shaw's favourite stand-bys.) But given a Larry Doyle and a Peter Keegan—or even a Sergius and a Bluntschli—Shaw can guarantee a high level of dramatic conflict. And conversely, plays without such characters—*You Never Can tell, Captain Brassbound's Conversion, Misalliance, Getting Married*—the list is a long one—never really get off the ground.

Major Barbara has one of the strongest lists of characters in Shaw. Barbara's mother, Lady Britomart (apparently based on Murray's mother-in-law) is a dragon:

LADY BRITOMART [*squaring herself at him rather aggressively*] Stephen; may I ask how soon you intend to realise that you are a grown-up man, and that I am only a woman?

STEPHEN. [*amazed*] Only a . . .

LADY BRITOMART. Dont repeat my words please: it is a most aggravating habit. You must learn to face the facts of life seriously, Stephen. I really cannot bear the whole burden of our family affairs any longer. You must advise me: you must assume the responsibility.

Stephen Undershaft, her son, is a serious-minded prig who takes a tone of high moral disapproval of his father's business. Barbara possesses her mother's strength of character, but is a great deal more intelligent. Light relief is provided by Charles Lomax, the fiancé of Barbara's sister Sarah, a vague, brainless, upper-class young man. (I have always suspected that he was the original inspiration for Wodehouse's Bertie Wooster.)

It is a tradition in the Undershaft cannon business that it should not be passed from father to son, but that each Undershaft should adopt a bastard to succeed him. At the end of the play Cusins reveals that he is, in a technical sense, a bastard—since his father married his deceased wife's sister in Australia, and the marriage is illegal in England—and agrees to become the next Andrew Undershaft.

For anyone unfamiliar with the play it sounds as if Shaw has set himself an almost insoluble problem, dramatically speaking— how to get Barbara to give up the Salvation Army for the cannons, how to get Cusins across the 'abyss of moral horror' that lies between himself and the munitions business. It sounds an impossible sleight of hand. In fact, Shaw demonstrates that it is not only possible, but inevitable. And, in a sense, he takes up where he left off in *John Bull's Other Island*. In that play Keegan asks Larry what right they have to spend their lives sneering at Broadbent's practical realism and doing nothing, and Broadbent interjects: 'But you know, something must be done.' Precisely. But what? Barbara has stumbled on the Salvation Army, and it satisfies her need to 'do'. Cusins, who fell in love with her at a street-corner meeting—assuming her to be 'a woman of the people'—is as naturally idealistic as Barbara, but is too self-critical—and has too much sense of humour—to be a convinced salvationist. He admits that he joined the Salvation Army to worship Barbara, but his true allegiance is to Dionysus. Barbara becomes disillusioned about the Salvation Army when she realises it is financed by people like her father and Bodger the whisky king. There is no need for Cusins to be disillusioned, since he was never really involved. The question remains: how can two, basically religious idealists find a way to express their idealism in a society in which the real power lies in the hands of Bodger and Undershaft? For Shaw, the answer is self-evident: stop preaching in a corner, and enter the race for power with Bodger and Undershaft. The core of the play is contained in its final scene, the long argument between Cusins and Undershaft— after Cusins has accepted the succession—about the moral question of being a manufacturer of cannons. Undershaft's central point is that poverty is the greatest crime:

UNDERSHAFT. I save [my workers'] souls just as I saved yours.

BARBARA [*revolted*] You saved my soul! What do you mean?

UNDERSHAFT. I fed you and clothed you and housed you. I took care that you should have money enough to live handsomely—more than enough; so that you could be wasteful, careless, generous. That saved your soul from the seven deadly sins.

BARBARA [*bewildered*] The seven deadly sins!

UNDERSHAFT. Yes, the deadly seven. [*Counting on his fingers*] Food, clothing, firing, rent, taxes, respectability and children. Nothing can lift these seven millstones from Man's neck but money; and the spirit cannot soar until the millstones are lifted. I enabled Barbara to become Major Barbara, and I saved her from the crime of poverty.

CUSINS. Do you call poverty a crime?

UNDERSHAFT. The worst of crimes. All the other crimes are virtues beside it. . . .

Yet even expressed in these terms, the argument sounds wildly paradoxical. Shaw himself was always totally opposed to war, no matter how much he might favour revolution. And a note that Shaw wrote for a new production of the play in 1929 makes it fairly clear that he was no admirer of Undershaft and Lazarus:

'When the war came, Undershaft and Lazarus did not do so well as was expected of them . . . and after a frightful slaughter of our young men through insufficient munitions the Government had to organise the business. . . . But the moment the war was over, Undershaft and Lazarus came back with all their newspapers shouting that they had saved the country, and that the national factories were sinks of corruption and incompetence. They then plunged into an orgy of overcapitalisation followed by repudiation . . . so that every blunder and swindle on their part left the public more impressed . . .'

But what Shaw has in mind gradually becomes clearer in the final argument.

UNDERSHAFT. . . . What do we do here when we spend years of work and thought and thousands of solid cash on a new gun or an aerial battleship that turns out just a hairbreadth wrong after all? Scrap it. Scrap it without wasting another hour or another pound on it. Well, you have made for yourself something that you call a morality or a religion or what not. It doesn't fit the

facts. Well, scrap it. Scrap it and get one that does fit. That is
what is wrong with the world at present. It scraps its obsolete
steam engines and dynamos; but it wont scrap its old prejudices
and its old moralities and its old religions and its old political
constitutions. Whats the result? In machinery it does very well;
but in morals and religion and politics it is working at a loss that
brings it nearer bankruptcy every year.

The problem is created by an industrialised and highly central-
ised society. Chesterton and Belloc wanted to de-industrialise
and decentralise, to return to the 'acre and a cow' ideal of the
Middle Ages. Shaw recognised that there is no way back; it has
to go forward. Industrialisation has many disadvantages; but it
is an inevitable step on the evolutionary road, because it aims at
higher living standards, at freedom from the 'millstone' round
man's neck. But what is to be the religion of the new society?
Barbara herself recognises that there is an entirely new problem
here: that the 'salvation' of well-fed men and women is more
difficult than the salvation of the poor of West Ham. As Undershaft remarks: 'It is cheap work converting starving men with a
Bible in one hand and a slice of bread in the other. I will undertake to convert West Ham to Mahometanism on the same terms.'

But what is this religion of the future, of industrialised society?
This is a question that neither Barbara nor Shaw himself can
answer. The first necessity is to scrap the orthodox state religion
that calls itself Christianity, and that Shaw calls 'Crosstianity'
because its central tenet is that men have been redeemed by the
death of Jesus on the cross. At the present stage of evolution,
there is no point in men believing they are saved. This is a passive
attitude, and a point has come where man must recognise that
he must take his evolution—that is to say, his religion—into
his own hands. At the end of the play Barbara says: 'Let God's
work be done for its own sake: the work he had to create us to do
because it cannot be done except by living men and women.' A
woman of Barbara's idealism and force of character must try to
save souls as a great artist has to create. It makes no difference
whether there is a 'demand' or not; it is only her business to
express the god-power she feels flowing in her, to testify to her
sense of a meaning and purpose behind human existence. As to
Cusins, he can only sense that the religion of the past is some-

how dead, the religion that told men they only had to be good and they would be saved. He sees that man's task is not to be good but to be god. To accept the power that Undershaft places in his hands seems to be a natural step towards this goal; but he is a long way from seeing the goal.

Major Barbara is Shaw's most extreme and complete statement of his position, a position that began as a revolt against the defeatism of the romantics. The basic romantic position is that spirit is trapped in matter, that its situation is finally tragic. Shaw like Nietzsche, could say, 'I have made my philosophy out of my will to health.' Yeats accuses Shaw of a compromise with materialism; Shaw accuses Yeats of the escapism of immaturity, and asserts that Yeats will be forced to end by agreeing with him, because there is no other way. The romantic believes that the occasional moments when he feels godlike and reconciled to existence are an illusion; the music of Beethoven, the poetry of Shelley, is not telling us something about the real world, 'this dim vast vale of tears', but about an ideal world, the true home of the human soul. The feeling of conquest produced by the music of Wagner vanishes the moment we step out into the street. Shaw was romantic enough to refuse to accept this. It should be possible to impose these romantic ideals on the real world—as Morris believed. He was aware that it was not entirely a new idea:
UNDERSHAFT. . . . Remember the words of Plato.
CUSINS [*starting*] Plato! You dare quote Plato to me!
UNDERSHAFT. Plato says, my friend, that society cannot be saved until either the Professors of Greek take to making gunpowder, or else the makers of gunpowder become Professors of Greek.
CUSINS. Oh, tempter, cunning tempter!

But in practice neither Plato nor Socrates approximated to the ideal of the philosopher-king; Socrates virtually committed suicide, since he had plenty of time to escape. Shaw is the first philosopher since Plato to approach the idea with total consistency. But Shaw made one miscalculation. He thought he was living at the end of the romantic era. He was not; he was living in the middle of it. The philosophy that took over from romanticism was called existentialism, but it was only a slightly disguised form of romanticism, dressed up in philosophic terminology. After Verlaine and Rimbaud, Dowson and Yeats, came Eliot,

Joyce, Heidegger, Sartre, Mann, Hesse, Kafka. Cultural history left Shaw standing by the side of the road; romantic pessimism still had a long way to run, as Nietzsche accurately foresaw. (He predicted two more centuries of 'nihilism'.)

The message of *Major Barbara* looks deceptively simple; that the end justifies the means. Undershaft's factory estate is full of well-fed men living in decent homes—the result of the 'death and destruction' industry. And Undershaft says: 'I had rather be a thief than a pauper; I had rather be a murderer than a slave. I dont want to be either; but if you force the alternative on me, then, by Heaven, I'll choose the braver and more moral one.' He explains: 'I moralised and starved until one day I swore that I would be a full-fed free man at all costs; that nothing should stop me except a bullet, neither reason nor morals nor the lives of other men. . . . I was a dangerous man until I had my will: now I am a useful, beneficent, kindly person.' As to the 'morality' of manufacturing cannons, Cusins goes into this in his final scene with Barbara:

BARBARA. You know that you will have no power, and that he has none.

CUSINS. I know. It is not for myself alone. I want to make power for the world.

BARBARA. I want to make power for the world too; but it must be spiritual power.

CUSINS. I think all power is spiritual: these cannons will not go off by themselves. I have tried to make spiritual power by teaching Greek. But the world can never be really touched by a dead language and a dead civilisation.

Up to this point the argument is admirably clear and consistent; but here it suddenly takes a rather odd turning:

. . . The people must have power; and the people cannot have Greek. Now the power that is made here can be wielded by all men.

BARBARA. Power to burn women's houses down and kill their sons and tear their husbands to pieces.

CUSINS. You cannot have power for good without having power for evil too. Even mother's milk nourishes murderers as well as heroes. This power which only tears men's bodies to pieces has never been so horribly abused as the intellectual power, the imaginative power, the poetic, religious power that can enslave men's souls. As a teacher of Greek I gave the intellectual man weapons against the common man. I now want to give the common man weapons against the intellectual man. I love the common people. I want to arm them against the lawyers, the doctors, the priests, the literary men. . . . I want a power simple enough for common men to use, yet strong enough to force the intellectual oligarchy to use its genius for the general good. . . .

And it is at this point that one begins to suspect that clear thought has given way to the need to convince the audience before the curtain comes down. 'The people must have power.' But Shaw knows as well as anyone else that most people do not want power. In fact, he knew *exactly* how many people do not want power, for he says in Chapter VI of *Everybody's Political What's What:*

'Many years ago I began investigating classification by asking H. M. Stanley, the journalist who explored Africa in search of Livingstone, what proportion of his men he found capable of leadership when he had to leave them in charge of his expedition for a while. He replied instantly and positively 'Five per cent'. I pressed him as to whether this was an offhand guess or an exact figure. He said, again without hesitation, that it was an exact figure.'

Stanley died in 1904, the year before Shaw wrote *Major Barbara.* Shaw knew about the 'dominant five per cent' long before modern biology stumbled upon it.

Shaw goes on, in the same passage, to point out that if Stanley had needed a Julius Caesar he could certainly not have reckoned on one man in twenty; that the Caesars, Michelangelos and Shakespeares are born only once in fifteen generations. Shaw's interest as an evolutionist and a playwright was in the Caesars and Shakespeares, the Undershafts and Cusineses, not in the common man. And then there is this curious jump in logic from the wielders of the power of imagination, poetry and religion to the 'lawyers, doctors, priests . . .' At no other point in his work does Shaw speak about the *abuse* of the power of intellect, imagination, religion. In *Candida*, when Morell asks Eugene if the responsibility of being a poet does not make him tremble, Marchbanks answers: 'It does not make me tremble. It is the want of it in others that makes me tremble.'

As soon as we begin to wonder about Cusins, it is natural to wonder about Barbara too. When it was announced that Shaw intended to write about the Salvation Army there was apparently some slight alarm in religious circles about the idea; the Lord Chamberlain was even doubtful about licensing the play until Granville Barker assured him that the line 'My God, why hast thou forsaken me' occurs in the Psalms as well as in the Gospels. The doubts were justified; Shaw's attitude to the Salvation Army was bound to be negative, since Booth's Salvationism was fundamentally a Revivalism of the same type as Moody and Sankey's. The play is a deliberate contrast between this backward-looking, old-fashioned revivalism and his own evolutionism, in which man must somehow learn to recognise the god in himself. Shaw could no more have become emotionally committed to Salvationism than Cusins or Undershaft can. In that case what is Barbara doing in the Salvation Army? The play is named after her; she is its 'heroine'; yet she fails to make the impact she is obviously supposed to. Her disillusionment with the Salvation Army in the second act can be very moving in performance, but Shaw's real opinion of it is expressed by Undershaft: 'Come, come, my daughter! Dont make too much of your little tinpot tragedy.' And when Barbara admits that her spirit is still troubled, Undershaft tells her: 'You have learnt something. That always feels at first as if you have lost something.' It is Undershaft and Cusins who really dominate the play. Barbara is an enthusiastic idealist who lacks the qualities of intellect and imagination that are the essential qualities of a Shaw hero or heroine. Shaw may admire the saintly enthusiast, but it is a rather abstract admiration, for the Shaw play is essentially the drama of intellect and intelligence. Barbara's religious enthusiasm may be a more desirable quality than her mother's aristocratic aggressiveness or Stephen's priggish conservatism, but it is not enough to place her on the level of the kind of people Shaw really admires. (Even George Fox in *Good King Charles* is intelligent and sympathetic rather than enthusiastic.) She is not even the play's religious centre of gravity; Undershaft comes closer to being religious in the sense that Shaw admired; when Barbara introduces him to Peter Shirley as a

Secularist, Undershaft says: 'Not the least in the world: on the contrary, a confirmed mystic.' Again, when Lady Britomart rebukes Barbara: 'Really, Barbara, you go on as if religion were a pleasant subject. Do have some sense of propriety', Undershaft says: 'I do not find it an unpleasant subject, my dear. It is the only one that capable people really care for.' All of which makes it seem that Major Barbara is not really essential to the play in which she is supposed to be the central character; like Lady Cicely Waynflete—and like St Joan in the later play—she is another attempt of Shaw's to create the kind of woman he felt *ought* to be a heroine.

This recognition makes the main argument of the play all the more difficult to grasp. Undershaft can make it sound unambiguous enough; for example, when Stephen asks him whether so much pampering is really good for the character of the workers:

UNDERSHAFT: Well you see, my dear boy, when you are organising civilisation you have to make up your mind whether trouble and anxiety are good things or not. If you decide that they are, then, I take it, you simply don't organise civilisation, and there you are, with trouble and anxiety enough to make us all angels! But if you decide the other way, you may as well go through with it.

Civilisation comes first; but if he is really so concerned about civilisation, what is he doing manufacturing cannons? It is the argument of *Mrs Warren's Profession* over again: that escaping poverty is the first duty of anyone who belongs to the dominant five per cent. But Vivie Warren's question is even more pertinent here: 'But why . . . that business? Saving money and good management will succeed in any business.' What one begins to suspect here is not exactly confusion, but that the apparent clarity gives an impression of questions completely solved, when in fact they are not half solved. Edmund Wilson has pointed out one of Shaw's most characteristic tricks:

'It depends on a technique which he has mastered of functioning on three distinct planes and of shifting from one to another. His air of certainty, his moralist's tone, his well-drilled sentences, his regular emphasis, all go to create an impression of straightforwardness. But actually the mind of Shaw is always fluctuating between various emotions which give rise to various points of view.

'The mechanics seem to be somewhat as follows: at the bottom of Shaw is a commonsense sphere of practical considerations; above this a plan of socialism . . . and above this, a poet-philosopher's ether from which he commands a longer view of life, *sub specie aeternitatis* and where the poet allows himself many doubts which neither the socialist nor the bourgeois citizen can admit. Shaw has never really taken up his residence for any length of time on any one of these three planes of thinking. The socialist, for example, denounces war; but when England actually goes to war, the respectable householder backs her. The moralist denounces marriage; but the conventional married man always advises young people to get married. The socialist takes sword in hand to battle for a sounder society based on a redistribution of income; and the long-view philosopher-poet comes to sap the socialist's faith with misgivings as to the capacity for intellect and virtue of the material of common humanity as contrasted with philosopher-poets. The poet gets a good way above the earth in the ecstasy of imaginative vision; but the socialist reminds him that it is the duty of art to teach a useful social lesson, and the householder damps the fires of both by admonishing them that the young people in the audience oughtn't to be told anything that will get them into trouble. The result is that reading Shaw is like looking through a pair of field glasses of which the focus is always equally sharp and clear but the range may be changed without warning.'*

Is this the answer to the curious ambiguity of *Major Barbara*—that the poet-philosopher and the socialist are in conflict? that the poet has a Nietzschean enthusiasm for vitality and power, even if it involves war, while the socialist wants civilisation—and therefore peace—at any cost?

This explanation certainly comes closer to explaining the play; but it is still inadequate. Wilson sees *Major Barbara* as being about the confrontation of the saint and the practical man, as with Keegan and Broadbent in *John Bull's Other Island*; but in that case, why has Shaw made Undershaft a mystic?

It is necessary to stand back and view the play as a part of Shaw's total career. He declined to accept the Yeatsian antithesis between the poet and the practical man, asserting that a poet who

* *The Triple Thinkers,* 'Bernard Shaw at Eighty'.

had the courage and the vision would eventually acquire the
qualities of the practical man without losing any of his own.
Yeats makes one of his characters ask:

> 'What portion of the world can the artist have
> Who has awakened from the common dream
> But dissipation and despair?'

Shaw's reply would be: In that case, he has not awakened
enough; he is only half awake. Let him wake up fully and he will
see himself as a part of a greater purpose that aims at altering the
common dream until it becomes the dream of poets.

This carries him into an attempt to go beyond Keegan and
Larry Doyle in a new stage of the dialectical movement. Broadbent is Doyle's antithesis; Keegan is an attempt at a synthesis
that embraces both, (hence, presumably, the long speech on
efficiency). But Keegan is really no advance on Don Juan,
another poet-philosopher who proposes to spend his eons in
contemplation. The poet philosopher is reincarnated in Cusins,
who wants to make spiritual power through translating Euripides,
and he is made to recognise that all power is spiritual power, that
the poet's business is to aid the forward march of civilisation,
not to look back nostalgically to the past. At the end of the play,
Cusins promises a new synthesis: the poet who has apparently
gone over to the side of the man of business, but only in order to
give himself the power of action, of influencing civilisation. But
then, what of Shaw's earlier recognition that Wotan cannot
resort to the forces of the law without losing half his integrity?
Would Cusins not be better off to try to create spiritual power
by translating Euripides, or by perhaps writing his own plays,
as Shaw actually did, rather than become a cog in the wheel of
big business? Shaw stated his own aim clearly in *Everybody's
Political What's What*: 'Only the fictions of fine art gave me any
satisfaction; and it became my chosen job *to bring these fictions to
life* [my italics], and meanwhile to live as a Bohemian, as a rebel, as
an enemy. . . . The precept "Love one another" was impossible
with human society divided into two detestably unloveable
classes.' Cusins's step in becoming a partner of Undershaft and
Lazarus will certainly bring the millennium a step closer in the
sense that it will contribute to abolishing the gap between the

two detestably unloveable classes; but his real business, like Shaw's, is to somehow bring the fictions of fine art to life.

In trying to carry his ideas to a new level, Shaw has involved himself in a self-contradiction. Don Juan speaks of 'helping life in its struggle upwards'. How can this be done in practice? By accepting that the poet-philosopher must become a political force. *Major Barbara* is an attempt to dramatise this idea; but it does not turn out to be the synthesis that Shaw aims at. In fact, it turns out to be a kind of dead end. Where does he go from here? He can only look back to Don Juan's promise of a 'mind's eye', to the notion of an evolutionary leap. For the time being, there is no way forward. . . .

8 CUL-DE-SAC

Major Barbara was a considerable success at the Court Theatre in November 1905, the audience at its first performance including the Prime Minister, now a Shaw devotee. It became the most discussed play of the season, and ran for six weeks—the limit allowed for any play by Barker and Vedrenne. (Vedrenne, a good businessman, was all for letting Shaw plays run until they stopped making money, but Barker talked about 'that boa constrictor, the long run', and insisted on the six-week limit.) Its run was terminated by the general election in which, as already mentioned, twenty-nine Labour candidates were sent to Parliament. Success was complete.

Now he was suddenly a literary celebrity, other celebrities wanted to meet him. Shaw was inclined to stick on his own ground; he declined most invitations to other people's houses. Charlotte would issue a counter-invitation to lunch. In her biography of Charlotte, Janet Dunbar expresses it bluntly: 'Shaw, in his own phrase, liked to "coruscate", and Charlotte was content to be a good hostess, and allow him to indulge his natural vanity —for this was how she had come to regard his strong vein of exhibitionism.' What must be borne in mind is that this exhibitionism was not a natural character trait, inherited or imitated from parents. It had been cultivated almost theoretically, in the teeth of natural shyness; it sprang from the same roots as *Major Barbara*: the belief that a poet should discipline himself to face a social role. Shaw was subject to fairly frequent revulsions, when he fled to Cornwall, or looked around for a home in the country.

In 1906 they discovered the Rectory at Ayot St Lawrence, a small village in Hertfordshire, near Welwyn, and although Charlotte began by renting it on a short-term basis, it became their home for the rest of their lives.

On one of their visits to Mevagissey, in Cornwall, Shaw was asked for another play for the Court. He had no ideas; but Charlotte reminded him of an incident at St Mary's Hospital, when they had been calling on Sir Almroth Wright, a doctor who had invented a new method for treating tuberculosis. An assistant had asked Wright if they could add another patient to their list, and Wright asked 'Is he worth it?' Shaw had remarked at the time that it was a good subject for a play; then he forgot about it. Now, at Charlotte's suggestion, he settled down to work on *The Doctor's Dilemma*. His doctor has only room for one more patient on his list, and he has to choose between two men: a brilliant but scoundrelly artist, and a mediocre but decent local practitioner. The situation is complicated by the fact that the doctor has fallen in love with the artist's wife.

In a purely theatrical sense *The Doctor's Dilemma* is the culmination of Shaw's career as a playwright. From *Widowers' Houses* onward he had shown himself to be a master of the dramatic form, capable of writing a play that, no matter how controversial its content, held the attention of audiences for exactly the same reasons as a play by Pinero or Wilde. *Man and Superman* was a radical departure, in that it allowed equal weight to the drama *and* the ideas. *John Bull's Other Island* and *Major Barbara* are not 'well-made plays' in the sense that all his previous ones had been, in that they have no neat and theatrical ending; they both tail off in talk. But since, in both cases, the talk completes the *dialectical* movement of the play, they produce a satisfying sense of the well-made play raised to a higher level of intelligence.

The Doctor's Dilemma (1906) is a return to the well-made play of earlier days, in that the talk all takes place in the first act; the remaining four acts follow a line of straight dramatic development. And the talk of the first act is among the best in any Shaw play; a number of doctors call on Sir Colenso Ridgeon to congratulate him on his knighthood. None of them says anything that is particularly memorable; all of them talk out of sheer egotistic exuberance, with the exception of Ridgeon himself, and Blenkinsop, the unprosperous general practitioner who is suffering from tuberculosis. Shaw is at his best with the clash of egos between the successful doctors:

WALPOLE . . . Sir Patrick: how are you? I sent you a paper lately about a little thing I invented: a new saw. For shoulder blades.

SIR PATRICK [*meditatively*] Yes: I got it. It's a good saw: a useful, handy instrument.

WALPOLE. [*confidently*] I knew youd see its points.

SIR PATRICK. Yes: I remember that saw sixty five years ago.

WALPOLE. What!

SIR PATRICK. It was called a cabinetmaker's jimmy then.

Sir Ralph Bloomfield Bonington—B.B.—is one of Shaw's best inventions:

SIR PATRICK . . . In the privacy of our family circle, sir, my father used to declare his belief that smallpox inoculation was good not only for smallpox, but for all fevers.

B.B. [*suddenly rising to the new idea with immense interest and excitement*] What! Ridgeon: did you hear that? Sir Patrick: I am more struck by what you have just told me than I can well express. Your father, sir, anticipated a discovery of my own. Listen, Walpole. Blenkinsop: attend one moment. You will all be intensely interested in this. I was put on the track by accident. I had a typhoid case and a tetanus case side by side in the hospital: a beadle and a city missionary. Think of what that meant for them, poor fellows! Can a beadle be dignified with typhoid? Can a missionary be eloquent with lockjaw? No. NO. Well, I got some typhoid anti-toxin from Ridgeon and a tube of Muldooley's anti-tetanus serum. But the missionary jerked all my things off the table in one of his paroxysms; and in replacing them I put Ridgeon's tube where Muldooley's ought to have been. The consequence was that I injected the typhoid case for tetanus and the tetanus case for typhoid. [*The doctors look greatly concerned. B.B., undamped, smiles triumphantly*] Well, they recovered. THEY RECOVERED. Except for a touch of St Vitus's dance the missionary's as well today as ever; and the beadle's ten times the man he was.

One thing that immediately becomes clear even from this single speech is how much Shaw enjoyed writing the play. The first act bounces along like a Rossini overture. The whole play has such vitality that one is inclined to overlook its lack of weight compared to its predecessors. But upon closer examination this is the most striking thing about *The Doctor's Dilemma*: that for the first time for more than a decade Shaw had written a play that was not about his central theme: evolution. It is certainly not about natural Christianity; Ridgeon virtually condemns Louis Dubedat to death (that is, to Bloomfield Bonington) because he is in love with his wife. Dubedat was apparently based upon Edward Aveling, a dedicated socialist who was nevertheless completely unscrupulous about women and money. Aveling committed at least one murder; he persuaded his mistress, Eleanor Marx, that they should make a suicide pact, and watched her take the poison; then hastened out of the house to provide himself with an alibi. (He became her heir.) One of Marx's recent biographers has described him as 'morally insane'. Although Dubedat dies exclaiming: 'I believe in Michael Angelo, Velasquez and Rembrandt' (parodying Wagner's story *An End In Paris*) he could scarcely be described as a 'higher evolutionary type'.

It is typical of Shaw's lack of interest in romance that Ridgeon doesn't get the girl in the end; she simply tells him she has married somebody else, and he is left reflecting that he has murdered a man for nothing. Her faith in her husband's integrity and genius is untouched; she only thinks Ridgeon is slandering his memory when he tells her the truth.

All this makes *The Doctor's Dilemma* more 'unpleasant' than any of the three *Unpleasant Plays*. It is oddly negative. It is also the first case of Shaw refusing to toss the audience some kind of a happy ending. (The impresario Charles Frohman remarked of *Major Barbara*: 'Shaw's very clever; he always lets the fellow get the girl in the end.') The fact that Ridgeon does not marry Jennifer and cannot even convince her that her husband was a scoundrel, produces an odd frustration in the audience, which in turn emphasises that Ridgeon is no hero either. A happy ending might have removed this odd flavour of bitterness, but it would be irrelevant to the theme of the play, the 'doctor's dilemma', the moral dilemma which is intended to give the play weight and substance.

It was after *The Doctor's Dilemma* that Shaw had occasion to make a speech to the drama critics. He told Hesketh Pearson: 'My first new play to be done at the Court was John Bull's Other Island. The critics denounced it as no play at all and said that the actors did their best with impossible parts. Then came Man and Superman. This was voted dull and uninspired compared with its predecessor. Major Barbara followed, and the critics promptly burst into raptures over Man and Superman. But Major Barbara was duly described as a masterpiece when its successor The Doctor's Dilemma was dismissed as a feeble joke in bad taste. So I seized the first opportunity at a public dinner when all the leading dramatic critics were present. "I want to make a suggestion to the Press," I said. "I don't ask you to stop abusing me. It gives you so much pleasure to say my plays are no plays and that my characters are not human beings that I would not deprive you of it for worlds. But for the sake of Vedrenne and Barker, not to mention the actors, may I beg you to reverse the order of your curses and caresses? Instead of saying that my latest play is piffle, the one before it brilliant, why not acclaim the latest one as a masterpiece compared with the disgusting drivel I had the impertinence to serve up last time? . . ." '*

The result of this, according to Pearson, was that the critics now declined to take Shaw seriously on any level, and reviewed revivals of *Arms and the Man, Caesar and Cleopatra* and *The Devil's Disciple* as if they were comic operas. Shaw was now successful in the sense of having an immense audience and influential friends; but he was never successful with the critics or with England's literati. The critics were not interested in his evolutionism; for them, this was merely 'ideas', and had no place on the stage. They insisted on judging Shaw's plays purely as plays, and finding them somehow fraudulent. In a volume called *Tricks of the Trade* published in 1917 J. C. Squire puts the current view of Shaw in a parody of a play about Mahomet. Shaw walks into the middle of his own play, explaining to Mahomet: 'The truth is that I came here for the simple reason that though I have frequently

* *Extraordinary People,* p. 245. It is worth remarking that Pearson is quoting Shaw from memory. When Pearson attempts to reconstruct something that Shaw said, it usually comes out in this odd Pearsonese; the antithesis of 'curses' and 'caresses', and words like 'piffle' or 'disgusting drivel' sound more like Sir Thomas Beecham than Shaw.

put my own name into my characters' mouths, I have never hitherto actually introduced myself as a person in one of my plays. After all, when you come to think of it, my habit of expressing my sentiments through invented characters has been utterly fantastic. And besides, some of these confounded actors have made hay with the parts by trying to turn them into other people. . . . I wasn't born in order that a lot of stupid mummers should have an opportunity of parading their temperaments in public.'

When one considers the variety and range of Shaw's characters, from Lickcheese to Bloomfield Bonington, from Mrs Warren to Adolphus Cusins, it is impossible to see what the critics meant by claiming that all his characters were disguised versions of himself, or even that they all express Shaw's ideas. On the other hand, any one who has ever been involved with the machinery of publicity knows its chief drawback: that it is a highly selective distorting mirror; it chooses certain facets of a personality and inflates them until they dominate everything else.

Now what had happened to Shaw should be very clear. He knew that he had more to say than any of his contemporaries, with the possible exception of Wells. He believed that it deserved to be said loudly enough for everyone to hear it. For twenty-five years he practised the self-advertisement that he felt appropriate to the importance of what he had to say, and tried to make it palatable with humour and paradox; but the success was small compared to the effort. Then, overnight, he achieved what he wanted; suddenly he was the centre of the stage, with the spotlights on him. And it was some time before he realised that the publicity had defeated its own purpose. In one important respect Yeats was right and Shaw was wrong. Yeats wrote:

'. . . truth flourishes where the scholar's lamp has shone
And only there . . .'

Shaw disagreed; if you believed in truth, you shouted it from the roof-tops. But in the midst of this immense, unprecedented success what had happened to the 'truth', to the insights of the poet-philosopher? Where was the audience who would understand what he was saying, and perhaps even carry it further? The Shaw who was known to the public was no more than an enormous wooden puppet with a few well-known mannerisms. And—most difficult of all to understand—the plays and prefaces were read as if they were the products of this puppet.

If all this had happened to Shaw fifteen years earlier it would probably have had the effect of turning him into an introvert. What had this new public to do with his obsession with the 'higher evolutionary type' and his relation to society? But Shaw was fifty in 1906; it was too late to change direction. The 'hermit' of *Immaturity* had become a public figure, but one who had lost control of his public image. In the days of music and drama criticism, his self-advertisement had achieved scarcely any effect, except to give him an agreeable kind of notoriety with a small circle. Most people in England had never heard of Bernard Shaw. This sudden fame was like an amplifying system that turned every word into a shout, and every shout into a deafening roar. The rebel who lectured at street corners and 'coruscated' for the benefit of admiring young actresses was suddenly a member of the establishment. When he went to stay with the Webbs, he had dinner with the Prime Minister and a selected handful of M.P.s. (Wells was also present.) Rodin modelled his head. His plays reached Czechoslovakia, Poland, Holland, Germany, Denmark, Finland, France, Belgium, Canada, even Japan. *The Bookman* came out with a special Bernard Shaw number.

It is possible to see, then, that *Major Barbara* represents a *cul-de-sac* in Shaw's life as well as his thought. The gospel of Andrew Undershaft declares that if society is to be saved the poet-philosopher must become the philosopher-king. But fundamentally Shaw was no more cut out to be a philosopher-king than Yeats was. He was a born artist; or perhaps it would be more accurate to say a self-made artist. There are many artists —writers, musicians, actors, painters—who are primarily interested in the impact they make on the public. Others are so absorbed in the work of the mind that the 'circuit' is virtually complete when their ideas are on paper or canvas. They derive a pleasure from creating in solitude, feeling cut off from other human beings. (Shaw knew the feeling well enough to quote two stanzas of Byron's *Childe Harold* on the importance of solitude —quite gratuitously—in *The Apple Cart*.) The more the artist accustoms himself—particularly when young—to deriving pleasure from the work itself, the more the public impact of his work becomes irrelevant. The mathematician is perhaps the most extreme form of this temperament, for it is obviously impossible for him to work with one eye on the public. Shaw had created five long novels by the age of twenty-seven, without the smallest sign of public interest. Independence of public opinion had been an ideal from an early stage, the ability to stand alone. Even Robert Smith of *Immaturity* possesses it. Marian says of Edward Conolly in *The Irrational Knot*: 'What would you not give to be never without a purpose, never with a regret . . . to take pleasure in trifling lazily with the consciousness of possessing a strong brain.' It is this pleasure in possessing a strong brain that gives his best work its unique flavour; there is a power-house quality about it, a driving thrust. This kind of drive achieves its best results when there is a certain resistance. By 1906 there was very little resistance, except from critics who brought entirely irrelevant accusations.

Shaw was still at the height of his powers. It was impossible that he should produce downright bad work. What he actually did over the next eight years was to produce a number of plays upon more-or-less social subjects—marriage, parenthood, phonetics—and a great many 'tomfooleries'—*Overruled, Fanny's First Play, Great Catherine, Augustus Does his Bit,* and others. Only two works of this period, *Blanco Posnet* (1909) and *Androcles and the Lion* (1911–12), return to his fundamental subject, evolution; and these, in fact, say nothing that has not already been said better in earlier plays. He was in a *cul-de-sac.*

The most difficult thing to grasp about Shaw is also the most important thing for understanding the world celebrity that he remained for the rest of his life: that he was a dual personality, fundamentally self-divided. In a quite basic sense, he was still Robert Smith of *Immaturity*, covered up with a public façade. He never became a genuine extravert: that is, a person who likes people because he understands them and is sensitive to their moods. The composer Feruccio Busoni remarked in a letter to his wife: 'Shaw loves people *theoretically*'; (his telegraphic address is "Socialist, London").' It was an acute observation, but not quite accurate. Shaw did not love people, theoretically or otherwise. The artistic temperament is naturally aloof, detached; it may be basically kindly and courteous, as in the case of Henry James; but it looks at life from the other side of a plate of glass. Yeats emphasised his alone-ness and detachment:

> 'There is not a fool can call me friend,
> And I may dine at journey's end
> With Landor and with Donne.'

This kind of Olympianism would not have been consistent with Shaw's chosen profession of artist-philosopher and worldbetterer; but his temperament was nevertheless shy and aloof. This was why he remained unmarried for so long; he found it impossible to feel close enough to another human being to offer to share his life. (The same applied to Yeats, who was fifty-two when he married.) And even when he had developed the G.B.S. personality he remained curiously out of touch with people, strangely clumsy in his social relations. Busoni described a meeting with Shaw in a letter to his wife:

'Yesterday afternoon, G.B.S. came to tea (which he did not drink). He is now 63, very tall. . . . He talks too much and cannot cloak his vanity. He began at once by shooting off one of his witty darts. Maudi [Maude Allan, the dancer]* was saying that she had just come out of a nursing home. "I wonder that you are still alive," said G.B.S., "for in a hospital they throw you out into the street before you are half-cured, but in a nursing home they don't let you out until you are dead. . . ."

'During tea he spoke chiefly about music, and evidently wished to display his knowledge. He loves Mozart with understanding. "Mozart was my master, I learnt from him how to say important things, and yet remain light and conversational." "How do you make that tally," I asked, "with your admiration for Wagner?" "Oh, there is room for many different things in the world. And it was necessary at that time to protest against senseless misunderstandings. But I confess, much as I love Tristan, I could wish that Tristan might die a little sooner."

---

* Aficionados of crime might be interested to know that she was the sister of the San Francisco murderer Theodore Durrant, hanged in 1895.

'. . . I said "It would attract me to try and write music for the scene in hell in 'Man and Superman'." "That would be a waste of work," (said S.) "because it could bring in no profit." "That is not what attracts me," I said. "Oh, but you *must* reckon with that; everybody has to reckon with it. Of course, I am now a famous artist," (he added half jokingly), "I can allow myself to ride hobby horses." Now that was not very nice, and still less tactful.

'He talks so much and so quickly that the result is very unequal; he often says things like an impudent youth, things which are not weighed and proved, and not wise; and for his age, not dignified. As a musician he is still an amateur . . . what stamps the amateur is joy in his own discoveries and pleasure in different things which do not belong to one another.

'His tone is almost unbearably inconsiderate (softened by humour and liveliness) . . .'*

All this makes very clear that Shaw was basically as gauche and clumsy as he had been in his early days at the Lawsons when he had walked up and down the Embankment for half an hour before ringing the doorbell. Obviously, he did not intend to imply that Busoni—himself a world-famous pianist, only ten years Shaw's junior—was too poor and unknown to ride hobby-horses; it was sheer tactlessness and failure to express what he *did* mean. 'I have no doubt the Lawsons found me discordant, crudely self-assertive, and insufferable,' he wrote of himself at twenty-one; he was still much the same at sixty-three. 'I am now a world famous artist.' It was Robert Smith looking with astonishment at his bearded face in the mirror, and trying to convince himself.

This same insensitivity was responsible for his often stormy relations with Wells. Wells had joined the Fabians in 1903, although he found Wallas, Webb, Olivier and the rest too stuffy and pedantic to suit his own excitable temperament. Unlike Shaw, Wells never troubled about a public façade. His formative years had not been spent as a struggling artist but as a science student under T. H. Huxley. At the age when Shaw was writing

* *Busoni's Letters to his Wife,* London 1938. I am indebted to the composer Ronald Stevenson—who is engaged on a biography of Busoni—for drawing my attention to this passage.

his novels Wells was teaching in appalling private schools and periodically coughing blood. The sheer immensity of the universe revealed by science enchanted him to such an extent that he had no time to think about his personality and the impression he made on people. Like Shaw, he had the philanderer's temperament; but this developed late, for Wells married young, and then separated from his wife and lived with one of his students. He wrote *The Time Machine* during a long period of illness, and it made his reputation when he was twenty-eight. As with most men of genius, his immaturity lasted a long time—well into his thirties, and he never lost a schoolboy tendency to fly into a temper and call people names. In 1906 he startled the Fabians by reading a paper called 'Faults of the Fabians' at a meeting. Full of grandiose schemes for world-socialism, Wells felt that the 'Old Gang'—Shaw, Webb, Wallas, etc.—were too cautious and intellectual; they should think in terms of an enormous Fabian Society with branches all over Britain, a large fund for propaganda purposes, and so on. The younger Fabians agreed enthusiastically, and debates raged for months, into 1907, with Wells periodically losing his temper and abusing Shaw as a sexless biped and an intellectual eunuch, and finding equally appropriate insults for every member of the 'Old Gang.'* At the final debate on whether to censure the 'Old Gang' and adopt Wells's policies, Shaw was selected to demolish Wells. He did this by simply telling the Society that if they supported Wells's onslaught, the 'Old Gang' would walk out and form a new society. It was the William Morris technique, and Shaw later turned it to good account in *The Apple Cart*. The story of Shaw's ultimate demolition of Wells has been told many times as an example of Shaw's use of wit on the public platform. Shaw said:

'Mr Wells in his speech complained of the long delay by the "Old Gang" in replying to his report. But we took no longer

---

* Shaw told Pearson, after Wells's death, that the famous Fabian row was not simply a matter of disagreements about policy. Bland and Wallas both suspected Wells of having designs on their daughters. When Bland warned his daughter against Wells she apparently countered by telling him that Wells had described Bland as an incorrigible philanderer. This was true; but it was hardly tactful of Wells to say so. The resulting row gradually involved all the Fabians.

than he. During his Committee's deliberations, he produced a book on America. And a very good book too. But whilst I was drafting our reply, I produced a play.'

At this point, Shaw paused with his eyes on the ceiling and waited, then said finally: 'I paused there to enable Mr Wells to say "And a very good play too." ' The audience laughed for several minutes, and Wells, seeing that no more serious business would get done, withdrew his amendment. 'Keats was snuffed out by an article,' writes S. G. Hobson, who relates the incident,* 'Wells was squelshed by a joke.'

What the incident reveals, more than anything else, is the reputation Shaw had built up for himself. His 'joke' was not even a joke; it was a quip, which may have occurred to him on the spur of the moment, and it does not rate particularly highly as a stroke of humour. Nevertheless, every Shaw biographer has told the story as a demonstration of Shaw's platform brilliance. It is not even true that Shaw 'squelshed' Wells. It was his threat of the mass resignation of the 'Old Gang' that swung the vote. Wells was far from being squelshed; the Society members elected him to the executive committee, and he topped the poll.

An article Shaw wrote on Wells in *The Christian Commonwealth* in 1909 gives an account of the Fabian row,† but is mainly of interest as an example of Shaw's tendency to say things that were 'not weighed or proved'. He begins: 'Wells is a spoiled child. His life has been one long promotion. He was born cleverer than anybody within hail of him. You can see from his pleasant figure that he was never awkward or uncouth or clumsy-footed or heavy-handed as so many quite personable men have been when they were mere cubs. He was probably stuffed with sweets and smothered with kisses until he grew too big to stand it. . . . He won scholarships, and had hardly turned this success over his tongue to get the full taste of it when he tried his hand at literature, and immediately succeeded. The world that other men of genius had to struggle with, and which sometimes starved them dead, came to him and licked his boots.' In fact, Wells's childhood had been harder than Shaw's, and before he became successful he knew the kind of real hardship that Shaw had never tasted His

* *Pilgrim to the Left,* London 1938.
† Reprinted in *Pen Portraits and Reviews,* p. 279.

mother was a housemaid who married the gardener; when a
china shop they opened went bankrupt, and Joseph Wells broke
his leg, Sarah Wells became a housekeeper and supported her
children herself. Wells started to earn his own living at fourteen,
and a year later he was apprenticed to a draper, where he spent
two miserable years. Scholarships and various teaching positions
followed, until a serious breakdown in his health decided him to
try journalism. By comparison with Wells, it was Shaw who was
the spoilt and pampered one. Some of Wells's attacks on Shaw
were unfair; but one can see why he accused Shaw of 'practising
the woman's privilege of wanton incoherent assertion'. But Shaw
had gained his reputation by this kind of effrontery, and, as
Busoni noted, he never broke himself of the habit of 'saying
things like an impudent youth'.

All this may explain why Shaw's reputation began to decline
almost as soon as it was established. The age was not ready for
his optimistic evolutionism, and the only aspect of Shaw that
was understood was the flamboyant personality. Besides, he had
arrived late, and the next generation was already knocking at the
door. As long ago as 1902, the twenty-year-old James Joyce had
called on Yeats in London and told him irritably that he did
not talk like a poet but like a man of letters—meaning by that
that Yeats was too full of ideas. For Joyce, literature should be
akin to music; it should produce strange and powerful effects on
the feelings, not on the intellect. In 1909 a twenty-four-year-old
American poet, Ezra Pound, arrived in London, full of ideas
about the nature of poetry that were closely akin to Joyce's. It
was Pound who, in an essay on Joyce, was to dismiss Shaw as 'a
ninth-rate coward'. A young philosopher, T. E. Hulme, came
under the influence of Bergson after being sent down from
Cambridge; like Shaw, he came to feel more and more strongly
the reality of the spiritual values represented by the Church, and
like Blake he had an intense dislike of mere rationalism. But a
certain authoritarian tendency led him to place increasing
emphasis on man's sloppiness and need for discipline, so that he
ended by preaching the need for a return to Christian dogma—

particularly the dogma of original sin. Pound was influenced by Hulme; so, in turn, was another young American, T. S. Eliot, who came to Europe shortly before the war in which Hulme was killed. Eliot agreed with Hulme that it was time for a new age of classicism and discipline . . . and as time went by, he also came to agree with him about religion. In fact, Eliot's profoundly religious temperament differed from Hulme's and Shaw's mainly in being altogether less vital. He was a hypochrondriac by nature, and seems to have suffered most of his life from various guilt feelings. His religion had a narrow, almost morbid intensity that was closer to Pascal or Kierkegaard than to Hulme, and he could see no real difference between the vague humanism of Bertrand Russell and Shaw's evolutionism; both seemed to him typical products of the sick modern mind.

These men were the rising influences in the decade before the First World War, and there were many others: D. H. Lawrence, E. M. Forster, Dorothy Richardson, Virginia Woolf, Wyndham Lewis, Aldous Huxley—most of them differing from the generation of Chesterton, Bennett and Wells by reason of a disciplined intellectualism. They were not 'simplifiers' in the way that Shaw and Wells seemed to be; their view of reality was subtle, complex, and tinged with pessimism.

It would have been impossible for Shaw and Wells to foresee this in 1908; they were too preoccupied with *their* revolution. And this in itself seemed so momentous that it was perhaps excusable that they thought it would be the last for some time. What had happened is that they were reaching a completely new public of intelligent readers. Carlyle and Ruskin had written for the middle classes; and apart from these 'prophets', Victorian writers were not intellectuals; Dickens, Thackeray, Trollope, George Eliot, Meredith, Hardy—they all stuck to mirroring the age. Then, in the last decade of the nineteenth century, there was a sudden movement towards popular education. A young pupil of H. G. Wells's, Alfred Harmsworth, started a magazine called *Answers to Readers' Questions*, full of informative paragraphs on every subject under the sun. Its success was tremendous; Harmsworth went on to become a press baron and a millionaire; one of his most successful ventures was issuing an encyclopaedia in weekly parts that was cheap enough for any worker to buy.

Popular series of the classics were being published on every hand, and made fortunes. And it was this new educated public, hungry for ideas and information, that bought the books of Shaw and Wells, and found them altogether more exciting than old-fashioned novelists like Bennett and Galsworthy. And since there was obviously no possible reason to anticipate a reversal of the trend, Shaw and Wells seemed justified in being optimistic about the future. They were the men of the moment, and their moment looked like lasting for a long time.

In the 1890s, on completing *Arms and the Man*, Shaw had remarked to Henry Salt: 'Mozart is bigger than Wagner as I am bigger than Ibsen.' He explained the aim of his comedy: 'I want the people to go away from my plays feeling a little bigger than when they came to them. To have laughed themselves out of littleness.' Kate Salt answered acutely: 'You have it in you but I doubt if you have the courage. It needs a kind of courage . . . a courage you do not possess. You are more likely to run away from the really big effort and find sport in little things. It is so much more amusing. There is something feline [in you].' Salt duly recorded this in his diary. When we consider Shaw's output between 1906 (the year of *The Doctor's Dilemma*) and 1913, Kate Salt's words take on a prophetic ring. Shaw proceeded to find sport in little things.

But before speaking of the plays of this period, it should be admitted that they are disappointing only in comparison with what went before, and what came later. If Shaw had written nothing else, *Getting Married* (1908) and *Misalliance* (1910) would be two of the most interesting plays of the twentieth century. They are unapologetic 'discussion plays' with a minimum of plot; the talk is as good as ever, the dramatic incident as absurd and amusing. Shaw was out to prove that he could make a play out of the materials of a debate, and his success was complete. The example of *Getting Married* set Granville Barker writing *The Madras House*, also about marriage, and in some ways a better play than either of Shaw's. Barker was not a humorist, and he was influenced by Henry James; to compare his plays with Shaw

H

is like comparing a string quartet with a Rossini overture. Shaw was immensely disappointed when Barker—whom he treated as a son—married an American woman who hated the theatre and who persuaded him to stop writing plays. Barker is still one of the great underrated playwrights of this century.

Getting Married takes place in the Bishop's palace on the morning of Bishop's daughter's wedding. Someone has sent the bride and groom-to-be a pamphlet on the marriage laws, with the consequence that they decline to go through with it. There follows a discussion in which everyone tries to suggest how the marriage contract could be improved, but they fail to reach agreement. The Mayor's wife goes into a trance, in which she speaks with the voice of the 'Eternal Feminine'. Then the play comes back to earth as the young couple announce they have married after all.

It is tempting to say that as an artist, Shaw was hurtling downhill on a toboggan, and there is perhaps some truth in it. But it is only necessary to read half a page of *Getting Married* to be drawn into it, and to recognise that Shaw was not really conceited in comparing himself to Mozart. The texture is light, but the gaiety is irresistible. It is a divertimento with more serious undertones, and as such, it is perfectly successful. But it must be admitted that the attempt to drag the play to a level of high seriousness in the trance speech is little short of embarrassing. On a first reading, it looks as if Shaw included it out of bravado—to demonstrate that he can break all the rules, move from comedy to seriousness and back again without effort. Closer study reveals its importance. In this play about marriages and divorces—Shaw's 'domestic level'—he wants to include the wider vision of the poet-philosopher, woman as an instrument of evolution, searching for 'a father for the Superman'. 'When all the stars sang in your ears and all the winds swept you into the heart of heaven, were you deaf? were you dull? was I no more to you than a bone to a dog?' This is the theme that is the core of all D. H. Lawrence's work. But in this Shavian discussion play, in which none of the characters rise much above the level of *You Never Can Tell*, it is nevertheless out of place.

The ending of the play suddenly brings into focus for a moment the problem that Shaw was evading. St John Hotchkiss is a young man about town, a self-declared snob, who is still one of the most intelligent characters in the play. He is in love with Mrs George—the Mayor's wife. Mrs George invites him back to her home, but when he explains: 'If I were an eighteenth century marquis I could not feel more free with a Parisian citizen's wife than I do with regard to Polly' [Mrs George] she quickly withdraws the invitation. 'I'm looking out for a friend and not for a French marquis.' He reassures her: '. . . once I cross the threshold of your husband's house and break bread with him . . . this marriage bond which I despise will bind me as it never seems to bind the people who believe in it.' In short, we are back to natural Christianity. Hotchkiss will not betray his host because, although he believes himself to be an irresponsible rake, some force of deeper seriousness is gradually coming to birth in him. This is the subject Shaw *should* have been writing about, instead of manufacturing comedies on topics of the day.

Most of these comments also apply to *Misalliance* (1910), the play about parents and children. This time the scene is a country house belonging to a successful underwear manufacturer John Tarleton, whose daughter, Hypatia, is about to marry an intelligent but spoilt young man. When discussion palls, Shaw tends to make something happen quite arbitrarily—an aeroplane crashes in the garden and brings in two new characters, a young man waving a revolver emerges from the Turkish bath and proposes to shoot Tarleton. One of the characters in the aeroplane is a Polish lady acrobat, to whom all the men immediately make immoral proposals. It is she who makes a speech that might have come out of Act 3 of *Man and Superman*:

'Old pal, this is a stuffy house. You seem to think of nothing but making love. All the conversation here is about love-making. All the pictures are about love-making. The eyes of you all are sheep's eyes. You are steeped in it, soaked in it: the very texts on the walls of your bedrooms are the ones about love. It is disgusting. It is not healthy.'

She is an attempt to return to the level of seriousness of *John Bull's Other Island* and *Major Barbara*. But then, she is only an acrobat; her discipline is purely physical. It also has a suicidal element; her family have a tradition of risking their lives once a day.

But she helps to focus what is wrong with the Shaw of this period. The Tarleton house is really no better than Heartbreak House of the later play; the people are living the stifled, pointless lives of the rich lady in *The Waste Land*:

> '. . . What shall we do tomorrow?
> What shall we ever do?'

It is a curious thing, which inclines one to believe in that elusive abstraction, the *zeitgeist*. The Victorian age, the age of prosperity and optimism, was turning sour and stale. The enormous spiritual energies that had produced Carlyle and Ruskin and Morris and the Oxford Revival were running low; the peace and prosperity seemed an anti-climax. And even Shaw, one of the most vital men of the age, was subject to the malaise. There was something stifling and exhausting in the air, like a subtle gas. It seemed to happen towards 1910, and became steadily more oppressive. Some of the vitality has leaked out of Wells in *The New Machiavelli* (1911) and *Marriage* (1912); there is a feeling of repetition and futility. The breezy optimism of Chesterton, which had been so triumphantly convincing in *The Man Who Was Thursday* (1908) has begun to degenerate into a tiresome mannerism in *The Ball and the Cross* (1910) and *The Innocence of Father Brown*; which bring to mind the epigram that a pessimist is a man who has to live with an optimist. H. H. Munro ('Saki'), who had specialised in depicting 'high society' in the manner of Oscar Wilde, produced in 1912 a curious, bitter novel, *The Unbearable Bassington*, which is intended to be light and witty, and ends by creating something very like horror. Saki was another who died in the war. In his case, it might be argued that the pose of shallowness was simply producing revulsion, like a child who has over-eaten at a party and ends up being sick. This hardly applies to Shaw, who had always recognised the importance of the religious impulse, and whose *Blanco Posnet* was intended to be a religious tract. In spite of his efforts, he seemed to be hypnotised by the trivial, like everybody else. *Misalliance* does not end. It simply grinds to a halt:

TARLETON. Well, I—er [*he addresses Lina, and stops*]. I—er [*he addresses Lord Summerhays, and stops*] I—er [*he gives it up*]. Well, I suppose—er—I suppose theres nothing more to be said.

HYPATIA [*fervently*] Thank goodness!
and the curtain descends.

In his next play, *The Dark Lady of the Sonnets*, Shaw writes about Shakespeare with what the critics probably called 'characteristic Shavian irreverence', but which comes closer to silliness. It is true that this was a *pièce d'occasion*; but *Fanny's First Play* was not. It was presented anonymously at the Little Theatre in 1911, and was so successful that it was transferred to the Kingsway theatre, where it ran for 622 performances—still a record for a Shaw play. The secret of the authorship—kept up until it was published in 1914—may have contributed to this success. (But Shaw made no very serious attempt to keep it secret; it was advertised as being by Xxxxxxx Xxxx.) It is a play within a play. A Miss Fanny O'Dowda has written a play at Cambridge, and her father is rich enough to put it on in his house and pay London critics to come down and see it, without telling them who wrote it. When the play—again about parents and children—is over, the critics discuss who might have written it. One guesses Granville Barker, another Pinero. The third, who suggests Shaw, triggers a discussion of Shaw that enables the author to put his grievances against the critics.

VAUGHAN. Rot! . . . Poor as the play is, there's a note of passion in it. . . . Now Ive repeatedly proved that Shaw is incapable of a note of passion.

BANNAL. Yes, I know. Intellect without emotion . . .

VAUGHAN. Well, at all events, you cant deny that the characters in this play are quite distinguishable from one another. That proves its not by Shaw, because all Shaw's characters are himself: mere puppets stuck up to spout Shaw. . . .

BANNAL. There can be no doubt of that: everybody knows it. But Shaw doesnt write his plays as plays. All he wants to do is to insult everybody all round and set us talking about him.

TROTTER [*wearily*] And naturally, here we are all talking about him. For heaven's sake let's change the subject.

GUNN. . . . What I've always told you about Shaw is. . . .

BANNAL. There you go. Shaw, Shaw, Shaw! Do chuck it. If you want to know my opinion about Shaw——

The others interrupt him with shouts of 'We don't', and when the uproar has died down, all begin at once: 'Shaw . . .'

All this could be defended, of course, by pointing out that the whole play is a joke, and that it was a sufficiently good joke to run for 622 performances. But it is undeniably a self-advertising joke; Shaw was again walking the razor edge between vanity and humour. To the rising generation that included Pound, D. H. Lawrence and Hulme, the play must have seemed little more than the cavortings in public of an intensely self-satisfied clown.

And during the next three years Shaw seemed intent on supplying his critics with ammunition. *Androcles and the Lion* is one of his shortest plays, and seems to be an attempt to prove that it is possible to write a religious drama in terms of farce. In the opening scene Androcles and his nagging wife are approached by a lion in a forest. Androcles tells his wife to run away while the lion eats him. Then he notices that the lion has a thorn in his paw, and takes it out while keeping up a patter of baby-talk, 'Oh, musnt frighten um's good kind doctor, um's affectionate nursey.' Then he and the lion waltz around the stage, while his wife wakes up from a faint and shouts: 'Oh, you coward, you havent danced with me for years.' Then the play becomes serious, with Christians being marched to Rome to be thrown to the wild beasts. Lavinia, a young aristocrat who has become a Christian, asks the captain why they are being persecuted.

THE CAPTAIN [*unmoved and somewhat sardonic*] Persecution is not a term applicable to acts of the Emperor. The Emperor is the Defender of the Faith. In throwing you to the lions he will be upholding the interests of religion in Rome. If you were to throw him to the lions, that would no doubt be persecution.

The Christians again laughed heartily.

CENTURION [*horrified*] Silence, I tell you!

Lavinia is one of Shaw's best portrayals of the religious temperament. The captain wants her to marry him and urges her to burn the incense to Diana, pointing out that it doesn't matter by what name God is called. She explains her point: 'Oh, do you think that I, a woman, would quarrel with you for sacrificing to a woman god like Diana, if Diana meant to you what Christ means to me?' It is the problem of the higher evolutionary type in an irreligious society. She explains that if they succeed in persuading her to sacrifice to Diana, 'I should believe more in Diana than my persecutors have ever believed in anything.'

And in the next act, before she is due to be thrown to the lions, there is another exchange with the captain which is the core of the play. The captain asks her: 'Are your Christian fairy stories any truer than our stories about Jupiter and Diana, in which, I may tell you, I believe no more than the Emperor does, or any educated man in Rome?'

LAVINIA. Captain; all that seems nothing to me now. I'll not say that death is a terrible thing; but I will say that it is so real a thing that when it comes close, all the imaginary things—all the stories, as you call them—fade into mere dreams beside that inexorable reality. I know now that I am not dying for stories or dreams. . . . It is since all the stories and dreams have gone that I have no doubt at all that I must die for something greater than dreams or stories.

THE CAPTAIN. But for what?

LAVINIA. I dont know. If it were anything small enough to know, it would be too small to die for. I think I am going to die for God. Nothing else is real enough to die for.

THE CAPTAIN. What is God?

LAVINIA. When we know that, Captain, we shall be gods ourselves.

Shaw had already touched upon this theme in a curious little play called *The Glimpse of Reality* (1909), set in Renaissance Italy, in which a spoilt young nobleman has a similar awakening: 'There is nothing like a good look into the face of death: close up: right on you: for shewing you how little you really believe and how little you really are.' Even in the midst of his least serious period Shaw never lost sight of this realisation. *Androcles and the Lion* gives the impression of a man struggling to get back to his most serious level. But after the dialogue between Lavinia and the Captain the farce returns. Ferrovius, an enormous muscular Christian, finds at the last moment that he cannot die without a fight; and his fight is so successful that he kills all the gladiators. The Christians are pardoned by the Emperor, all except Androcles, who is thrown to the lion. The lion recognises him, and they waltz around the arena. Shaw mentioned in an appendix to the play that when the play was performed in Berlin the Crown Prince walked out, 'unable to endure the . . . very clear and fair exposition of autocratic imperialism'. It would be a safe guess that the Kaiser walked out in disgust at what he took to be the play's determined silliness.

(In justice to Shaw I should comment that a film version made by Gabriel Pascal in 1952 was remarkably successful; the element of farce seemed perfectly calculated for cinema audiences, and the transition from farce to the serious was aided enormously by the element of realism that can be given by the camera—as well as by some additional material written for Ferrovius by Hollywood writers. This raises the speculation that *Androcles* was not aimed at the usual Shaw audience but at the audience who still filled the music halls to laugh at Marie Lloyd and Little Tich. It was certainly extremely successful when first presented in London, running for fifty-two performances at the St James Theatre in the autumn of 1913.)

Pygmalion, written immediately after *Androcles*, ran for 118 performances in the April of 1914, and has continued to be Shaw's most popular play. It certainly demonstrates that Shaw was still at the height of his powers at fifty-six. The play is better than anything he had written since *Major Barbara* simply because it once again has a Shaw hero; together with Jack Tanner and King Magnus, Higgins is one of his most typically Shavian creations. In *The Concise Cambridge History of English Literature* George Sampson has the interesting comment that *Pygmalion* 'fails at the end because its author lost courage'. At first sight, and in view of Shaw's appendix to the play, in which he explains why Eliza could never marry Higgins, this comment may sound unperceptive. Surely it was only Shaw's realism that made him grasp that Eliza and Higgins are totally unsuited to one another? But then, on closer examination, one realises that Mr Sampson has a point, even if not quite the one he intended to make. The relation between a male professor and female student has a strong element of the father-daughter relation in it, and such a relationship is often a satisfactory one for marriage—which no doubt explains why so many male professors marry their students.

(The reverse—a female professor marrying a male student—is far rarer, because the mother-son relationship occurs less frequently as a basis for marriage.) Since Shaw's attitude towards women was completely unpaternal, he was unable to envisage Eliza marrying Higgins, although for a different type of writer—Ernest Hemingway, for example—it would have seemed inevitable. Shaw was a good enough dramatist to have made Eliza marry Higgins, if it *had* seemed natural; (as it stands, the play simply tails off) but he was *unable* to present it as dramatically convincing. The present ending tells us a great deal about Shaw.

The run of success had been long and unbroken, ever since that first night of *John Bull's Other Island*, and success seemed to have brought dramatic decline. But his luck was running out. Like the luck of the rest of Europe.

The year 1913 brought him a defeat and humiliation that rankled for the rest of his life.

Back in 1898, Shaw had written *Caesar and Cleopatra* with Mrs Patrick Campbell in mind as Cleopatra. She was then thirty-four years of age, eight years Shaw's junior. 'Mrs Pat' was beautiful, tempestuous, and very feminine. In 1912, just after finishing *Pygmalion*, Shaw asked her to listen to the play—and two years later, she created the part of Eliza. Shaw found the forty-eight-year-old woman as fascinating as she had been when he had praised her in his days as a drama critic. She never made any attempt to conceal her age; even in 1906 she mentioned her son of twenty-two and daughter of twenty in a letter to Shaw. And as early as 1906, when they were corresponding spasmodically, she was signing herself 'Your Stella Beatrice C.' This did not indicate any intimacy; she was simply a born flirt who used her charm automatically. Offering her the part of Eliza was something of a breakaway for Shaw; many of his earlier heroines—including Ann in *Man and Superman*, Jennifer in *The Doctor's Dilemma* and Lavinia in *Androcles*—had been written for Granville Barker's wife Lillah McCarthy. Only a week after reading her the part of Eliza, Shaw was beginning a letter to her 'Beatricissima'. There can be no doubt that she had fluttered her eyelids to good effect,

and Shaw, after fourteen uneventful years married to a woman
whose strong point was not sexual allurement, suddenly began to
think nostalgically of the old Fabian days when no woman could
resist him. Here was Wells, who had been married even longer
than Shaw, behaving in a manner that had become the scandal of
London—although it would be some years before he openly put
photographs of his mistresses on the mantelpiece. And Stella
had graduated—without prompting—to addressing him as 'darling' in her letters, and in the postscript of one of them promised
coquettishly: 'Perhaps someday, if you are very good and behave
properly at rehearsal I will write you a love letter.' To Shaw, and
to anyone else, who might have read their letters, it must have
seemed clear that Stella was infatuated with Shaw—or, at least,
strongly attracted—and would not object to a love affair. And
Shaw, as romantic as ever, could see no good reason to decline
the offer. Stella asked about his sister Lucy, who was now
divorced and suffering from tuberculosis, and went to see her;
the two women became extremely friendly. What reason could
Stella have for such a move unless to work her way a little further
into Shaw's affections? Shaw, at fifty-six, would have been too
sensible to take the lead in pursuing Mrs Pat, but since it seemed
clear that she was offering herself as a bonus for the part of
Eliza, he abandoned caution. It was true that she seemed to be
extremely cautious, but her reasons seemed flattering enough.
On the 18th November 1912 she began: 'No more shams—a real
love letter this time—then I can breathe freely,' and went on to
explain: 'I havent said "kiss me" because life is too short for the
kiss my heart calls for. . . . All your words are as idle wind—
Look into my eyes for two minutes without speaking if you dare!
Where would be your 54 years? [she was flattering; he was
fifty-six] and my grandmother's heart? and how many hours
would you be late for dinner?' In short, she seemed to imply,
he was married and she was afraid of getting her emotions any
more deeply involved; she ended by saying: 'I wouldn't let any
man kiss me unless I was sure of the wedding ring.' In April of
the following year he was writing from Ireland: 'So if you are
idly curious as to whether I am still in love with Stella, the
answer is yes yes yes yes yes . . .'—the 'yes' repeated twenty-nine
times. Her letters were signed 'My love to you' but they contained

no affectionate phrases. Perhaps Shaw ought to have taken warning from this. He was committed too far, and was feeling slightly ashamed of himself. Webb called his infatuation 'a clear case of sexual senility'—which it might have been if he had not felt so certain that Stella wanted an affair—and Charlotte had overheard a telephone conversation between Shaw and Stella that had thoroughly upset her.

The truth was that Stella was thinking about marriage, and although she may have toyed with the idea of marrying Shaw, she could see that he was too settled in his domesticity with Charlotte—he had told her so several times. She was also attracted by George Cornwallis West, a romantic playboy type, far more eligible than Shaw, being in the process of getting divorced, and brother of the Duchess of Westminster. If she became Shaw's mistress, and West found out, it would be the end of the possibility of marriage. She made what she decided was the correct choice. In August 1913 she went to Sandwich to recover from a minor operation, telling Shaw clearly: 'You know I must be alone by the sea.' But for Shaw it seemed foolish to miss this opportunity of finally consummating the affair, especially as she had just admitted: 'It's getting difficult not to love you more than I ought to . . .' He pursued her to Sandwich, and immediately received a brief note: 'Please will you go back to London today—or go wherever you like but don't stay here . . . Please dont make me despise you.' It was a bombshell. Shaw had crawled out on a limb, probably giving Charlotte some excuse for his absence, and risking being noticed by the Press, and Stella had sawed off the limb. He moved along the coast to Ramsgate, and did his best to face it with bravado: 'Very well, go: the loss of a woman is not the end of the world.' But the length of the two letters he wrote her on the same day reveal the extent of the emotional hurt. He had the courage to be frank: 'You have wounded my vanity; an inconceivable audacity, an unpardonable crime.' She did her best to soothe him, asking: 'Do you think it was nothing to me to hurt my friend?' which must have galled him all the more. He simply did not possess the essential key to the mystery: the other man.

This was not the end of the relationship. He was too disciplined and too basically good-natured to break with her. There must have been some grim satisfaction for him later in knowing she had made the wrong choice. Although she married George Cornwallis West in April 1914, the marriage did not last. And although they continued to write on friendly, almost affectionate, terms, the 'betrayal' rankled too deeply for real forgiveness. If she had risked a break with West by allowing Shaw his consummation—even briefly—her later years might have been different. Her luck also began to run downhill with the war, in which her son was killed. Her 'temperament' made parts more difficult to get. In 1932 she wrote to suggest that their 'love letters' should be published, and he refused, giving every reason except the crucial one: that their relation never reached the stage of a love-affair.

It would be unfair to Shaw to say that the 'betrayal' of August 1913 turned him against Mrs Pat; in May 1915 he even authorised her to take 50 per cent of his author's royalties on *Pygmalion*. But when he met Mrs Pat's daughter he remarked: 'To her I am . . . only an absurd old josser whom her mother made a fool of.' She never acted in another Shaw play; he gave as his reason for declining her for *Heartbreak House* that no one would make more than £40 a week—a sum that the fifty-six-year-old Stella might have been glad of. Nevertheless, he continued to be kindly and helpful, even suggesting at one point that he should try to obtain a civil list pension for her. But the extent to which the betrayal rankled became apparent in 1929, when *The Apple Cart* was produced at Malvern. Mrs Pat wrote on June 7th, 1929: 'I went to the Selfridge Ball and met Miss Edith Evans, who gazed eagerly at me saying she was playing *me* in *The Apple Cart*.' *The Apple Cart* contains a very long first act, and a fairly long second act, the two being separated by a brief Interlude that seems to serve no particular purpose. In the Interlude King Magnus pays a visit to Orinthia, a beautiful young lady of the court with whom he apparently carries on a romantic but innocent relationship. She starts a quarrel and he placates her. Then she proposes that Magnus divorce his dull wife and marry her. When he declines, she exclaims: 'You have low tastes. Heaven is offering you a rose; and you cling to a cabbage,' and Magnus points out: 'What wise man, if you force him to choose between doing without roses and doing without cabbages, would not secure the cabbages?' Orinthia declares grandly that everyone knows she is the real queen, and asks if he would marry her if his wife died.

He tells her: 'My dear Orinthia, I had rather marry the devil.
Being a wife is not your job.' At the end of the scene she becomes
playful when he starts to leave to have tea with his wife, and tries
to hold him back by force; they end up wrestling on the floor.
The Secretary comes in and then hastily backs out, and enters
after knocking loudly. Orinthia says grandly: 'The king forgets
everything when I am here,' but the Secretary says, 'No explanations are needed. I saw what happened.' This final scene made
Orinthia's identity unmistakable; Stella had had a wrestling match
with Shaw on a similar occasion when he tried to return to
Charlotte.

In answer to Stella's indignant letter, Shaw explained sooth-
ingly that Orinthia's identity was a secret between them, and
Stella countered by asking how it could be a secret when Edith
Evans told her about it. (Shaw said Edith Evans 'guessed'—an
unlikely explanation.) Stella was too polite to point out that the
real element of travesty in the scene is that Orinthia is rejected
by Magnus, not vice versa.

At Stella's insistence, Shaw changed a few lines; but the scene
remained identical in outline. It is the only occasion on which
Shaw was known to take 'literary revenge'—although he had
made a character in *Immaturity* do the same thing in circumstances
that bear some resemblance to the Shaw-Stella situation. There
remains, of course, the possibility that none of Shaw's biographers seem to have considered: that Stella really did ask Shaw
to get rid of his 'cabbage' and marry her. The letters do not
support it—except for the phrase about refusing to kiss 'unless
I was sure of the wedding ring'; but then it was hardly the kind
of proposition she would put into a letter.

On June 28th, 1914, Mrs Pat was writing to Shaw to ask if
nothing could be done to lengthen the run of *Pygmalion*, which was
due to come off in two weeks although still playing to packed
houses. On the same day a young Serbian terrorist shot and
killed the Archduke Ferdinand of Austria and his wife at Sarajevo
in Bosnia. Although nobody wanted war the consequences
followed inevitably. Austria shelled Belgrade; Russia mobilised

to defend Serbia; Germany declared war on Russia and then on Russia's ally France, relying on a swift, violent campaign to finish them both off before they could complete mobilisation. France's frontier being too short for full-scale invasion purposes, the Germans decided to strike through Belgium. Britain had been chafing about the increase of the German navy for a long time—the truth was that Britain and Germany were both too powerful and expanding too fast not to clash sooner or later. In any case, Britain was committed to defending the sanctity of the Belgium frontier. Quite apart from the obligation to defend a small neighbour, there was the need to keep the sea coast of Belgium and France out of German hands; with that much Atlantic coastline, Germany could have reduced Britain to a second-rate trading power even if Britain decided to stay neutral. And so the whole of Europe rushed into war.

Shaw had seen the war coming; he knew too many people in the government and the Foreign Office not to be aware what was in the air. He wrote two articles on the topic of preventing it, one in March 1913, the other in January 1914. What he suggested was an alliance between France and Britain to unite against Germany if Germany attacked—which was what actually happened in the event—and a build-up of armaments and compulsory military service. When England entered the war in August 1914 Shaw went off to Torquay, and wrote a pamphlet, *Common Sense about the War*, which was published in due course in *The New Statesman*, the magazine started by the Webbs in 1913 as a Fabian vehicle.

To read this pamphlet (published in *What I Really Wrote About the War*) after two world wars makes it seem one of Shaw's most irrelevant pieces, even though Pearson describes it as the most courageous act of Shaw's career. The point he wanted to make hardly seems worth making: that Britain's high moral tone—defending 'little Belgium', etc.—was a fraud. He was intent on standing back and taking a detached, Swiftian view of human nature. His main points might have come out of a preface to *Arms and the Man*: 'War, as a school of character and nurse of virtue, must be formally shut up and discharged by all the belligerents when this war is over.' 'Militarism must not be treated as a disease peculiar to Prussia. It is rampant in England.'

'I see both nations duped . . . by their Junkers and Militarists into wreaking on one another the wrath they should have spent in destroying Junkerism and Militarism in their own country.' These sentiments are unexceptionable, although perhaps hardly tactful in a moment of national emergency. The comment: 'If the soldiers of every army engaged were wise they would shoot their officers and return home' was good socialism, but it was not particularly well-timed. And some of his comments were simply untrue. It was untrue that 'We began it, and if they met us halfway . . . it is not for us to reproach them.' More than half a century later it is as clear as it was then that the Kaiser began it. Militarism may have been rampant in England as well as Germany; but again, examination of historical evidence shows that it was ten times as rampant in Germany; England was unprepared for war. This latter point also disposes of another of Shaw's most controversial assertions in *Common Sense*, that if the Kaiser was to be sent to St Helena after the war the British Foreign Secretary Sir Edward Grey should be sent there too. Shaw's single valid point was that England entered the war because it could not afford to let Germany become master of the coastline of Europe; but even this does not make Britain's immediate reason—the pact with Belgium—a 'trumped-up excuse'.

What Shaw was doing, of course, was using the war as an excuse for some of his socialist anti-war propaganda, and employing his usual method of making outrageous and only half-true assertions in order to make everyone think. But it was the wrong time, and it revealed the odd kind of miscalculation that made him introduce Mrs George's 'visionary' speech into *Getting Married* or the waltzing lion in *Androcles*; it was the gaucheness and clumsiness of his early years operating on the international stage instead of in the Lawson's drawing room. Whatever the reasons, Britain was in her worst trouble since Napoleon, and it would obviously be a fight to the finish. Shaw's position was not really very different from that of everyone else. 'I felt I was witnessing the engagement between two pirate fleets, with, however, the very important qualification that as I and my family and friends were on board the British ships I did not intend the British section to be defeated if I could help it.' It is hard to see how he thought he was 'helping' the British section by his pamphlet; in fact, the

Germans and their allies immediately used *Common Sense* in their propaganda, and managed to cause some trouble for the French in the Middle East by citing Shaw to the Arabs and stirring up revolt against the French.

Henry Arthur Jones, an old friend of Shaw's, wrote furiously to his daughter: 'Shaw continues his crazy attacks. I never felt more angry with any man. He is trying to keep up the strife between Ireland and England. I do not think I can meet him in the future.' Jones was not entirely wrong. Shaw had nothing of real importance to say, but his old habit of self-advertisement was too strong; he had to keep on being a nuisance. When he later described his war controversies he made it sound as if it was a case of his intellectual integrity and common sense against the shouts of emotional patriots. On examination, this is found to be untrue. The trouble was that Shaw's curious self-absorption made him tactless, so that when other people were sharing a powerful emotion he continued to lecture and harangue. This had already been apparent at the time of the *Titanic* disaster in 1912; while the nation was shocked at the death of 1,500 passengers, many of them women and children, Shaw was writing to the *Daily News* about the 'explosion of outrageous romantic lying' in the reports of the disaster. It was Jack Tanner haranguing the Ramsdens about Violet's pregnancy: 'Poor dear brother! Poor dear friends of the family! Poor dear Tabbies and Grimalkins! Poor dear everybody except the woman who is going to risk her life to create another life . . .' The same thing was to happen again when a German submarine sank the *Lusitania* in May 1915, an American ship with civilian passengers; Shaw's immediate reaction was to point out that far worse things were happening at the front, and that perhaps it was not such a bad thing that civilians should get a taste of what it felt like to be in the front line. What was really annoying people was not whether Shaw was right or wrong, but the feeling of manic egotism that came through some of his assertions. An example can be found in one of the chapter headings of *What I Really Wrote About the War*: 'The Russian soldiers take my advice and return home.' The Russian soldiers had never heard of Shaw. Even the title, *What I Really Wrote About the War* provokes a desire to say 'Who cares?'

This was undoubtedly what triggered the violent reaction

against Shaw in the early part of 1915, and not his 'moral courage', as his biographers insist. He had nothing in particular to say in a time of national crisis, and he insisted on saying it. No doubt the patriots *were* annoying, but when all that had been brushed aside, the hard facts remained: the Kaiser wanted a war, and Britain had to fight or become a second-rate power. The only possible argument in the circumstances is that Britain should have been content to become a second-rate power; and it may be valid; however, Shaw did not raise this one. Dislike of him mounted. The Dramatist's Club sent him a letter asking him if he would care to resign, since members were staying away rather than risk meeting him; Shaw obliged. W. J. Locke suddenly rushed out of a meeting at the Society of Authors shouting: 'I will not sit in the same room with Mr Bernard Shaw.' Even *The New Statesman*, founded partly with Shaw's money, refused to publish his remarks on the *Lusitania* sinking. At a charity matinée many actors refused to be photographed with Shaw. His mail was suddenly full of abusive letters. Robert Lynd later remarked that the war was spoken of as a struggle between Britain, France, Russia and Belgium on one side, and Germany, Turkey, Austria and Bernard Shaw on the other. Even so, most eminent British writers refused to be stampeded into abusing Shaw. Sutro put the real objection when he said that Shaw's *Common Sense* was ill-timed, and Conrad also came close to the heart of the matter when he said that in questions of national tragedy, some dignity should be observed—that is, somebody should not immediately leap up and shout, 'Poor Tabbies and Grimalkins!'

We have no details about Shaw's reaction to his sudden reversal of his fortunes. The English had taken him to their hearts before the war for calling them sentimentalists and fools; now, quite suddenly, they were treating him as a traitor, much as they treated his fellow Irishman Roger Casement, hanged for treason in 1916. The Press suggested that his plays should be boycotted, and the public agreed; the only major Shaw play presented during the war was a revival of *Fanny's First Play* early in 1915, before Shaw's remarks on the *Lusitania* caused so much trouble. A one-act 'playlet', *The Inca of Perusalem*, reads like an attempt to regain favour with the English public; it is an inept piece of anti-German propaganda in which a typically Shavian maidservant impersonates a princess and bullies the Kaiser (the 'Inca'), finally rejecting his proposal of marriage on the grounds that he is too poor. (He admits that the war has bankrupted him.) The other one-act war 'playlet', *Augustus Does His Bit* (1916), is an equally unfunny satire on the British military mentality. No doubt soldiers as stupid as Lord Augustus Highcastle do exist, but no particular skill is needed to satirise them; Shaw is shooting a sitting duck. As with *How He Lied to Her Husband* and *Overruled*, it seems an aberration on Shaw's part that he bothered to write these; he seems like a nursery schoolteacher who has got into such a habit of baby talk that he uses it on adults.

In retrospect we can see that his unpopularity during the first two years of the war made no long-term difference to Shaw's career; revivals of his plays began as soon as the war ended. It is more difficult to grasp *that Shaw himself had no way of realising this*. All his reputation for brilliance and paradox had evaporated. His more violent adversaries regarded him as a loquacious and dangerous egotist; level-headed critics thought him a tactless fool. The reputation he had spent so long in building up had collapsed. For all he knew, it would never recover. He had seen the same kind of thing happen to Oscar Wilde, and Wilde was still an unmentionable.

But apart from this personal disaster there was the collapse of the world he had helped to build, the post-Victorian world with its religion of evolution and human progress. He had never been rashly optimistic about human progress; but with Wagner and Ibsen and Tolstoy and Wells and himself it *did* seem that the world might be entering a new intellectual era, that an intelligent evolutionism might replace the bankrupt forms of Christianity. And then, overnight, the world was in the middle of an immense war that proved that human nature had not changed in 2,000 years. Shaw had said as much in justifying the anachronisms of *Caesar and Cleopatra*; but in common with Wells and Tolstoy, he hoped otherwise. Besides, all his intellectual attitudes were geared to the prosperous self-satisfied England of the past twenty-five years. What relevance could *John Bull's Other Island* have in a Europe gone back to barbarism? As to *Major Barbara*, it now seemed a rather poor joke. The gospel of Andrew Undershaft had gone a little too far.

After a decade of 'tomfoolery' and intellectual acrobatics Shaw was suddenly brought back to earth. At sixty years of age it was time for a new start.

9 GLIMPSE INTO CHAOS

For Europe the war was an unmitigated disaster; but as far as Shaw was concerned, it is a pity that it didn't happen ten years earlier. It pulled him up short; it restored him to a level of seriousness he had not touched for nearly a decade.

Of course, it is pointless to speculate what would have happened to Shaw if the events of 1914 had been somehow averted; but the downward curve from *The Doctor's Dilemma* to *Androcles and the Lion* gives some indication. Shaw's chief trouble was that he was developing the opposite of what Keats called 'negative capability', the poet's capacity to remain wide open to new experience and new ideas. He had become so accustomed to talking, to 'performing', that he had ceased to listen. J. B. Priestley wrote of him: 'The performance was often brilliant, always touched with an intensely personal charm . . . But a performance, however dazzling, is not an adequate substitute for an exchange of ideas and opinions.' In this Shaw was the opposite of Wells, who, according to Priestley 'never bothered about a *persona*. He was with you, not performing at you.'* This also explains why Wells developed during the last decades of his life in a way that Shaw never did. The immense trilogy that is the apex of his life's work—*The Outline of History*, *The Science of Life*, *The Work, Wealth and Happiness of Mankind*—was all written after the war, and it reveals a mind pointing outwards, like an enormous radar sounder, at the universe. By comparison, Shaw's mind was closed. His development had always been more of an inward

* J. B. Priestley, *Margin Released*, pp. 164–6.

process, a deepening understanding of forces and impulses inside himself. His central problem was to understand the evolutionary urge that drove him, and to learn how to serve it. And after 1905, he seems to have subconsciously arrived at the conclusion that he had reached some kind of limit, that as far as these deeper purposes were concerned, there was no further to go.

To a certain extent he was right. Art is, after all, an attempt to resolve certain conflicts, to embrace certain opposites. In minor art the conflicts tend to be on a personal or merely social level, as in Wilde's plays. The greater the artist, the more the conflicts are those of the human condition itself, Carlyle's Everlasting Yes versus Everlasting No. I have tried to show how Shaw attacked this problem—the great Romantic problem—and how he produced a solution that was beyond the understanding—or at least, the sympathies—of his contemporaries. Dostoevsky's response to human suffering had been the desire to 'give God back his entrance ticket'. But this was based upon the Russian idea of a mystical, all-powerful God. Shaw's reply was that God has no alternative than to work through men. 'It was early days when He made the croup,' says Blanco Posnet. 'It was the best He could think of then; but when it turned out wrong on His hands He made you and me to fight the croup for him.' Dostoevsky made the sufferings of children a reason for rejecting God's universe; Shaw replied that this is another matter that is within the power of human beings.

What the war did was to cause Shaw to reopen his artistic books and reconsider the question of human suffering. His work had to be somehow broadened. What he perceived immediately was that the English tradition of which he was a part—the tradition running from Scott down through Dickens—is somehow resistant to this kind of broadening, for it is fundamentally a comic tradition. The European tradition, on the other hand, tends to be fundamentally tragic, from Greek drama to nineteenth-century romanticism. And shortly before the war England had become very aware of the Russian tradition; novels by Dostoevsky, Andreyev and Artsybashev were translated, Tchehov's plays were performed, while Diaghileff's ballet was the sensation of the theatrical season of 1913. Shaw's immediate reaction to his contact with this tradition was to write the playlet *Great Catherine*

(1913), a satire on the English in his silliest vein. The sobering effect of the war now produced a second 'Russian' play *Heartbreak House*, a play which gave him more trouble than anything he had done so far and took five years to write.

The most interesting thing about *Heartbreak House* is that it is, artistically speaking, Shaw's first failure since *The Philanderer*. So far, Shaw had always taken care to bite off no more than he could chew. What he wanted now was to produce an effect that he had never produced before: an atmosphere of futility and boredom with undertones of menace. The theme of the play was to be Europe just before the war, the emotional shallowness and drifting, the 'devaluation of values' that Nietzsche called Nihilism. The 'house party' structure had already been used in *Getting Married* and *Misalliance*. But this was to be a far more complex and concentrated play, for it was an attempt to portray all the important attitudes of mind of the period: Victorian idealism, Empire colonialism, the ruthless ethic of big business, the ineffectuality of romantic daydreamers. (In Germany Thomas Mann was doing the same thing on a far larger scale with *The Magic Mountain*, using a sanatorium as his symbol of a sick Europe.) It was all to crystallise around a Shaw hero, the half-mad Captain Shotover, whose basic aim is to achieve 'the seventh degree of concentration'. It was Shotover—based on the father of the actress Lena Ashwell—who provided the first germ of the play.

But then let us consider: what *would* Shaw's attitude be towards this European war? First of all, that it was largely a consequence of capitalism, nationalism and militarism, which he had already denounced in earlier plays. What did that leave him to say? Again, that the chief problem is that the imaginative man, the higher evolutionary type, fails to play his real part in the international drama. But he had not only said this before; he had even tried to outline a solution in *Major Barbara*. In short, Shaw had already said everything he had to say on the subject. And yet he wanted to reconsider it in the light of this world war.

In that case, what Shaw really wanted to do was to produce a 'mood' play, like Tchehov's, an English equivalent of *The Cherry Orchard*. But this was exactly what he was not equipped to do. Shaw's drama depends upon intellectual clarity, upon reasonable and articulate characters being able to discuss their problems. Moreover, Shaw's chief virtue as a dramatist, is that he can make things happen, even in discussion plays like *Getting Married* and *Misalliance*; and in his best plays the dramatic movement has a clean, direct flow. Tanner asks: 'Ramsden do you know what this is?, waving a sheet of paper, and from that moment everything in the play develops from the question. The Russian drama—or novel—deliberately avoids this kind of movement; it takes pleasure in emphasising the irrelevancies of everyday life; Oblomov sits on his stove, and nothing in particular happens.

All this means that what Shaw was attempting was an impossibility for his talent. What he actually succeeded in doing was creating a typical Shaw play with articulate characters and a great deal of activity, but which, unlike any of his other plays, very obviously fails to say what it set out to say. A great deal happens in the play, but none of it seems somehow relevant to a central theme. A young girl, Ellie Dunn, turns up at 'Heartbreak House', and tells her hostess about a romantic involvement with a handsome stranger in the National Gallery; she is obviously in love. A handsome stranger comes in, and Ellie introduces him as the man she has been talking about. Her hostess says: 'What a lark! He is my husband.' The coincidence is preposterous, but it gives the play a sense of movement. What comes of this romantic involvement between Ellie Dunn and Hector Hushabye? Nothing. It has served its purpose: to introduce Hector, the romantic daydreamer, who is capable of acts of courage, but who prefers to lie—and dream—about things he didn't do.

Most of the play has this arbitrary quality. Shaw once claimed that when he began a play, he had no idea of how it would finish. This is plainly untrue of most of his plays; but it seems to be true of *Heartbreak House*. It has the air of an improvisation. Every time the action flags, Shaw introduces a new character or some new event. Just as in *Misalliance* he introduced an aeroplane crash, so here he introduces a comic burglar when the action begins to flag, and the burglar turns out to be an old bosun of Captain Shotover and the husband of the nurse-housekeeper. It is all as absurd as the waltzing lion, but one gets the feeling that this time Shaw is not snapping his fingers at the audience, but trying to disguise his own uncertainty.

The real subject of the play is hidden away in some remarks of Captain Shotover. Ellie Dunn intends to marry the crooked businessman, Boss Mangan, because her soul needs to 'eat music and pictures and books and mountains . . .' and she cannot have them without money. Shotover tells her: 'You are looking for a rich husband. At your age, I looked for hardship, danger, horror and death, that I might feel the life in me more intensely.' And this is the deeper theme of the play—a theme that Shaw had never touched before and that, in a way, was contrary to his socialist faith. Shotover is a spiritually healthy person, who sought out danger because security is stifling and demoralising. And this is basically what is wrong with Heartbreak House—the Europe of *Misalliance* and Saki's *Unbearable Bassington*: it is suffocating in its own triviality, and its triviality produces a death-wish that has led to the war. For there can be no possible doubt that this *is* what Shaw is saying. At the end of the play there is an air raid (in which Mangan is killed); Hector turns on all the lights in the house. And when the raid is over, Hesione Hushabye says: 'I hope theyll come again tomorrow night,' and Ellie says: 'Oh, I hope so.' This is Rupert Brooke's reaction to the war:

> 'To turn, like swimmers into cleanness leaping,
>   Glad from a world grown old and cold and weary.'

Shaw himself was afflicted with no such death-wish. He once said: 'You may demand moral courage from me to any extent, but when you start shooting and knocking one another about, I claim the coward's privilege and take refuge under the bed. My life is far too valuable to be machine-gunned.'

One might expect that Shotover, as the play's most serious character, would provide a contrast to the sense of futility; but, on the contrary, he admits to Ellie that he spends most of his time drinking rum, and that his ideas are now 'echoes, nothing but echoes'. He abandoned all real hope of achieving 'the seventh degree of concentration' years ago.

As to the problem of the relation of the higher evolutionary type to a society run by Boss Mangans, the play seems to conclude that there is no answer—at least for the moment. Shotover wants to invent some weapon to give him the power of life and death over the Mangans: 'There is enmity between our seed and their seed. They know it, and act on it, strangling our souls. They believe in themselves. When we believe in ourselves, we shall kill them.' This is a long—and very strange—step from Tom Broadbent and Andrew Undershaft. Hector counters by pointing out that 'Mangan's son may be a Plato, Randall's a Shelley'; 'We are members of one another.' Then what is the answer, if the Mangans force us to 'kill the better half of ourselves every day to propitiate them'? Clearly there is no immediate answer. The situation is a deadlock, unless Mangan conveniently gets himself blown up.

It can be seen that the war has made Shaw aware of a new set of problems. *Heartbreak House* anticipates Eliot's *Waste Land* in its tone and in its analysis of the problem of a civilisation undermined by triviality and 'nihilism'. But Eliot arrived at the conclusion that the answer lies in a return to traditional Christianity, and Shaw was quite certain that it did not.

The really impressive thing about *Heartbreak House* is that it represents the first long stride forward that Shaw had taken in ten years—a stride in his actual *thinking*. *Major Barbara* declared that we must have civilisation at all costs, and that this is bound to involve increasing industrialisation and centralisation. Undershaft's men are well clothed and well fed; Barbara recognises that what they now need is food for their souls. What is more, she is aware that it is harder to 'convert' a well-fed man than a starving man. Why should it be? Because one of the chief human problems is laziness; a miserable man struggles and fights; a comfortable man relaxes and yawns.

So Shaw was aware even in 1905 that the problem was how a comfortable society could be kept aware of its evolutionary purpose—for this, after all, is the basic role of a church: that men involved in the trivialities of everyday living should be reminded of wider meanings.

Now Shaw faces the problem squarely. One of the problems of

a civilised and comfortable society will be a tendency to drift into boredom, to lose all sense of purpose.

CAPTAIN SHOTOVER. At sea nothing happens to the sea. Nothing happens to the sky. The sun comes up from the east and goes down to the west. . . . Nothing happens, except something hardly worth mentioning.

ELLIE. What is that, O Captain, my captain?

CAPTAIN SHOTOVER [*savagely*] Nothing but the smash of the drunken skipper's ship on the rocks, the splintering of her rotten timbers, the tearing of her rusty plates, the drowning of her crew like rats in a trap.

ELLIE. Moral: dont take rum.

SHOTOVER [*vehemently*] That is a lie, child. Let a man drink ten barrels of rum a day, he is not a drunken skipper until he is a drifting skipper. Whilst he can lay his course and stand on his bridge and steer, he is no drunkard. It is the man who lies drinking in his bunk and trusts to Providence that I call the drunken skipper, though he drank nothing but the waters of the River Jordan.

And Hector underlines the point by asking: 'And this ship that we are all in? This soul's prison we call England?' But what can be done about this failure of purpose that comes with comfort and prosperity? Those last lines of the play—Hesione's 'I hope theyll come again tomorrow night'—is a recognition that the war is a consequence of boredom and lack of real purpose as much as international tensions. The affluent society is inevitably the violent society. In other words, this civilisation, which is the necessary instrument of the evolutionary force, contains within itself the seeds of its own destruction. 'Civilisation cannot survive without adventure,' said Whitehead, perhaps Shaw's greatest living contemporary. That is why Shotover sought danger, hardship, horror and death, 'that I might feel the life in me more intensely'.

This was a new recognition for Shaw—in fact, for most of his contemporaries. It represented a complete change in the cultural climate, the immense leap between Ibsen's bourgeoisie, with their essentially moral problems, and the people of Michael Arlen's *Green Hat* and Aldous Huxley's *Point Counter Point*, for whom morals have become an irrelevancy. It is to Shaw's credit that he was the first person in England to see it clearly and write about it.

The Waste Land, Antic Hay, The Sun Also Rises, Vile Bodies, The Great Gatsby and the rest, came during the next decade. Shaw's curious historical intuition had served him well.

The war years produced one other important work: the preface to *Androcles and the Lion* (1916). The return to seriousness induced by the war seems to have led Shaw to re-read the Gospels, and to make certain discoveries about Jesus and Christianity. Some of these are bound to strike an orthodox Christian as blasphemous; but if one studies the Gospels in the light of Shaw's preface, it is hard to see how they can be denied. One of his more interesting conclusions is that at a certain point in his life, Jesus became insane, or at least, unbalanced and obsessed—specifically, when Peter exclaimed 'Thou art the Christ, the son of the living God!' Shaw also points out that Jesus announced that the Last Judgement would take place within the lifetime of people present at the crucifixion; another indication that he was less than omniscient. He was executed for the blasphemy of claiming to be God, not for his social or political opinions or for his doctrine of the forgiveness of sins. But perhaps the most revolutionary thing in this preface is Shaw's account of Paul:

'Suddenly a man of genius, Paul, violently anti-Christian, enters on the scene, holding the clothes of the men who are stoning Stephen. He persecutes the Christians with great vigor, a sport which he combines with the business of a tent-maker. This temperamental hatred of Jesus, whom he had never seen, is a pathological symptom that that particular sort of conscience and nervous constitution which brings its victims under the tyranny of two delirious terrors: the terror of sin and the terror of death, which may be called also the terror of sex and the terror of life. Now Jesus, with his healthy conscience on his higher plane, was free from these terrors. He consorted freely with sinners, and was never concerned for a moment, as far as we know, about whether his conduct was sinful or not; so that he has forced us to accept him as the man without sin. Even if we reckon his last days as the days of his delusion, he none the less gave a fairly convincing exhibition of superiority to the fear of death. This must have both fascinated and horrified Paul, or Saul, as he was called. The horror accounts for his fierce persecution of the Christians. The fascination accounts for the strangest of his fancies: the fancy for attaching the name of Jesus Christ to the great idea which flashed upon him on the road to Damascus, the idea that he could not only make a religion of his two terrors, but that the movement started by Jesus offered him the nucleus of his new Church. It was a monstrous idea; and the shock of it, as he afterwards declared, struck him blind for days. He heard Jesus calling to him from the clouds, "Why persecute me?" His natural hatred of the teacher for whom Sin and Death had no terrors turned into a wild personal worship of him which has the ghastliness of a beautiful thing seen in a false light.'

What Paul did was to invent a religion of redemption from Original Sin through the Vicarious Atonement. As Shaw points out: 'There is no record of Christ's ever having said to any man: "Go and sin as much as you like: you can put it all on me." He said "Sin no more," and insisted that he was putting up the standard of conduct, not debasing it . . . The notion that he was shedding his blood in order that every petty cheat and adulterer and libertine might wallow in it and come out whiter than snow cannot be imputed to him on his own authority. "I come as an infallible patent medicine for bad consciences" is not one of the sayings in the gospels.' In short, the religion which has passed for Christianity for 2,000 years was invented by St Paul, and is a travesty of what Jesus actually said. Paul said: 'Believe in Jesus and you will be saved.' Jesus said: 'Go away and save yourself; I can only tell you how to go about it.'

An attempt to summarise this preface makes one aware of the quality that makes Shaw great; he writes with a clarity and compression that means that he is already his own summary. His mind glows like a pressure-lamp, casting a white, even glare that exhilarates. And this was not a natural talent, a 'literary knack'; it was the result of a lifetime of discipline.

The end of the war found Shaw more famous than ever, now an established classic. This was perhaps inevitable. There were plenty of good writers in that generation—Bennett, Conrad, Galsworthy, Kipling, Gissing, Moore—but apart from Wells, none of them carried any intellectual weight. And Shaw and

Wells between them had converted England to the notion that an important writer must have a brain as well as emotions. His influence in this respect can be seen in the new generation: Eliot, Joyce, Pound, Huxley.

J. B. Priestley makes another interesting point in his auto-biography: 'In those days before film stars and "television personalities" . . . writers like Shaw, Wells, Bennett, were *news*, daily journalism's stand-by. (Even as late as the Twenties Bennett could declare—foolishly, in my opinion—that a successful novelist should be mentioned in one newspaper or another every day.) With no publicity departments working for them, their doings and saying were reported, week in and week out. Even people who never read a word they wrote knew all about them.'*

Shaw told Beatrice Webb in a letter in 1922: 'I grow old apace . . . I have lost all differentiated interest in women, and am bored by their redoubled interest in me.' He was apparently referring to the young women at the Shavian summer schools. An apocryphal anecdote of this period refers to the dancer Isadora Duncan (whose face Shaw described as looking 'as if it had been made of sugar and someone had licked it'), who is said to have suggested to Shaw that they have a baby, since a baby with his brains and her beauty would be a prodigy. Shaw is supposed to have replied: 'What if it has your brains and my beauty?'

The philosopher C. E. M. Joad—who has been undeservedly forgotten since his death in 1953—describes how he attended the Fabian summer schools in the years immediately after the war:

'In 1919 and the early '20s the School was held at a vegetarian establishment, Penlea, on the Devonshire coast near Dartmouth. Shaw, who was living intermittently in a chalet a hundred yards distant from the main building of the school, was engaged in playwriting. At luncheon I used to sit at his table excited by the proximity, thrilled to hear him ask for the salt, delighted to be able to pass it. But I found conversation difficult. Shaw's talk sprayed continuously like a fountain, but he never seemed to pay much attention to what anybody said to him in return; certainly, not to what I said, so that instead of the give and take of conversation, there was a Shavian monologue. Talk to which

* p. 164, op. cit.

you must listen without contributing is one of the best recipes for the production of boredom. . . . In Shaw's case it was only the extreme interest of the matter which prevented the almost unbroken monologue from producing its customary effect. To a large extent, this matter consisted of anecdotes of famous people. Shaw had met everybody worth meeting, and when he began, "once when I was staying with Hardy. . ." or "Meredith used to tell me..." or "I always tell Wells that his real trouble is . . ." I was enchanted.'

In fairness to Shaw it is doubtful whether any of the young people at the table had anything to say that might interest him, while his anecdotes of famous people show an amiable desire to give the young Fabians value for their money. Both Priestley and Joad testify to a gentle charm in his manner that would have been inconsistent with a manic desire to indulge his vanity. Shaw was perhaps not always tactful, but according to his own lights he was always generous, always considerate, always polite.

Joad goes on amusingly:

'In the afternoon Shaw could be seen bathing: it was an odd sight. His limbs seemed to me to be insufficiently geared up to their central directing agency, with the result that they appeared to be possessed of wills of their own, striking out each in its individual direction and operating with a fine idiosyncratic independence of one another. Shaw's dancing gave one the same impression; whether his partners shared it, I cannot tell; they were too respectful to say.'

This remark of Joad's perhaps explains why Shaw managed to have so many accidents. (He had written to Charles Ricketts in 1918: 'I have been knocked out for a week by ptomaine poisoning and a fall on my precious head down a flight of steps—a form of exercise that I have somewhat outgrown. Therefore, now that I have got over it, I find that it has bucked me up remarkably; and the bumps on my head are taken for intellect.') It makes it all the more amusing that Shaw should have taken so immediately to any new invention for transport; after his early bicycling days, he was one of the first people in England to buy a car, and later one of the first to take a trip in an experimental aeroplane. A balloon trip in 1907 to celebrate the first English performance of

Don Juan in Hell ended with a crash into the branches of a tree. (Shaw's driving was often disastrous because his first car had the accelerator between the clutch and the brake; ever after this, he was likely to cause disaster by accelerating at crucial points when he should have been braking; his wife or chauffeur had to be ready to turn off the ignition.)

Joad also describes Shaw's reading of *Back to Methusaleh* to the summer school:

'Shaw, who never appeared until midday, spent the mornings writing, and sometimes in the evening he would read to the assembled School what he had written. The reading was most impressive. Shaw sat in front of a reading-desk with a candle on either side of him, the rest of the hall being in darkness. Much has been written about Shaw's histrionic powers. . . . But anybody who has not actually heard Shaw read one of his plays can have no conception of the charm and power of his presentation.' In the light of this, it seems a pity that Shaw made no recordings of his own plays.*

Joad was later to write *Matter, Life and Value* (1929), an enormous and impressive attempt to work out the philosophical implications of Shaw's evolutionism; it is Joad's best book, and is still the best philosophical exposition of Shaw's ideas.

It was at about this time—1922—that Shaw met T. E. Lawrence, 'Lawrence of Arabia', who was taken to Shaw's flat by Sidney Cockerell. In due course Lawrence asked Shaw to read the manuscript of *Seven Pillars of Wisdom*. Charlotte read it and was excited; Shaw was persuaded to read parts of it, recognised that it was a good book, and advised Lawrence at exasperating length on punctuation. But Shaw failed to understand Lawrence or the *Seven Pillars*. Shaw was essentially a late Victorian, and Lawrence was in every way a figure of the new century. Admittedly, neither Shaw nor Charlotte possessed a vital clue—which has only emerged in recent years—to Lawrence's complex personality: that he was a textbook case of masochism who enjoyed being beaten, and felt profoundly guilty about it. But the neurosis is not necessary to the understanding of Lawrence's genius. He was a living example of one of Shaw's 'higher evolutionary types', who had become a leader of the Arab revolt against the Turks for

* C. E. M. Joad, *Shaw,* 1949.

exactly the same reason that Shotover sought 'hardship, danger, horror and death'. He was a man in the grip of a force he did not understand, a force that, in spite of his physical frailty, enabled him to survive three years of desert warfare. He wrote of the Arabs: 'Their less taut wills flagged before mine flagged, making me seem tough by comparison.' And this immense will drove him, in spite of a curious philosophy of renunciation and denial, to seek out obstacles to surmount. Shaw's description of Hamlet fits Lawrence perfectly: 'a man in whom the common personal passions are . . . superseded by wider and rarer interests, and . . . discouraged by a degree of critical self-consciousness.' There was no living man better qualified to understand Lawrence than Shaw; and yet, as his portrait of Lawrence in *Too True to be Good* shows, he failed completely. Shaw's contribution to *T. E. Lawrence by His Friends* shows it even more; what impressed Shaw about Lawrence were the legends about the Prince of Damascus, Lurens Bey, and so on. Shaw's strong point was not his insight into other people.

In the same way there is no evidence that Shaw understood the later development of his friend Granville Barker. Between 1919 and 1922 Barker wrote *The Secret Life*, a play that succeeds triumphantly and completely in doing what Shaw failed to do in *Heartbreak House*. The play is completely uninfluenced by Shaw; but the subject is the fundamental Shavian subject: men driven by an obscure impulse that they cannot understand, even though, on a conscious level, they consider themselves without beliefs. The play is the culmination of Barker's life work, and one of the most important works of the decade in which it appeared. It is still insufficiently known.* But at least Shaw should have seen that Barker had succeeded where he had failed.

The active association between Barker and Shaw had come to an end at the beginning of the war, when Barker went to America and met the millionairess, Helen Huntingdon. He later divorced Lillah McCarthy to marry her. The new Mrs Barker seems to have been a snob who hated socialism and hated the theatre; and since Shaw was always urging Barker to return to the theatre, she hated Shaw. (When the Labour Party came to power, Barker would have been given a peerage if his wife had

* At the time of writing (1968) it is out of print.

not forced him to abandon socialism, which, as Shaw remarked, 'must have been gall and wormwood to her'.)

Shaw tells a most curious story of the new Mrs Barker, which should be included here:

'Her hatred of me manifested itself in a most uncomfortable manner. In May 1925 there was a meeting at King's College in the Strand to hear Barker give an address on the theatre. A. J. Balfour was in the chair; I was down to second the vote of thanks. . . .

'After Barker had delivered his address, and Forbes Robertson proposed the vote of thanks, I rose to second it. The devil entered into me . . . I brought down the house by protesting that his retirement from active work in the theatre was a public scandal. . . .

'What happened then was most extraordinary. The moment when I got up to leave the platform I felt that my spine had been converted into a bar of rusty iron which grated on the base of my skull. The pain at the top and bottom of my spine was so frightful that I could not even bend down to get into a taxi. Somehow I reached home on foot, and when my wife arrived I was lying flat and helpless on my bed. The doctors could make nothing of it, and I really thought I was done for. I was brought down here to Ayot and after a while began to hobble about a bit; but I daren't go further than the garden gate; until one day, with a great effort of the will, I decided to walk down the road, come what might. Instantly and miraculously, the pain left me, and I recovered completely. I noticed that it was exactly one month to the hour since I had been stricken down.

'Some time later I met Lady —— (what's her name . . .?) . . . anyhow, she had been present at the King's College meeting, and I told her what had happened to me. That, she said, was easily explained. She had watched Mrs Barker, who was sitting exactly behind me, and who had been leaning forward in her seat while I was speaking, every muscle in her face and body rigid with hate. There was not the slightest doubt that she had bewitched me. And after hearing this I could conceive of no other explanation.'*

The anecdote sounds so strange that at first it is difficult to make any comment on it except that even men of Shaw's intellect

* Hesketh Pearson, *G. B. S. A Postscript*, 1951, pp. 159–61.

I

have their superstitions. In fact, it brings out an aspect of Shaw that has never been sufficiently stressed. From the atheism of the Moody and Sankey days, there had been developing in him an increasingly religious attitude. In the early plays, evolution is a blind force, like a sleepwalker, which has only succeeded partially in waking-up in man. It is often stupid and wasteful because it lacks consciousness. *Blanco Posnet* shows a subtle change in this notion; it now possesses a peculiar power to *compel* human beings to act according to its will; not simply 'higher evolutionary types' like Dick Dudgeon and Don Juan, but a corrupt sheriff and a vindictive prostitute. In *Heartbreak House*, when Ellie says that she has a 'horrible fear that my heart is broken, but that heartbreak is not like what I thought it must be', Hesione replies: 'It's only life educating you, pettikins.' The comment is so casual that it can easily be passed over. But what it implies is that negative events—like heartbreak—which Shaw would once have assumed to be an accidental product of evolution, are now somehow regarded as a positive shaping force in the hands of the 'power' that reforms Blanco and Feemy. The blind, groping life-force of *Man and Superman* has changed into something with more tricks up its sleeve than Shaw once gave it credit for. And so that his apparent credulity on the subject of bewitchment is only another indication of his increasing tendency to accept that 'there are more things in heaven and earth . . .'

Heartbreak House was followed by the play which, according to Shaw, 'is a world classic or it is nothing', *Back to Methuselah*. It may as well be admitted at once that, as Shaw's 'world classic', it is disappointing; it does not stand above his other plays as *Faust* or *War and Peace* or *Peer Gynt* stand above the other writing of their creators. But then it has to be admitted that this is somehow appropriate for Shaw. There is a remarkable consistency about his work; his comparison of himself with Mozart is accurate. With the exception of a few 'tomfooleries' nothing he wrote between *Widowers' Houses* and *Farfetched Fables* is a total failure, and the level is remarkably high. His work is a mountain range with no Everest peaks, and no deep valleys either.

Back to Methuselah is an extremely uneven play (or series of plays; it can either be regarded as an immense play in five acts, or as five rather short plays). Its final section, *As Far as Thought Can Reach*, is the summit of Shaw's work; at least two of its sections, *The Thing Happens*, and *Tragedy of an Elderly Gentleman*, are as bad as anything he ever wrote. In these sections one is continually aware of the strange failure of self-criticism that made him produce so many feeble jokes between *How He Lied to Her Husband* and *Augustus Does His Bit*. As a dramatist, Shaw had deteriorated badly since *Major Barbara*. But as a thinker he had continued to improve ever since *The Quintessence of Ibsenism*, as the *Androcles* preface shows. And since *Back to Methuselah* sets out to be a work of ideas rather than a dramatic masterpiece, its shortcomings as a play are easy to forgive. Judged as a work of ideas, it is undoubtedly the world classic that Shaw believed it to be.

In *Heartbreak House* Shaw had faced some of the practical problems of a civilisation midway between a moribund Christianity and the new evolutionism that must be the religion of the future. It was Shaw's belief that man is on the point of entering a new estate. He has evolved very slowly from the animal level, and the chief characteristic of an animal is its *passivity*. It is a slave of its environment, and its main problem is merely staying alive. Through the use of his intellect and his imagination, man has ceased to be passive. And when he discovered the organisation of enquiry called science, his relation to the universe changed abruptly; he was suddenly the master of immense fields of knowledge—which meant of immense areas of the universe. The change from slave to master was too abrupt; he has still not become psychologically adjusted to it. Even Isaac Newton, who was the first to glimpse these new vistas of power, spent his life writing an absurd commentary on the Book of Daniel, failing to see that the *Principia* had destroyed his right to accept the Bible as revelation.

According to Don Juan in *Man and Superman*, man is on the point of accepting the consequences of his mental powers, and beginning to *shape* his evolutionary destiny, instead of allowing nature to shape it for him. This will result in a new exploration of his limitations, psychological and physical, and the steady expansion of his freedom.

Now the religions of mankind have all been religions of passivity, in which the gap between the worshipper and the worshipped is as immense as the gap between a king and his slaves. Keegan summarised the religion of man's new estate: 'It is a temple in which the priest is the worshipper, and the worshipper the worshipped.' From the moment that scientific man first stumbled into his new estate, the religion that maintained a distinction between worshipper and worshipped was doomed. No matter how great his feeling of inadequacy and unworthiness, no matter how intense his longing for the old authority, his newly found reason is bound to demolish his old gods. No matter how frightened and miserable, man has to do without his Church and Bible and the rest of his creeds, and stand on his own feet, his own master and his own judge.

But now the problem arises. At the very most only 5 per cent of the human race possesses the kind of strength necessary to stand alone, and in practice the higher evolutionary types are only a tiny fraction of these. In *Heartbreak House* Shaw faced the social consequences of the disappearance of the old religion: artists with courage but without conviction, businessmen with a creed of 'Dog eats dog', ineffectual idealists exploited by the businessmen, intelligent girls who have accepted the need to sell out; and everybody suffering from boredom and wishing that something exciting would happen. And the result was a war that almost destroyed civilisation. Nietzsche had seen even further: that a century without religious conviction will be at the mercy of every charlatan and fanatic who offers to lead it out of the wilderness; he foretold the age of dictators.

And now, in the long preface to *Back to Methuselah*—again, one of his finest pieces of writing—Shaw begins by analysing the way in which this total loss of faith has occurred. His interest here goes beyond the mere collapse of the old religion; he is concerned with the active force of materialism and 'nihilism'. For the Science that has demolished the foundations of dogmatic Christianity has ended by setting itself up as a purely negative god. Having demolished religious faith, it proceeds to sow the ground with salt. Shaw's first task is to point out that the disappearance of dogmatic Christianity does not involve the disappearance of the notion of purpose in the universe. He is concerned with Darwin's theory of Natural Selection or Survival of the Fittest, and its implication that man could have reached his present stage of evolution by purely natural processes. Opposed to this is the view of the older evolutionists—Goethe, Erasmus Darwin, and Lamarck, who believed that species evolved because they wanted to. In Lamarck's view the giraffe grew a long neck by striving to reach the highest branches of trees. In Darwin's view some giraffes were accidentally born with long necks, and in times of food shortage, they survived when the others died off; and in due course reproduced their own kind, until all giraffes have long necks.

The truth is that Shaw was here tackling a problem that was simply too big for him. The most he could usefully assert was that there is no way of knowing whether Darwin or Lamarck is right. One view covers the known facts as well as another. And in Shaw's time, the reaction against dogmatic religion was so violent that scientists preferred a purely mechanical explanation of anything. The psychologist J. B. Watson set up a psychology in which man is reduced to a series of measurable reflexes and responses, and rejected such imponderables as consciousness and will as remnants of medieval superstition. More than fifty years later it is still the most dominant form of psychology in England and America.

The only way in which the vitalist view could be argued against the mechanistic one would be to demonstrate that the mechanistic view fails to account for some of the facts. Samuel Butler had attempted something of the sort in a series of books beginning with *Luck or Cunning?* with so little success that most reference works fail even to mention his anti-Darwin books. All that Shaw could do in his lucid and very amusing preface to *Back to Methuselah* was to explain clearly the difference between Creative Evolution and Survival of the Fittest, and state his own preference for Creative Evolution. 'When a man tells you that you are a product of Circumstantial Selection solely, you cannot finally disprove it. You can only tell him out of the depths of your inner conviction that he is a fool and a liar.' The march of science seemed to be against Shaw; the rediscovery of the work of the Abbé Mendel indicated that changes in species—called mutations—are due to changes in tiny particles called the genes. Genes determine the colour of your hair, the shape of your nose, the size of your feet; and therefore the length of the giraffe's neck. Even if an individual giraffe developed a longer neck by endless striving there is no way in which this long neck could be inherited by its children. If Shaw had known this he might have replied that there is no evidence that the genes cannot be somehow influenced by the human will, and the Darwinians would have replied that there is no evidence to the contrary either. It would again have been a deadlock.*

But the major point of this preface is that 'civilisation needs a religion as a matter of life and death', and that the answer may be to attempt to create a new religion by 'pooling' all the religious legends of the world, so that 'China would share her sages with Spain, and Spain her saints with China'. Since the essence of religion is always the same, whether in Mahometanism, Shinto-ism or Christianity, Shaw says, why do they not attempt a kind of merger? The weak point of this argument, of course, is that the strength of the Church in the Ages of Faith lay in its conviction that the legends were true. Saints may be able to grasp the spiritual essence of religion and ignore the trappings; most men need the trappings. If they have no inner compulsion that acts as an authority to discipline them into giving of their best, then they require an external authority; and this authority immediately loses its point if you explain that it is entirely symbolic and metaphorical.

It would seem, then, that Shaw has not solved the problem he stated in *Major Barbara* and *Heartbreak House*. But in the five plays that make up *Back to Methuselah*, he at least makes another over-all attempt to survey the workings of evolution in human

* It is only in recent years that a reputable Darwinian biologist, Sir Alister Hardy, has advanced the view that the genes might be influenced by 'psychic factors' (*The Living Stream*, 1965).

history. And his chief point here is the revolutionary one that man has somehow *chosen* death, and that there is no reason why he should not reverse the choice and live as long as he wants to—for example, for 300 years. For Shaw, at sixty-five, had become aware of another aspect of the problem: the absurd brevity of human life. He had spent the first fifty years of his life in 'literary struggles'; emerged to become a vital influence on his time; and then immediately proceeded to lose the powers he had taken so long to develop. 'Animal man' may find seventy-five years adequate for his purposes, since he lives passively, but intellectual man possesses foresight and purpose, both of which find themselves cramped in the present brief life-span, as musicians would find themselves cramped if there was a rule that no piece of music should last more than five minutes. Like a great symphonist, man possesses the power to think and plan in long, sweeping lines; he needs time in which to expand. Shaw contends that the leaders of civilisation, the statesman and artists and scientists, will have to live for at least 300 years if civilisation is to be saved. The present rulers and thinkers simply do not possess enough planning powers for long-term world organisation.

In what way has man 'chosen' death? In the first play, 'In the Beginning', Shaw shows how Adam, living on a more-or-less animal level, finds eternal life a boring prospect and decides that a thousand years will be ample; at the end of that time, he will die. Shaw is not suggesting that man actually did something like this at any point in his evolution. He is suggesting that the repetitive futility of animal existence leads to a subconscious desire to die. Life for an animal is inevitably limited; once it has mastered its environment and fulfilled its basic biological urges, living can become a matter of habit; and once habit takes over, vitality begins to wane. Vitality can only thrive upon *new* interests, new challenges. Since an animal's interests in the physical world are limited, its life is also limited, and a new, inexperienced animal has to come upon the scene and start all over again.

What man has done is to discover a direction in which his development can be, theoretically, infinite: the realm of knowledge. He can take the same delight in his intellectual activities that an animal takes in feeding or procreating, and his intellect is not subject to the same limitations as his body. Man has a direction in which he can expand infinitely, without limit; the more he knows, the more he is able to know, and the greater his power becomes. *If* we are willing to admit the hypothesis that death may be due to lack of desire to live, then the converse is also admissible: that a purposive desire to live longer may in fact lead men to live longer. It is certainly demonstrable that people who have lost the desire to live often die; and that a strong desire to live can prolong life.

And so in the second play of the 'pentateuch', 'The Gospel of the Brothers Barnabas', two biologists expound their theory that the 'mind's eye' that will turn man into a purposive creature will also steel his subconscious will to live for three hundred years. In a pendant to this section called 'The Domesticity of Franklin Barnabas' (published in *The Black Girl In Search of God*), Shaw states it very clearly:

CONRAD. I deny that [dying] is a biological law. It is nothing but a bad habit. We can live as long as we like. Do you know what people really die of?

IMMENSO.* Of reasonableness. They do not want to live for ever.

CONRAD. Of laziness, and want of conviction, and failure to make their lives worth living. That is why.

The brothers Barnabas are made to expound their doctrine to two politicians, based on Lloyd George and Asquith, and there is a great deal of heavy handed satire.

In the next play, 'The Thing Happens', some descendants of the politicians and the brothers Barnabas make the discovery that there are human beings who have lived far beyond the normal life span. This discovery is made accidentally, when the public records office is examining films of famous men who have died by drowning; the famous men all turn out to be the same man—who was forced to pretend to die or be regarded as a freak. When this discovery is made, the female Domestic Minister also admits that she is a 'long-liver'. She was Franklin Barnabas's housemaid; the male long-liver was his son-in-law; and the irony is that neither of them took the idea of living to be three hundred seriously. According to Shaw, it need not be willed consciously; the subconscious may do the work.

In the fourth play, 'Tragedy of an Elderly Gentleman', the

* Who is based on G. K. Chesterton.

world is now divided into long-livers and short-livers, and the
long-livers are all grouped together in the country that was once
Ireland. A party of short-livers have gone to consult the Oracle
about some unimportant political decision. The play is the least
successful one of the five, for once again it depends upon satire,
upon emphasising the stupidity of the short-livers when compared
to the long-livers. Shaw had been supremely successful in portray-
ing a 'higher evolutionary type' in Caesar and Peter Keegan;
in his long-livers, he seems to have lost his touch.

But whatever the faults of the earlier parts, the fifth play makes
up for them; 'As Far As Thought Can Reach' justifies its title.
The artist in Shaw rose perfectly to this climax of his creative
life. The time is 30,000 years in the future. Man is once again
living simply in nature, for he no longer needs gadgets to give
him power over nature. The method here is the same as in
previous acts: the contrast of maturity with immaturity; but there
is no longer any need for satire, for the immature ones here are
'children' (actually three-year-old adults) who will grow up
anyway.

I have said that *Back to Methuselah* contains very little 'drama'
in the sense of *Candida* or *The Devil's Disciple*. It is dramatised
exposition, explanation. In the first play the serpent explains
about death to Eve, and later Eve explains to Adam and Cain
how her hope for evolution lies in the artists and scientists, not
in the workers and fighters. In the second play the brothers
Barnabas explain their evolutionism to the politicians. In the
third and fourth plays long-livers try to explain themselves to
uncomprehending short-livers. It may seem that so much
explanation is the opposite of what we mean by drama; but, then,
all Shaw's best drama has been explanatory. He can dramatise
almost anything. (In *Everybody's Political What's What* he even
turns his explanation of the English party system into a playlet,
which is one of the most successful chapters of the book.) Now,
in the last play, his Ancients attempt to explain their total vision
of evolution to the 'children'. It is true that this play has met with
more criticism than any other part of the 'pentateuch'; without
exception, Shaw's biographers and commentators have been
repelled by his Ancients. But if the Ancients fail to convince, this
is not an artistic failure on Shaw's part; this play possesses the

sureness of touch that he always displays when he is working at white heat. The Ancients are a logical development of Don Juan's intellectual evolutionism, and an intellectual evolutionism is as unlikely to achieve popularity as higher mathematics. But the question about higher mathematics is not whether it can achieve general popularity, but whether it is *true* or not. The question with Shaw's Ancients is whether he is leaving important facts out of account, or whether it is his critics who are introducing irrelevancies. G. K. Chesterton thought that Shaw would be a better philosopher if he enjoyed Christmas; Shaw would have replied—perhaps did reply—that the force of evolution tends to drive men away from their pleasure in communal celebrations, and that it is a mistake to assume that the lonelier pleasures of the mind cannot be as intense as more 'human' activities. In effect, each is accusing the other of narrowness, and the reader's decision as to who is right is bound to depend on whether he is temperamentally closer to Shaw or Chesterton. Shaw is obviously in the authority, but this is as we might expect. One can only say of this last part of *Back to Methuselah* that for anyone who is in sympathy with Shaw's evolutionism, it is perhaps his greatest achievement.

As the play opens, the 'children' of this future time are preparing to assist in the birth of a 'baby', who is still inside an enormous egg. The 'baby', when she appears, is about twenty years old; Shaw explains that just as babies of the present day pass through thousands of years of evolution in the womb, so these babies of the future pass through the first twenty years of human life before they are born. They also mature at an enormous speed. A girl of four tells a youth of two that she has already outgrown their kissing and sweethearting because she finds them trivial:

THE YOUTH . . . You used to be vexed if I so much as looked at another girl.

THE MAIDEN. What does it matter what I did when I was a baby? Nothing existed for me than except what I tasted and touched and saw; and I wanted all that for myself, just as I wanted the moon to play with. Now the world is opening out for me. More than the world: the universe. Even little things are turning out to be great things, and becoming intensely interesting. Have you ever thought about the properties of numbers?

THE YOUTH . . . Numbers! ! ! I cannot imagine anything drier or more repulsive.

THE MAIDEN. They are fascinating, just fascinating. I want to get away from our eternal dancing and music, and just sit down by myself and think about numbers.

She tells him: 'Sleep is a shameful thing: I have not slept at all for weeks past. I have stolen out at night when you were all lying insensible . . . and wandered about the woods, thinking, thinking, thinking; grasping the world; taking it to pieces; building it up again; devising methods; planning experiments to test the methods. . . . Every morning I have come back here with greater reluctance; and I know that the time will come—perhaps it has come already—when I shall not come back at all.'

STREPHON. How horribly cold and uncomfortable!

THE MAIDEN. Oh, dont talk to me of comfort! Life is not worth living if you have to bother about comfort. Comfort makes winter a torture, spring an illness, summer an oppression and autumn only a respite.

For the rest of the act, Shaw plays variations on this theme of growing up. An Ancient assists in the birth of the baby, and explains the elementary facts of evolution. Then a sculptor opens an exhibition of his latest works, and causes violent indignation because they are all studies of the heads of Ancients. There is a particularly opinionated girl, Ecrasia—who sounds as if she might be modelled on someone Shaw had met at the summer school—who accuses the sculptor of having lost his talent. He tells her: 'Go and look at my busts. Look at them again and yet again until you receive the full impression of the intensity of mind that is stamped on them; and then go back to the pretty-pretty confectionery you call sculpture, and see whether you can endure its vapid emptiness.'

After this episode, a scientist, Pygmalion, tells them that he has succeeded in animating two living creatures, and there follows the only satirical episode in the play. The male and female creatures are typical human beings of our own time. When someone asks the man what he thinks, he answers 'I have not seen the newspaper today.' He goes off into a bombastic tirade in which he explains that he is a king and his companion a queen. Then they fall to quarrelling; Pygmalion tries to intervene, and the woman accidentally kills him by biting his hand. (This is one of the few illogicalities of the last act; Shaw's argument is that the coarser the form of life, the greater its power of physical survival—a lobster can re-grow a lost limb—and therefore the higher the form, the more easily it is killed.) An Ancient arrives, and the two creatures proceed to accuse one another of the death. The Ancient says: 'Let us see whether we cannot put a little more life into them,' and places his hand on the man's forehead. This time, when he asks the man 'Which of you shall we kill,' he answers: 'Spare her; and kill me.' She answers: 'Kill us both. How could either of us live without the other.' But the sudden 'evolutionary leap' has exhausted them both; the man collapses, saying: 'I am discouraged. Life is too heavy a burden,' and the woman says: 'I am dying . . . I am afraid to live.' They die with speeches and soft music—a deliberate parody of Shakespeare—and then the newly born child remarks: 'That was funny.' It is Shaw's most crushing comment on Shakespeare and his view of 'poor human nature'.

The tragedy of Pygmalion's death has made the children more capable of understanding, and the Ancients now try to explain the stages of human evolution. The first step away from the animal came with man's capacity to create works of art. 'Art is the magic mirror you make to reflect your invisible dreams in visible pictures. You use a glass mirror to see your face; you use works of art to see your soul. But we who are older use neither glass mirrors nor works of art. We have a direct sense of life.' In other words, they have developed the 'mind's eye' that enables them to grasp the purpose of life directly. They are no longer creatures who live without understanding why; the subconscious evolutionary drive has become fully conscious in them.

Man outgrows works of art and turns to contemplation. 'I had rather walk up a mountain and down again than look at all the statues Martellus and Arjillax ever made,' says Acis. 'It leads . . . to the truth that you can create nothing but yourself.' The She-Ancient explains: 'When I discarded my dolls as he discarded his friends and his mountains, it was to myself I turned as to the final reality. Here, and here alone, I could shape and create. When my arm was weak and I willed it to be strong,

I could create a roll of muscle on it; and when I understood that, I understood that I could without any greater miracle give myself ten arms and three heads. . . . One day, when I was tired of learning to walk forward with some of my feet and backwards with others and sideways with the rest all at once, I sat on a rock with my four chins resting on four of my palms, and four of my elbows resting on four of my knees. And suddenly it came into my mind that this monstrous machinery of heads and limbs was no more me than my statues had been me, and that it was only an automaton that I had enslaved.'

The ultimate aim of this power of self-creation is the total and complete mastery of matter. The Ancients live indefinitely, but sooner or later they die by an accident. They have total control of their bodies, but no power to do without the body. And this is their final goal, 'redemption from the flesh', 'the vortex freedom from matter . . . the whirlpool in pure intelligence that, when the world began, was a whirlpool in pure force.' And life, which began its invasion of matter through unicellular organs, will be master of the material universe.

When the Ancients have left them alone, the children discuss what they have been told; but few of them even begin to grasp it; they declare they would prefer to commit suicide before they reach the 'adult' age of four. One by one, they drift off to their beds. The artistic Ecrasia is rejected by two of the males, and goes off saying: 'After all, I can imagine a lover nobler than any of you.' Even she possesses the embryonic power that will raise her to superhumanity: the power of the imagination that brings independence of the material world.

The play ends with a dialogue between the ghosts of Adam, Eve, Cain and the serpent, and a final long speech from Lilith, the earth mother, in which she says: 'They have accepted the burden of eternal life. They have taken the agony from birth; and their life does not fail them even in the hour of their destruction.' The ending is dramatically impressive, but perhaps unnecessary after what has gone before. Shaw's natural instinct was to end his plays as impressively as possible, but the result was not necessarily better than when he simply allowed them simply to come to a halt, as in *Misalliance* or *Pygmalion*.

Dramatically speaking, *Back to Methuselah* is less than a masterpiece, and this is simply because it fails to conform to the basic Shaw formula: the clash of egos. When Shaw has a hero to write about he also portrays his other characters with conviction, particularly the people who counterbalance the hero—Mrs Dudgeon, Roebuck Ramsden, Lady Britomart. When there is no hero his treatment of the other characters tends to degenerate into rather clumsy satire. The politicians of *Back to Methuselah* are absurd caricatures. Shaw would counter by replying that real politicians are caricatures. But one only has to compare Shaw's politicians with Barker's in *The Secret Life* to see how it can be done.

The truth is that Shaw, at sixty-five, was no longer very interested in people as such. His early novels are full of quite ordinary people, fairly well observed and portrayed; this is also true of *Widower's Houses* and *Mrs. Warren's Profession*. These plays have a certain feeling of weight that comes from real life. Cokane and Sartorius, Mrs Warren and Sir George Crofts, may be 'Shaw characters', but they are also recognisable as living types. As his skill as a dramatist increases, Shaw becomes less and less concerned about living types, and *John Bull's Other Island* and *Major Barbara* display Shaw at the height of his powers, delighting in his power of creating convincing caricatures. But the scene in Barbara's Salvation Army shelter already shows a falling-off in his ability to sketch real people; Bill Walker, Rummy Mitchens and Snobby Price are not well-observed cockneys, any more than the cowboys of *The Shewing Up of Blanco Posnet* are well-observed Westerners. The characters of *The Doctor's Dilemma*, *Getting Married* and *Misalliance* are simply amiable Shaw caricatures. *Pygmalion* shows an improvement, simply because Higgins provides it with a centre of gravity; and when there is a major Shaw character 'coruscating' in the middle of the stage, the caricatures become perfectly acceptable. But when there is no central character, it is impossible not to notice that Shaw has lost sympathy with his creations as individuals; they are there merely to represent something that he wants to dramatise.

I have pointed out that one must make a clear distinction between Shaw as an artist and Shaw as a thinker. Shaw as an artist deteriorated after *The Doctor's Dilemma*; Shaw as a thinker showed no signs of flagging right to the end. His powers as a thinker increased as his power as an artist decreased. The preface to *Man and Superman* is unimportant compared to the play, but *Androcles and the Lion* and *Back to Methuselah* are well below the standard of their prefaces. The exception here is the last play of *Back to Methuselah*, which is, in effect, a dramatised preface.

It must be accepted that from now—1921—until the end of his life thirty years later Shaw has ceased to be a creative force as a dramatist. He has lost interest in people to an extent that makes it difficult for him to produce a recognisably real person. But he can still dramatise ideas so vividly that the audience fails to recognise the unreality of the characters. Unfortunately, this is only true when he *is* dramatising ideas, as in *The Apple Cart* and *In Good King Charles's Golden Days*. When he is not, the result can be almost painful.

When one looks back over Shaw's lifetime from this mountain-top of *Back to Methuselah* it is hard to deny that he was one of the greatest men of his time, possibly the greatest. It had been a very long road, from the child who was so delighted with Torca cottage, from the teenager who wanted to become a second Michelangelo, from the beardless, clumsy youth who arrived in London and almost drove his mother mad by thumping *Tristan* on the piano. He did not complete his first play until he was past the age at which Mozart and Byron died, and he had passed the age at which Shakespeare died when he reached the height of his powers. By that time he had accomplished more than most men accomplish in a lifetime; in effect, he now went on to add another lifetime to the first.

At the end of this long pilgrimage he has reached a conclusion that contradicts most of what has passed for philosophy since the beginning of civilisation. There has been a general agreement that life as apprehended by thought is tragic. Happiness is an emotional—or physical—state. When thought brushes aside the emotions and sees life without chloroform, so to speak, it is recognised as fundamentally alien to human aspirations. But in *Man and Superman* Don Juan explains that he took Woman 'without chloroform', and recognised that *in spite* of his freedom from illusions, he was impelled by a positive and creative force. Again, in *Back to Methuselah*, Strephon complains that life is difficult, and the Ancient replies: 'Life is not meant to be easy, my child; but take courage: it can be delightful.' If Shakespeare found life tragic, that is because his characters are all on the level of the two 'creatures' made by Pygmalion, who declare their names are Ozymandias and Cleopatra. According to Shaw, life is only seen as tragic when viewed through clouds of immaturity and emotion. There is not a permanent 'balance' between life and nature, by which life has its flowering, and then dies. Life is fighting a battle that it will one day win. As to the final argument of the philosophers, that no matter what his hopes and aspirations, man dies, Shaw replies: Not necessarily. It must be acknowledged that his optimism is logical and consistent. There are no questions that he shirks.

According to Shaw, then, it is thinking that keeps man alive. This is partly because a man who thinks possesses a discipline and self control that are not possessed by emotionalists. In this respect, the moral essence of Shavian philosophy is expressed in the section of the preface to *Back to Methuselah* called 'The Greatest of these is Self-Control':

'As there is no place in Darwinism for free-will, or any other sort of will, the Neo-Darwinists held that there is no such thing as self-control. Yet self-control is just the one quality of survival value which Circumstantial Selection must invariably and inevitably develop in the long run. Uncontrolled qualities may be selected for survival and development for certain periods and under certain circumstances. For instance, since it is the ungovernable gluttons who strive the hardest to get food and drink, their efforts would develop their strength and cunning in a period of such scarcity that the utmost they could do would not enable them to over-eat themselves. But a change of circumstances involving a plentiful supply of food would destroy them. We see this very thing happening often enough in the case of the healthy and vigorous poor man who becomes a millionaire by one of the accidents of our competitive commerce, and immediately proceeds to dig his grave with his teeth. But the self-controlled man survives all such changes of circumstance, because he adapts himself to them, and eats neither as much as he can hold, nor as little as he can scrape along on, but as much as is good for him. What *is* self-control? It is nothing but a highly developed vital sense, dominating and regulating the mere appetites. To overlook the very existence of this supreme sense; to miss the obvious inference that it is the quality that distinguishes the fittest to survive; to omit, in short, the highest moral claim of Evolutionary Selection: all this, which the Neo-Darwinians did in the name of Natural Selection, shewed the most pitiable want of mastery of their subject, the dullest lack of observation of the forces upon which Natural Selection works.'

This 'highly developed vital sense dominating and regulating the mere appetites' is certainly essential for longevity; but it is not the final factor; far more important is the sense of evolutionary purpose, and this must be given by thought. Shaw has here a certain logic on his side; for a glance through a biographical dictionary of philosophers, scientists and mathematicians shows that they are far more long-lived, as a group, than poets, musicians or artists. It is curious that Shaw, who completely lacked any scientific or mathematical ability, should choose mathematics as his symbol of the mind's capabilities. Chloe asks Strephon: 'Have you ever thought about the properties of numbers?' and Martellus later quotes with approval the dictum of some unknown philosopher: 'Leave women and study mathematics.' Shaw's last play, *Buoyant Billions* (1947) ends with a long speech in praise of the mathematical faculty which promises man 'an intellectual ecstasy surpassing the ecstasies of saints'. Obviously, Shaw was not thinking of mathematics as such; figures tell us nothing about the human soul or the universe; he would probably have agreed with Wittgenstein that all mathematical propositions are tautologies (i.e. that to say one and one equals two is the same as saying that one and one equals one and one). Shaw uses mathematics as a symbol of completely disinterested thinking, *divorced from all the other appetites*, of thinking for its own sake.

And it is this that enables us to summarise Shaw's strength and his weakness. Certainly, as far as he personally is concerned, the point is proved by his own career. As an artist he was past his prime at fifty-two; as a thinker, he was still in his prime at eighty-two; the *Intelligent Woman's Guide to Socialism* (written at seventy-two) and *Everybody's Political What's What* (written at eighty-eight) are better books than the *Fabian Essays* of his thirties. On the other hand, it must be acknowledged that in spite of this, Shaw was not, in the strictest sense of the word, a thinker. 'Shavian philosophy' came to birth slowly and intuitively. After *Man and Superman* it marked time for nearly twenty years, until the profound disturbance of the war caused him to reappraise his ideas. I have pointed out that the important preface to *Back to Methuselah* makes no real attempt to prove its point by considering the evidence that was available to him; in fact, its first version was written in 1906, and Shaw made no attempt to bring its biology up to date, either when he rewrote it in 1921, or when he revised it for the World Classic edition in 1944. After *Back to Methuselah*, Shaw ceased to develop as a thinker. T. E. Lawrence was impressed at the way Shaw read Doughty's enormous and difficult *Arabia Deserta* when in his seventies; but Shaw made too few efforts of this kind. There was no reason why his thinking should have stopped. Most philosophers are stimulated to thought by assimilating the work of other philosophers and disagreeing with them. This is not evidence of lack of originality; it is the way the philosophical tradition operates. All philosophers do their best thinking 'intuitively', but their intuition works upon a mass of material provided by other philosophers. A philosopher who tried to keep his thinking entirely original and intuitive would get very little thinking done. Philosophically speaking, the period of Shaw's adult lifetime was one of the most exciting in the history of philosophy: Kierkegaard, Nietzsche, Bergson, William James, Husserl, Russell, Whitehead, Heidegger, the Vienna school and the neo-Kantians. The relativity theory and the quantum theory transformed physical science. Whitehead alone produced enough important work between his sixty-fifth and eighty-fifth years to last most philosophers a lifetime. Shaw could have done the same if he had made the same intellectual effort that he had made to master Karl Marx and Jevons. But instead of obeying his own injunction to 'study mathematics' (i.e. to *think* creatively), he preferred to repeat the things he said many times over. They were 'echoes, nothing but echoes'.

Back to Methuselah was not only a sign of a creative rebirth; it was also conclusive evidence that Shaw was still one of the most serious voices in modern literature. In 1921 the new generation was not much in evidence. A few people recognised Pound's *Mauberley* (1920) and Huxley's *Crome Yellow* (1921) as portents, but it would be another year before *Ulysses, The Waste Land* and *Antic Hay* demonstrated that the new generation had definitely arrived. Meanwhile the 'old gang' was more influential than ever. Galsworthy's *Forsyte Saga*, finished in 1921, was obviously destined to become a modern classic, while no one doubted that Bennett and Hugh Walpole had already achieved that status. Wells's *Undying Fire* (1919) was perhaps his best novel yet, while *The Outline of History* (1920) startled everybody by selling two million copies, and making Wells a rich man. Shaw was also about to achieve the greatest commercial success of his career with *St Joan* (1923), which also brought him the Nobel Prize.

The subject had again been suggested by Charlotte; and, as with *The Doctor's Dilemma*, the play is a *tour de force* of hard work rather than of inspiration. There were two reasons why the play could not be the masterpiece he wanted to make it. One was that it had a heroine rather than a hero. Shaw had only once before attempted to make a woman the centre of a play—in *Captain Brassbound's Conversion*—and it is his one total failure in a period of near-masterpieces. Shaw's theory about women—at least, of the kind of women he approved of—was that they are really men with a few minor physiological differences. But in real life Vivie

Warren and Barbara Undershaft would probably be lesbians; and Lady Cicely Wayneflete comes fairly close to it. If Shaw had attempted to make Vivie Warren or Barbara Undershaft the real 'heroes' of their plays, *Mrs Warren's Profession* and *Major Barbara* would have failed as completely as *Captain Brassbound*. For better or for worse, Shaw was not a feminist by instinct. He cannot really bring himself to believe in his female 'heroes'.

The second reason that *St Joan* is not a masterpiece is that Shaw had outgrown his interest in this kind of manifestation of the religious instinct a long time ago. The period of his interest in the Christian Church as a manifestation of the evolutionary force runs from about 1895 to 1905. If he had written *St Joan* at the same time as the essay 'On Going to Church', it might have been as great as *Caesar and Cleopatra*. But he could already see, by the time he wrote *Major Barbara*, that saintliness and religious enthusiasm are no substitute for intelligence. If Shaw had written a play about a religious heroine who is also formidably intelligent, it would have carried the full charge of his deepest conviction. Shaw's real *forte* is to write about men of intelligence. He cannot portray a Christian with any conviction because he obviously feels that belief in the vicarious atonement is incompatible with the highest kind of intelligence; the Bishop in *Getting Married* is perhaps his least memorable 'hero'. Ultimately, his sympathy with religious enthusiasm is rather theoretical; he sees it as an expression of the same sense of meaning that is found in philosophy, art and science, but he is a little suspicious of the kind of enthusiasm and single-mindedness needed to become really religious. Shaw always liked to believe that people are more reasonable than they really are, from Jesus to George Fox, from Napoleon to Hitler; but when brought face to face with religious enthusiasm, he had to recognise that there is always a touch of Moody and Sankey about it.

This is why *St Joan*, for all its determined seriousness, is not a masterpiece. It is a skilful compendium of Shavian tricks: the apparent irreverence of Baudricourt's cry of 'No eggs!' and the Maid's Yorkshire accent, the monumental seriousness of the trial scene, Stogumber's horror at seeing her burned, the final scene with Joan's ghost crying, 'How long, oh Lord, how long?'; all this seems to imply that once again, Shaw is far more serious than one might at first assume. But for anyone who knows the cast of Shaw's mind, it is impossible not to notice that he has basically more sympathy for the Inquisitor than for the saint, and feels more at home with political realism than religious enthusiasm. Shaw is here doing what he once accused Shakespeare of doing in *Anthony and Cleopatra*, straining all the sources of his dramatic rhetoric to try to lift it into tragedy. But there is a contradiction here. In order to write a convincing tragedy, one must believe that life itself is tragic. And then the death of Medea or Deirdre or Macbeth reminds us that life is a 'brief candle', that the bravest spirit will finally be extinguished, that while we are pitying Othello, we are all in the same boat. Shaw had always refused to respond to tragic situations with the standard pity and terror; his response was more likely to be a kind of anger, and the determination to do something about it. Unnecessary death is not tragic; it is stupid. Caesar, reviewing his own past severities, says: 'What a fool I was then! To think that men's lives should be at the mercy of such fools!' This is a healthy *rejection* of the tragic view, the feeling that the 'tragedy' was a stupid accident, and that he won't allow it to happen again. Shaw's view of religious persecutions had been made clear in *Androcles* and its preface: that it is not a matter of good people being persecuted by wicked people, but of naive religious enthusiasts versus uninspired but honest politicians. Shaw's attitude to these enthusiasts is the same as his attitude towards unworldly poets: that if society is to be saved, they will have to *learn* to combine political realism with their religious fervour. Shaw had already created his own St Joan in Major Barbara, and she has to learn to come to terms with the secular forces. In every possible way, therefore, *St Joan* is a retrogressive step. It is a manufactured tragedy, without any real core of Shavian philosophy, as *You Never Can Tell* was a manufactured comedy. There can be no more complete proof of the general failure to understand Shaw than the widely accepted belief that this is one of his greatest plays.

The human mind is like farm land, it needs to be fertilised if it is to continue to be fruitful. In childhood and youth there is never any problem about this because experience itself does the fertilising. Intelligent people continue to develop long beyond unintelligent ones because their minds are also fertilised by ideas; that is, by experience that comes through books or works of art. If we consider Shaw in his most fertile period—between the ages of twenty and fifty—the most impressive thing about him is his capacity to digest new experience, both physical and mental. The sheer range of his interests led one of his biographers to make the incorrect assertion that Shaw was a man of immense erudition. In fact, compared with Wells or Aldous Huxley, he read very little.

The problem with this last period of Shaw's life—and it was, after all, a third of the total—is that he apparently ceased to ingest new experience. There is nothing in Shaw between *Heartbreak House* and *Buoyant Billions* to suggest that his mind had been fertilised by a single new idea or experience. The *Androcles* preface seems to represent his last great burst of assimilative activity.

Shaw's later works have many virtues; there is not one of them of which we can say—as of *Great Catherine* or the *Playlets of the War*—that it would have been better for his reputation if he had never written it. One day, someone will write a detailed study of the plays from *Too True to be Good* to *Why She Would Not*, and it will be an important addition to Shaw criticism. But it must be admitted that they all have an odd closed-in quality that makes them quite different from *Candida* or *Man and Superman*. They are the products of a mind *turned in on itself*, the same mind that can be seen in Stephen Winsten's two books of Shaw's table talk, repeating things he has already said.

It is significant that although the latter part of Shaw's life was as eventful as his earlier years—more so in many ways—none of his biographers have devoted more than a very small section of their books to it. This is because Shaw did not display the power of self-renewal displayed by his friends Wells and Yeats. He sustained his *vitality* to an incredible extent; but the G.B.S. *persona* had become a suit of armour that had rusted on him.

If this is regrettable, it is perhaps understandable. Although Shaw was to say modestly in *Everybody's Political What's What*: 'I dare not claim to be the best playwright in the English language;

but I believe myself to be one of the best ten, and may therefore perhaps be classed as one of the best hundred'* he was, in fact, fully aware that he was among the best two. What is more, thousands of other people accepted it. In 1927 Sir Barry Jackson (who had presented *Back to Methuselah* over five nights at Birmingham in 1923) founded the Malvern Festival, largely for the performance of 'England's second Shakespeare.' It was an unheard-of honour for a living author. As long ago as 1912, Charlotte had selected passages from his works for a Shaw anthology—again, the kind of thing that was often done for the safely dead like Ruskin or George Eliot, but seldom for the living. In 1927 there was even a calendar with a quotation from Bernard Shaw for every day of the year. In 1929 there was a *Shaw Dictionary and Bibliography* by Lewis and Violet Broad. He was a national institution in much the same way that Dickens had been—and as Wells, for example, never became. And no one could accuse him of selling out to the establishment. In 1927 he was defending Mussolini in a pamphlet, pointing out that 'the brutalities, retaliations, assassinations and counter-assassinations which accompany eternal struggle of government against anarchy are not peculiar to Fascism. . . . The murder of Matteoti is not more an argument against Fascism than that of St Thomas à Becket is against Feudalism.' He also defended the Russian revolution and, as Pearson points out, the Russians treated him as if he were Karl Marx in person when he visited their country in 1931. Shaw's approval of dictators has often been criticised, but it must be seen as part of his belief that the twentieth century represents a new stage in history when national leaders will develop a new sense of world-responsibility. For Shaw history was, as he said, the perpetual struggle of government and public spirit against anarchism and selfishness. In fact his next play, *The Apple Cart* (1929)—the first of the plays written especially for Malvern— states this belief of his with a vigour that conveys the impression that his powers are unimpaired. The play is about the struggle between King Magnus, a 'constitutional monarch' of England at some date in the future, and his socialist cabinet, who think he is not constitutional enough. The Prime Minister states the thesis of the play, that 'one man that has a mind and knows it

* Chapter 6.

can always beat ten men who havnt and dont'. The first act, the long wrangle between the cabinet and the king about whether he is to be permitted to go on making speeches, is Shaw's most successful 'discussion' since *Don Juan in Hell*. Shaw is here in his element, doing something he profoundly enjoys doing. The king's long speech demanding some degree of freedom is as long as the Inquisitor's speech in *St Joan* but it has none of the same feeling of being a 'set piece'; it is Shaw speaking with his own voice.

The play led many people to wonder why Shaw, the lifelong socialist and republican, had shown a king defeating his socialist cabinet; and in his preface Shaw mentions that it was banned in Dresden as a blasphemy against democracy. But it is perfectly consistent with his political beliefs. Shaw the evolutionist saw that life *is* organisation; he never tried to repudiate this aspect of civilisation. He also saw that evolution for the individual means evolution from egoism towards a sense of public responsibility, the willingness to undertake the organisation of society. His socialist cabinet are all party-men; not one of them has any real sense of public responsibility; and at the end of the play, two of his cabinet announce that they will retire because 'politics is a mug's game'.

But life was becoming quieter for Shaw; in his seventies he preferred it that way. In 1927, when the Adelphi Terrace building was due to be demolished, they moved to Whitehall Court, behind Scotland Yard, a place where Charlotte had no house-keeping problems at all, since they only had to walk downstairs to the restaurant or have their meals sent up. They did a great deal of travelling to warmer climes. *Too True to be Good* was conceived in 1931 between Corsica and Sardinia, and his 'story' *The Black Girl in Search of God* in Africa in 1932. The Standard Edition of his works began to appear in 1931, and it was also in this year that the publication of his correspondence with Ellen Terry gave Mrs Pat the idea of publishing theirs; any scrap of paper in Shaw's handwriting was publishable.

Too True to be Good is not a good play but it should be classed among Shaw's most interesting plays in that it is his only attempt, apart from *Heartbreak House*, to come to grips with the new world that had replaced the Victorian era. Shaw was an anachronism in this world, the 'jazz age' that was permeated by a Tchehovian feeling of despair and futility. He did not understand the world of Evelyn Waugh and Ernest Hemingway and Joyce's *Work in Progress*; he was incapable of grasping this poetry of spiritual bankruptcy, or D. H. Lawrence's attempt to find true values again in sex. (Although he told General Smuts at a luncheon party that every schoolgirl of sixteen should read *Lady Chatterley's Lover*, he later admitted to Winsten that he had never succeeded in reading Lawrence.) But in *Too True to be Good* he made an attempt to catch the mood of this Waste Land generation. It is a play about boredom. A rich young lady is suffering from some imaginary disease when a burglar breaks into her bedroom. She overpowers the burglar—an ex-clergyman, disillusioned by the war—but then decides it would be exciting to steal her own jewels and run away with the burglar and his accomplice to North Africa. They want freedom and pleasure; but without a sense of purpose, they are completely bored by their freedom. The play is weirdly unreal, without continuity, and C. B. Purdom explains this by advancing the hypothesis that it is supposed to be a dream of the rich girl as she lies in bed with a temperature. The truth is that Shaw was not trying to *say* anything, to express his own convictions; he was merely commenting on the things going on around him. The problem here, as in *Heartbreak House*, is that he has no emotional sympathy for this mood of despair, and the stage tricks he uses to keep the play moving (an Arab attack, for example) are all on the same level as the waltzing lion of *Androcles*. The clergyman's father appears, and makes a long speech about being a Freethinker who has lost his faith in Free Thought. 'Nothing can save us from a perpetual headlong fall into a bottomless abyss but a solid footing of dogma; and we no sooner agree to that than we find that the only trustworthy dogma is that there is no dogma. As I stand here I am falling into that abyss, down, down, down. We are all falling into it. . . .' Shaw often claimed that he was a mere amanuensis, writing at the dictation of the *zeitgeist*; in this case, he seems to have accidentally tuned to the same wavelength as Heidegger and Sartre. The burglar's long speech at the end of the play struck many people as an admission of despair: 'I am ignorant: I have lost my nerve and am intimidated: all I know is that I must find the way of life, for myself and all of us, or we shall surely perish. And meanwhile my gift has possession of me: I must preach and preach and preach no matter how late the hour and how short the day, no matter whether I have nothing to say. . . .' But he was only trying to record what he saw around him; the mind that conceived *Man and Superman* and *Back to Methuselah* could hardly find itself with nothing to say.

In South Africa in 1932 Shaw made his old mistake of putting his foot on the accelerator instead of the brake; the car bounced over a bank, through some barbed wire, and stopped in a field. Shaw was unhurt, but Charlotte, sitting in the back with the luggage, was badly bruised and jolted; her spectacle frames were driven into her eyes, her wrist sprained and her ribs and back severely bruised. This emergency, like the war, seemed to have a salutary effect on Shaw; while Charlotte slowly recovered, he started re-reading the Bible continuously from the beginning, and was struck by the evolution of the idea of God that it reveals. *The Black Girl in Search of God* would probably have been better in the form of a preface, like the one to *Androcles*; but he decided to make a story of it, a kind of *Pilgrim's Progress*. The black girl meets a series of old gentlemen who claim they are God, the vengeful God of Abraham and Noah, the argumentative God of Job; she rejects each one, and a few pages of her bible crumble away each time. She meets Koheleth, who tells her that to know God she must be God, and Micah, who tells her that she must trust entirely in God. She answers reasonably that God has given her a mind so that she can trust in herself and think for herself. She meets Jesus, and tells him that his commandment to love one another is 'like the pills the cheap-jacks sell us: they are useful once in twenty times perhaps, but in the other nineteen they are no use'. She sees various founders of religions carrying their churches on their backs, and talks with a modern scientist and a group of modern freethinkers. She also meets Jesus again, this time posing for an artist who is modelling the crucifixion, with Mahomet sitting by having a discussion with them. (Shaw had admitted that he would have preferred to write a play about Mahomet rather than St Joan, but was worried in case some Arab fanatic should decide to assassinate him for blasphemy.) Mahomet speaks of the majesty and oneness of God, but it is the artist who says that Allah is a bungler. 'I tell you Allah made this hand of mine because his own hands are too clumsy.' Next she meets Voltaire in his garden, and he also tells her that men must strive to become god-like, and meanwhile get on with God's work as best they can. Finally, an Irishman—Shaw himself—comes into the garden to dig potatoes, and tells her that God is 'not properly made and finished yet'. 'There's somethin in us that's dhrivin at him, and there's somethin out of us that's dhrivin at him, that's certain . . .' For him, God is an 'eternal but as yet unfulfilled purpose'. She ends by marrying the Irishman and raising a family.

Shaw's little fable sold 20,000 copies in its first year, and caused a furore out of all proportion to its modest merits. Libraries banned it and clergymen attacked it. The uproar must have astonished Shaw, who had always been convinced that he was living in the midst of a secular age. It may also have taught him why his own actual influence was so small; that it would be a long time before the world caught up with him. He had been saying precisely this for fifty years, and no one had noticed.

For anyone who thought that *Too True to be Good* indicated that Shaw was losing his power to shape a play, *On the Rocks* (1933) must have come as a surprise. As its title reveals, we are still in the bankrupt Europe of *Heartbreak House*, but the development is as clearly handled as any of the early plays. The Prime Minister faces a national crisis with mobs in the streets throwing stones. His wife persuades him to see a lady doctor, who tells him that his only trouble is 'that very common English complaint, an underworked brain'. She packs him off to a sanatorium with the complete works of Marx, and he returns with a revolutionary programme of nationalisation that only the Labourites reject. All his conservative colleagues are pleased, for various reasons, but in the end the Prime Minister decides that he is not the man to impose the revolution on England, and the unemployed break into Downing Street singing 'England arise'. But in spite of the play's remarkable vigour, the final effect is again one of despair, or at least of hope suspended. Its preface is one of the best of Shaw's later ones, with an excellent dialogue between Jesus and Pilate, which seems to belie Shaw's assertion in a letter to St John Ervine's wife that 'my bolt is shot, as far as any definite target is concerned'. But it is certainly true that all the plays of his last twenty years seem to go nowhere. And this is not because Shaw's brain was impaired, but because he was unfortunately underworking it.

This spectacle—of a man of Shaw's greatness losing his sense of purpose—is a sad one, and there is no point in dwelling on it. In one of the later prefaces he remarks jokingly that he looks like fulfilling his prediction that men will live to be 300. But that was not the central point of *Back to Methuselah*. Its point was that life is dependent upon an unbroken will, and that will is dependent upon the sense of purpose, and that the sense of purpose is maintained by creative mental activity. What Shaw should have been doing was asking himself questions about the next step in human evolution, and scrutinising the work of philosophers, biologists and psychologists to see whether there were any signs of the 'mind's eye' appearing. According to his own theory, the spearhead of European culture should have been developing a profounder self-consciousness, a new and more urgent sense of meaning. T. S. Eliot, now the most influential writer in the English-speaking countries, had paraphrased one of Shaw's own remarks in *For Lancelot Andrewes* when he wrote: 'It is doubtful whether civilisation can endure without religion.' Eliot had solved the problem by embracing the Church of England. Shaw knew this was no answer; but instead of straining his eyes for the emergence of the new religion, he was contented to reflect 'the despair of Europe'.

The plays of his last years can be mentioned briefly. *The Simpleton of the Unexpected Isles* (1934) is as confused as *Too True to be Good*, and is based upon Blake's notion: 'A Last Judgement is necessary because fools flourish.' The 'simpleton' is a clergyman who married two beautiful Polynesian girls and convulses the British Empire. But before any action can be taken against him an angel appears (rather arbitrarily) and announces the Last Judgement, when 'the lives which have no use, no meaning, no purpose, will fade out'. It will not be the end of the world, but a new beginning, with only the higher evolutionary types. The medical profession vanishes to a man, and the Stock Exchange and the House of Commons are left with only a few members. Lawyers and clergymen, oddly enough, are immune. The play ends with a reassertion of faith in life, 'which is always unexpected'. It is an interesting daydream—the total disappearance of all people who refuse to do the will of the evolutionary force— but it raises again the same question as the dialogue in *Heartbreak House*, in which Hector admits that 'human vermin' cannot be killed off because 'we are members of one another'. In his old age Shaw was becoming steadily less tolerant of the vermin, and the preface to *On the Rocks* begins with a plea that they be exterminated.

The Millionairess (1935–6) is again about the 'dominant 5%' (about whom Shaw writes in his preface). Again its thread of plot is tossed in rather arbitrarily; the millionairess agrees to give up her fortune and seek another one, in order to satisfy the demands of an Egyptian doctor she wishes to marry. She immediately accumulates another fortune. Shaw's point again appears to be a refutation of his socialism: that even if incomes were re-distributed, the world would be back in its old position in a short time. In fact, as Shaw explains in his preface, the problem of the tyranny of 'bosses' can only be solved by improving society so that none of the dominant 5 per cent can fail to achieve self-expression. Then, with one 'boss' in every twenty people, there will be something more like an even balance.

Geneva (1938) was written just before the Second World War; it toys with the idea that the dictators—Hitler, Mussolini and Franco—should be summoned to an international court to defend their policies. Significantly, Stalin—who had just finished one of his worst purges—was not among the dictators, although communism is represented by a commissar. Unfortunately, the play has nothing interesting or constructive to say about dictators. It really seems to be the dying flicker of Shaw's dramatic talent. And then, as usual, he sprang a surprise, and produced *In Good King Charles's Golden Days*, which is almost as good as *The Apple Cart*, and certainly his best play since that time. The reason for its vitality is quite clear; Shaw had obviously been reading some history, and subjecting his mind to new stimuli. The resulting play has no particular purpose, and no plot, but its characters are so alive, and the dialogue so good, that this hardly matters. He is simply exercising a talent he has spent a lifetime acquiring, and putting a number of his 'higher evolutionary types' on stage together. They include Charles II, Sir Isaac Newton, George Fox, and the painter Sir Godfrey Kneller. (Shaw wanted to use Rembrandt, but the dates wouldn't fit.) Shaw was writing about the sort of people who interested him, instead of about unpleasant bores to whom he felt irritably superior; the result is almost a masterpiece. It seems to demonstrate again that if Shaw had searched more assiduously for a direction—as Wells did—there might have been no falling-off in his final period.

If Shaw had died after *Geneva* it would have seemed appropriate; a new age was beginning, an age in which he could not possibly have a part; he was hanging on like an actor who has spoken his lines but cannot bear to make his exit. And the gentle downward slope of that last decade would have been a convincing argument for those critics who reject his notion that man ought to live longer. *Good King Charles* demonstrates that it is always a mistake to make generalisations about a living man, no matter how predictable he seems to be.

But still Shaw lingered on. Now it seemed clear that nothing new could be expected of this man who was ninety in 1946. And then, as a final magnificent gesture of unpredictability, Shaw produced a coda to his life's work that was a reaffirmation of everything he had stood for. For this is the most startling thing about the 'tomfooleries' of his last years, *Buoyant Billions* (1947), *Farfetched Fables* (1948) *Shakes versus Shav* (1949), and *Why She Would Not* (1950), written in the year of his death. Shaw had suddenly emerged from the pessimism of the thirties; there is no more boredom and despair. He brings to mind the ancient Chinamen of Yeats's *Lapis Lazuli*, contemplating tragedy with a supernatural gaiety:

> 'Their eyes mid many wrinkles, their eyes,
> Their ancient, glittering eyes, are gay.'

Buoyant Billions starts off promisingly with a young man telling his father that the only profession he wishes to follow is that of 'World Betterer', the profession of Marx, Lenin, Stalin, Ruskin, Plato, Luther and (a final plug for an old friend) William Morris. 'To me, living in a world of poor and unhappy people is like living in hell.' For a moment Peter Keegan's voice sounds again. And it is appropriate that we should be reminded of the great period of *Man and Superman* and *John Bull's Other Island*, for there is a new optimism here. 'Hiroshima and Nagasaki are already rebuilt; and Japan is all the better for the change. When atom splitting makes it easy for us to support ourselves as well by two hours work as now by two years, we shall move mountains and straighten rivers in a hand's turn. The problem of what to do with our spare time will make life enormously interesting.'

It must be admitted that after this excellent beginning the play rambles from act to act with the 'sweet indecision' that Shaw had noticed in the lady fiddlers sixty years earlier. Shaw's taste for exotic settings—which has been noticeable since *Too True to be Good*—appears in the next act, in which the World Betterer turns up in Panama, and meets a white woman who lives in a forest hut. She is the daughter of Old Bill Buoyant the Billionaire, and like the World Betterer, she has decided to turn her back on respectability. She ends by driving him away by calling up reptiles with her saxophone.

What is immediately noticeable about the play so far is that although Shaw had obviously lost his ability to give a play any continuity from act to act, he had not lost the power of holding the audience's attention with whatever he chooses to put on stage. The dialogue between Junius (the World Betterer) and Clementina utilises the old clash-of-egos technique, and one reads on simply to find out who will end by browbeating the other.

The remaining acts have even less continuity. The scene shifts to London, to the home of Old Bill Buoyant, and a drawing room that has been converted to look like a Chinese temple—presumably simply for another interesting change of scene. The Buoyant family are meeting to discuss taxes and death duty when Clementina rushes in, explaining that she thinks she has fallen in love with the man she met in Panama, and has decided to flee—like Jack Tanner. Junius enters shortly afterwards, having tracked her down, and his explanations about his feelings for her are much the same as Cusins's about Barbara—that it is an irresistible urge beyond his understanding. In a final act, she agrees to marry him, and Secondborn, one of the sons, ends the play with the great speech on mathematics as an intellectual passion. He also has the typically Shavian line: 'I don't want to be happy: I want to be alive and active.'

Shakes versus Shav, a puppet play written for Malvern, has very little to recommend it, but it is a reaffirmation of Shaw's evolutionary optimism in the face of Shakespeare's pessimism:

SHAV. You were not the first
    To sing of broken hearts. I was the first
    That taught your faithless Timons how to mend them.

In *Man and Superman* Don Juan had made a statement that sounds like an evolutionised version of Nietzsche's eternal recurrence: 'Granted that the great Life Force has hit on the device of the clock-maker's pendulum, and uses the earth for its bob . . . that in the unthinkable infinitude of time the sun throws off the earth, and catches it again a thousand times as a circus rider throws up a ball. . . .' Now again, his Shav makes the same point:

'I say the world will long outlast our day,
    Tomorrow and tomorrow and tomorrow
    We puppets shall replay our scene . . .'

The *Farfetched Fables* make almost no pretence to continuity, but it could be described as another attempt, in the manner of *Back to Methuselah*, to see into the future. In the first two sketches, science is the villain and men are as destructive as ever. A lighter-than-air poison gas destroys its inventor and depopulates London. But in the third sketch, science has taken a more constructive step by learning how to classify human beings according to their abilities, and the matron at the classification centre has become so skilled in her work that she instantly recognises a man who claims to be a genius as a fool, and a man who claims to be a fool as a genius.*

In the fourth fable a man is dictating a textbook of elementary biology for infant schools, and he describes how the world turned from meat-eating to vegetarianism, and then how a vegetarian athlete made the discovery that human beings can live on air and water, since 'it was already known that the vigils and fasts of saints did not weaken them when their spiritual activity was intense enough to produce a state of ecstasy'. After this 'the world became a world of athletes, artists, craftsmen, physicists and mathematicians instead of farmers, millers, butchers, bartenders, brewers, and distillers'. In the fifth fable sex has ceased to be a physical activity; geneticists perpetuate the race in the laboratory. (One might almost suppose that this fable was intended to enrage the post-war D. H. Lawrence cult; but Shaw was probably unaware of its existence.) In the sixth fable a schoolteacher of the future tells her class that certain human beings succeeded in getting rid of their bodies as our ancestors succeeded in getting rid of their tails and fur. The class is inclined to be sceptical until an angel appears who explains that he is one of the Disembodied Races who has made himself a body in order to find what it is like. 'Curiosity never dies.' The class remain sceptical about him—which Shaw obviously feels to be the right attitude—and the teacher ends by telling the class to read the Book of Job, in order to observe that God can put ten times as many unanswerable questions to man as man can put to him.

Even in his last 'playlet', *Why She Would Not*, Shaw managed to repeat an old theme in a new way; it is again about 'bosses'. A

---

* C. B. Purdom is of the opinion that this scene is also intended as a satire on science, but this interpretation is clearly mistaken. Shaw here shows science taking a practical step towards 'weeding out the nonentities' and isolating the dominant 5 per cent—themes he had already discussed in *The Simpleton of the Unexpected Isles* and *The Millionairess*.

K

tramp saves a young lady from a ruffian, and she offers him employment in her father's factory. He says he is unemployable and cannot do regular work; however, if they will allow him to come in whenever he likes and see if there is anything he can do, he will take the job. The firm is old, and its present owners are inefficient and sentimental about the past. The young man— whose name is, significantly, Bossborn—proves to be a ruthless organiser who sacks old retainers and replaces them with an adding machine. He advises the young lady to pull down the old family mansion, and build a modern house in its place and although she is mortally offended, she ends by doing as he suggests. In the last scene, she explains that she could never marry him because she is afraid of him; he apparently can make people do things they have no intention of doing. He replies: 'I coerce nobody: I only point out the way.'

SERAFINA. Yes: your way, not our way.

BOSSBORN. Neither my way nor yours. The way of the world. Some people call it God's way.

It is a reassertion of the theme of *Major Barbara*—expressed, perhaps, in a deliberately uncompromising way. Shaw was old, and inclined to assert his beliefs in a take-it-or-leave-it manner. His 'evolutionary force' seems almost as ruthless as Darwin's Natural Selection. Bossborn is a success, not because he is a bully or a born leader, but because he accepts his role as an instrument of a force greater than himself. And, significantly, he bears many resemblances to Edward Conolly, the hero of Shaw's second novel, written when he was twenty-four. He is calm and efficient; in each of his scenes with Serafina, he goes off calmly and decisively, so that the last scene—when she dismisses him as Marian dismissed Conolly—echoes the last scene of the novel. Shaw had discovered the Shavian hero at twenty-four; seventy years later the image was unchanged. He was a writer of remarkable consistency.

Towards the end of his life, Pearson asked Shaw if he missed any of his old friends. Shaw answered: 'I don't miss anyone except myself.' 'Yourself?' 'The man I used to be.' It was true. He had not reckoned in the physical failure, and the boredom of continuing to live with failing powers. His Ancients had lived on by thinking; but the truth was that Shaw had never really been a thinker, and now he had nothing to occupy his mind. On September 10th, 1950, he tripped and broke a leg while pruning a tree, and in hospital, the will to live became a will to die. '. . . it's so silly when all I want is to die, but this damned vitality of mine won't let me'. He hated the hospital and the constant washings and attention, and was glad to be back home. In October he was back at Ayot St Lawrence, now failing. He slept a great deal, and died in his sleep on the morning of November 2nd, 1950. Perhaps the loneliness of being a man who had outlived all his friends was the decisive factor in destroying his will to live. His old age might have been happier with children and grandchildren.

POSTSCRIPT: 'MY OWN PART IN THE MATTER'

This book has given me more trouble than anything I have ever written. As I struggled with the first version in 1965, I became aware of the problem: I was *too* familiar with Shaw. I came across his work when I was thirteen; since then I have read him so continuously that I suppose I know him as well as Keats knew Shakespeare or Dr Johnson the Bible. I tried to write my first book about him at fourteen; it was called *The Quintessence of Shavianism*. I came across it the other day, and winced at some of the judgements; but it certainly demonstrates that I had read all Shaw's plays by the time I was fourteen. At sixteen I tried my own hand at a play; it was to be a sequel to *Man and Superman*, about the relation between Jack Tanner—now twenty years older —and his son; determined to outdo Shaw, I made the first act longer than the whole of *Man and Superman*. Fortunately, the manuscript has been lost. After this, I tried a one-act radio play about Shaw (thinly disguised under another name); after his death my hero finds himself in hell, and immediately proposes to convert the place into a holiday resort. It was a feeble little joke, and after the B.B.C. had rejected it I sent it to Shaw. In due course his secretary returned it with one of his printed post-cards, which explained that not only had Mr Shaw no power to help authors to find publishers, but that his recommendation might well ruin a book's chances of acceptance. I had written Shaw a twenty-page letter with the manuscript, explaining that I considered myself his natural successor; possibly it is now sitting in Shaw's files in some American university library. I hope not.

I made no further attempt to communicate with Shaw, and I was in France when he died in 1950. In my haversack I had a copy of *Ulysses*, and Shaw's Collected Plays.

In 1956 my first book, *The Outsider*, began with an epigraph from Shaw—Keegan's remark about not feeling at home in the world—and ended with a long quotation from the *Methuselah* preface. A month after the book appeared Shaw's centenary came up, and a Sunday newspaper asked me if I would write an article about him. I noticed that mine was the only article that appeared that weekend that spoke of Shaw as a great writer; and even then the editor took care to commission another article from an Oxford history don who dismissed Shaw as an outdated exhibitionist.

This centenary, incidentally, caused me some trouble with *The New Statesman*, the paper Shaw had helped to found. The literary editor had suggested that I write regularly for the paper, and my first commission was an article about Shaw's influence on me. The Sunday newspaper objected to my writing a second piece on Shaw for the centenary, even though its approach would have been completely different. My relations with *The New Statesman* ceased forthwith.

Many of the critics of *The Outsider* seemed to feel that my advocacy of Shaw was a curious blind spot, an adolescent enthusiasm that I would outgrow. (A schoolmaster had told me that most intelligent teenagers have a Shaw phase, but that it never lasts much beyond twenty.) To underline my attitude, I included Shaw in a gallery of religious figures—Boehme, Pascal, Swedenborg, Newman—in my next book. I suspect this may have been not the least of the reasons for the hostile reception of *Religion and the Rebel*. In a short film on Shaw in which I took part about this time I stated it as my opinion that Shaw was probably the most important European writer since Dante. I do not think that I would modify this opinion now; even though, as can be seen, I have a clear view of Shaw's defects, both as a writer and a human being. In more recent years I have tried to pay Shaw a more solid tribute by taking up his suggestion—at the end of the *Methuselah* preface—that younger hands should try writing parables of creative evolution, the result being a rather bulky novel, *The Philosopher's Stone*.

Now, obviously, it would be impossible to be a lifelong admirer of Shaw without expanding and developing some of his ideas. The main trouble with the second version of this present book (written in 1966–7), was that I tried to adopt a more directly personal approach, and discuss and criticise his ideas in the main body of the book. This made for even more confusion than the earlier attempt. This is why, in this final version, I have tried to concentrate on Shaw's development as a thinker, and to keep 'discussion' to a minimum. This postscript is an attempt to summarise all things I have not been able to say in the rest of the book. With all due modesty, I must therefore follow Shaw's example in the *Methuselah* preface, and speak of 'my own part in the matter'.

I had seen the film of *Caesar and Cleopatra* when it was first released in 1945 but it failed to arouse my curiosity about Shaw. It was hearing the third act of *Man and Superman* on the B.B.C. Third Programme—I think it was during its first week—that made me read everything Shaw wrote.

I had done a certain amount of thinking for myself by then. At the age of eleven I had made the discovery of science, and I read Jeans's *Mysterious Universe*, Eddington's *New Pathways in Science*, and Einstein's book on relativity. What was so exciting at first was that this world of science was so completely different from the world of childhood, with its trivialities and boredoms and its emotional upheavals. In science, if you asked a question clearly enough, the answer seemed to follow inevitably. In real life, nothing was ever so certain. Your mother liked a certain person; your father said he was a weakling and a scrounger; who was right? At Christmas, or after seeing a Walt Disney film, you felt the world as pure affirmation, an enormous happy benevolence; but on a rainy Saturday afternoon in October you looked back on such moments as a man with a hangover and an empty wallet looks back on his night on the town. Yet the moments of intensity seem to imply quite clearly that the poor quality of our lives is due to slackness of the will, and our proneness to self-pity and defeat. Which insight is to be trusted? According to science, all questions are answerable if you go about it in the right way.

And then, almost immediately, came disillusion. Scientists had no idea of whether light was made of particles or waves; it behaved like both. They had no idea of how the universe came into existence, or where space ends; all they *did* know is that it is exploding. And the theory of relativity said you could never know whether the earth is moving at all, since Michelson and Morley's attempt to establish the existence of a fixed ether has failed. I could understand what Faust meant when he said that all his studies had led him to recognise that we can know nothing. My discovery of philosophy at about this time—through a book by Joad— seemed to confirm this. It was as if the universe was laughing at man's absurd attempt to be anything more than an insect.

This vertiginous state of philosophical nihilism, combined with the usual upheavals of puberty, plunged me into a state of almost permanent depression. And one of the worst things about it was that no one seemed to understand if I tried to talk about it. I suspected that I was the first person in the world ever to pursue these questions to their logical limit, and to see that all human life is illusion from beginning to end. Life simply moves, that is all. Water runs downhill, but nothing has been achieved when it reaches the bottom. There was a feeling that this knowledge had placed me outside the human community.

All this explains why that first evening of listening to *Don Juan in Hell* produced a sensation like a thunderbolt. It was the most total and shattering intellectual impression of my life to that date. So there *was* somebody else in the world who was aware of the question, and I was no longer a man with a unique disease. What was even more astonishing, Shaw was clearly optimistic. I found it hard to understand the grounds for this optimism. The notion that the purpose of life was to understand its own existence seemed to me to be based on a verbal misunderstanding. Supposing it understood its own existence?—that would still leave the problem of what to *do*. Still, there could be no doubt that Shaw had grasped the question. He expressed my basic fear in one sentence: 'Shall man give up eating because he destroys his appetite in the act of gratifying it?' For my feeling that all values were negative—mere responses of the body—made it seem that eating was the most futile of human activities.

I can still remember my feeling when I woke up the next morning—that a revolution had taken place. The nihilism was also still there—it persisted for many years to come—but there was also a restoration of my faith in the value of thinking. Merely to listen to Shaw's performance was to want to join in, to produce books and plays of ideas. My sequel to *Man and Superman* was an attempt to confront Shaw's optimism with my own nihilistic relativism; for I still felt that, logically, there was no answer to the problem of ultimate meaninglessness.

Between the ages of sixteen and eighteen Eliot and Dostoevsky influenced my approach far more than Shaw. The main trouble with evolutionism was that it seemed so *remote*. What I wanted was an answer to the problem stated by Ivan Karamazov in the Pro and Contra chapter, the problem of human pain and futility, the problem of evil, the problem that made Van Gogh shoot himself in the stomach after writing: 'Misery will never end.' I read and re-read Shaw until I know most of it by heart, but I also read and re-read the *Seven Pillars of Wisdom* and Nijinsky's Diary and the account of the Turkish massacre of Armenians called *Auction of Souls*. The mind is normally like a fire that has been stoked up with damp coal; it smokes and splutters. And then at certain moments the fire seems to burn through and the red glow seems capable of consuming anything. It is only in such states that the problem of evil seems to be solved. Saints and mystics were clearly people who had experienced such states and found the smoky dullness of everyday consciousness intolerable thereafter. That raised a new question. In the Middle Ages a man could retire to a monastery or his cave on the Aran Isles and try to concentrate his will. But this required a certain 'fixing' of the will, a fundamental commitment to a direction, a monastic dedication. How is this possible in this society of disc jockeys and Coca-Cola? Don Juan can talk of 'helping life in its struggle upward'—but *that* is life, that traffic in the Strand at half past five in the evening. Where does one begin?

From the age of eighteen—when I spent a few months in the R.A.F.—to twenty-three I moved around from place to place, too dissatisfied to stay anywhere for long. There was a marriage that lasted eighteen months, two spells in France, a change of lodging every month or so, even a period when I slept outdoors. My library travelled around with me—the *Bhagavad Gita*, St John of the Cross, Ruysbroeck, Traherne, *The Cloud of Unknowing*, Scupoli, William Law, the *Seven Pillars*; but if I had to travel light I would be contented with the complete Shaw plays, bound in waterproof canvas to withstand nights in the open. I agreed with Keegan that a man has to stand completely alone, alienated from his civilisation, if 'the times are out of joint'. I was tempted at times to become a Catholic and enter a monastery, but when it came to the point I could not pretend to swallow their absurd superstitions.

As I now saw it, the central question was one of religion. A religion could be regarded as a kind of canal or ditch, dug for the purpose of channelling man's fugitive spiritual energies, which might otherwise turn his mind into an unhealthy swamp. All men have clear flashes of creative energy in the midst of the endless distraction of everyday life. In a society like ours these flashes are wasted, and even the more abundant creative energies of artists and poets are likely to waste themselves in searching for a form. The problem of religion is also the problem of form. The actual content of a religion is to be found in the insights of saints and mystics; but the Church, with its dogmas and commandments, is the building that protects and preserves these flashes of meaning as an art gallery protects the pictures or a library the books. The building is now falling down, and the sensible thing would be to build another. But nobody knows where to begin. Shaw points out that in science you can take the truth and leave the legend behind—you can accept the law of gravitation without believing that Newton sat under an apple tree—and says that the same should be true of religion. But as soon as you try to unstick the legends from the truths of religion the whole thing collapses.

In the Christmas of 1954, when I was twenty-three, I sketched out *The Outsider* in a room in New Cross, and wrote it at intervals during the next eight months or so. It was a statement of this problem of religious man in a secular age. Surprisingly enough, although most of the writers I discussed were pessimistic in tone —Sartre, Kafka, Eliot, Dostoevsky—I discovered that Shaw and his own formulations of the problem remained relevant throughout. This was one thing of which I was quite certain: that the tendency to dismiss Shaw as someone who was too Victorian to understand the depth of the problems expressed by Eliot and Kafka, and too stupid to grasp the complexity of those analysed by Sartre and Heidegger, was simply a misapprehension by people who were too lazy or prejudiced to actually read Shaw. I had soaked myself in him too thoroughly to make the same mistake.

The Outsider certainly solved my immediate problem of how to live in a 'botched civilisation', by earning me enough money and reputation to make a certain isolation possible; I moved to a country cottage and started my second book. I had beaten Shaw by some twenty years in gaining a reputation. But this meant that I immediately encountered the problem that he avoided until he was fifty: the problem of publicity, of notoriety. This certainly strengthened my feeling that the Shavian torch had been handed directly to me. And since, in spite of his painful clarity, he had failed to make himself understood, I saw it as my task to *make* him understood. This was why he occupied a central place in my second book. When this appeared, I was at least relieved of the problem of too much acclaim. I also realised, with a certain wry amusement, that I had failed exactly where Shaw had failed. My restatement of his central problem, in terms that should have been comprehensible to people brought up on Eliot and Joyce, had fallen flat. Clearly, the English would not have Shaw on any terms. Meanwhile, the Royal Court Theatre presented plays by Osborne, Becket and Ionesco, and announced a new theatrical revival. Significantly, the only play that could have been described as Shavian—Nigel Dennis's *Cards of Identity*—had a very short run, and was not revived.

In 1956 I argued with T. S. Eliot about Shaw, pointing out that even on a purely artistic level he deserves to be considered a great writer. Eliot only said he found Shaw unreadable, and recommended me to read D. H. Lawrence, whom he had found unreadable a quarter of a century earlier. Herbert Read was the only important convert to my view of Shaw as a major figure.

But slowly, very slowly, as I lived quietly in Cornwall and attacked the philosophical problem from different angles, I began to see the outline of a solution. It was at about this time that Teilhard de Chardin's *Phenomenon of Man* came out, and his evolutionism became fashionable; but I cannot pretend that Teilhard influenced me. It was in Wells that I found a clear formulation of the problem which, I later realised, was very close to Teilhard's. Wells pointed out that for all animals that have so far existed, life has been little more than a struggle with environment; life has always been 'up against it'. Then man made a curious discovery; that by disengaging his mind from his environment, and thinking about apparently irrelevant subjects like physics and mathematics, he could gain a new degree of power over his environment. And soon a new kind of man appeared, a man with an immense appetite for this activity of the mind, dissociated from purely physical problems. This new type of man —who had become suddenly prevalent in the nineteenth century— actually finds the problems of animal existence a bore; he wants to do away with them completely. Says Wells in his *Experiment in Autobiography*: 'I do not now in the least desire to live longer unless I can go on with what I consider to be my proper business' —the business of creative intellectual (or imaginative) activity.

Thus far Wells. It was from there that I took off. For here, at the very beginning, we confront a paradox. Wells says: 'I am sick of irrelevancies. Let me get back to my proper work.' His secretary says: 'Very well. Hand the irrelevancies over to me, and get on with your proper work.' And what happens? Confronted with a clear desk and a sheet of blank paper, he stares out of the window and says 'What now?' then wonders if it is too early to walk down to the club for a whisky. . . . Man—at least, Wellsian man, if I might coin a phrase—knows quite clearly what he *doesn't* want, but he has no comparable certainty about what he *does* want. He has been a creature of the physical world for so long that he finds the world of the mind exhausting, and sometimes he cannot even muster the energy to dive in. Teilhard calls the physical world the 'biosphere', and the world of the mind the 'noosphere', and explains that man is in the process of making the change from one to the other just as if he is a land animal turning into a fish. Wells reverses the image, and compares man to the earliest amphibians who wanted to become land animals; but they had fins instead of legs, so that a short period on land was enough to exhaust them; they had to get back to the comfortable, sustaining medium of the sea—in our case, this irrelevant physical world and its problems. In Teilhard's terms the problem is: is there any way in which the land-animal can hasten the process of becoming a fish? In Wells' terms: is there any way of hastening the process of growing legs instead of fins?

There, then, is already a clearer statement of the problems than Shaw achieved in *Man and Superman* or *Back to Methuselah*, and it leaves us with our faces turned towards a solution, even if it is still invisible. Shaw recognised that the Webbs, for example, were a step in the right direction; but the problem is still implicit, for the material of which the Webbs fashioned their mental lives —facts and statistics—would not ultimately satisfy a Wells or Shaw. But 'thought' has got to be thought *about* something. And so the problem of Wells sitting at his desk and doodling on his sheet of paper is still unsolved. What *ought* he to be thinking about?

And now I come to what, I think, is my own particular contribution to the matter. We know that our capacity for living 'mental' lives is small; you only have to try to read a long book in one sitting, or watch television for too long, to notice that you get an odd feeling of claustrophobia, of spiritual dyspepsia. This seems to prove the point that we are amphibians who get tired of the land. . . . But does it? If I have got hold of some book that I have wanted to read for years, and I determine to read it slowly and carefully in one sitting, I can go on for ten hours without getting tired. It is only if I get impatient and careless, and try to read the book with only half a mind, as it were, that I begin to 'run down'. And, on a different level, this is the same thing that has often been noticed by explorers under harsh conditions: that they can draw on surprising reserves of strength if they know they *have* to survive.

In the same way Kenneth Walker has described how he used

to leave his Harley Street surgery in the early evening in a state of total exhaustion; motor the twenty miles or so to Welwyn, and spend the evening performing strenuous Dervish exercises with a group of Gurdjieff's followers; and yet when he left at midnight he felt so full of energy that he didn't want to sleep. So his earlier exhaustion was *not* real, even though it appeared to be so to the enquiring everyday consciousness. We have vast reserve energy tanks which become available under crisis, when the will wakes up. It is the flooding of consciousness with these energy tanks that produces the sexual orgasm and the ecstasies of saints. Ramakrishna, for example, had the trick of flooding his consciousness with these energy tanks—the Hindus call it *samadhi* —which he learned accidentally by attempting to commit suicide. The sudden crisis had the effect of awakening his 'true will', and he never lost the trick.

In short, there is an *unconscious* factor at work here, a factor below normal consciousness, and yet connected to it. Kenneth Walker believed himself to be exhausted, and in a sense, he was; yet the energy that later flooded his consciousness came from *inside* himself, and *he* released it. It was the philosopher Edmund Husserl who invented a word for this kind of subconscious operation of the will; he called it *intentionality*. I am inclined to believe that when I look at a thing, it merely walks in through my eyes and implants itself on my brain. In other words, I will see it whether I want to or not. This is only half true. I cannot *refuse* to see it if it is in front of me and my eyes are open. But it *is* quite possible for me to look at an object and not see it, because my mind is elsewhere. In order to see something, I must fire my mind at it as I would fire an arrow at a target. I do this 'firing' so automatically, for the most part, that I am not aware of doing it. That is why I think that seeing is a purely mechanical process. It isn't. It is *intentional*, and the intention behind it can be conscious or below the threshold of consciousness. If I am trying to pick out a distant object through a pair of binoculars, the effort is very conscious; I may even have to ask someone to stop speaking so I can concentrate on 'firing' my attention. As I type this page, the effort of focussing the words is quite sub-conscious. Conscious intentions become subconscious ones: that is to say, habits. When I have finished my work for today, I shall have to take a hot bath and a glass of wine to relax. I have written this postscript so far in a single sitting, and my attention has got so used to concentrating that I shall have to distract it with physical sensations before it will un-concentrate.

Man is more complex than any other animal because he has this two-tier system of mind. But this is only partly true. *All* organisms, even the simplest, need the two-tier system to some extent, or they could not survive. My friend Robert Ardrey drew my attention to an instance of this that is of considerable interest. Two scientists, J. B. Best and I. Rubinstein, were doing experiments to find out how much planaria could learn. Now the planarian worm is one of the most primitive of all organisms—it has no brain, nervous system, stomach or anus. And yet it seems to be capable of learning.

Planaria need water to live. Best and Rubinstein put a number of them in a closed tube which had a fork in it. The water could be drained out of the tube by means of a tap. And when the water was drained out, the alarmed planarian worm would rush off down the tube in search of water. Soon, he could come to the parting of the ways, and he would discover that one road was lighted, and the other dark. If he chose the lighted road, he would find water; if he chose the dark one, he wouldn't. In a very short time, a large percentage of the worms were making straight for the lighted fork every time their water supply was drained off.

But now a strange thing happened. For no apparent reason, the fully trained worms now began choosing the dark passageway. And then they did something even odder; when their water was drained off, they just lay still, as if saying, 'Oh God, not *again*'. They actually preferred to die rather than go off in search of water.

The investigators were baffled, and finally, one of them came up with the apparently mad suggestion that perhaps the worms had learned *too easily*, and were bored. They devised an experiment to test this hypothesis. They had two tubes, one made of rough plastic, one of smooth—so the worm could feel it with its belly. In one of these, the water was to be found down a lighted passage. In the other, it was to be found down the dark passage. It was a 'double ambiguity' problem they had to solve. The experimenters now started off with a new batch of worms, and kept moving them from one tube to another. This time, the worms took a lot longer to learn, and a much smaller percentage of them succeeded. But that small percentage *did not regress*. They would continue to make straight for the water supply every time their water was drained off, no matter how often the process was repeated.

Why? Consider what happens if someone persuades a business-man to finance a restaurant, and after a few months, the business looks like failing. The proprietor explains that this is because they haven't yet become fashionable, and persuades the businessman to lend him more money. And now, if the business is still unsuc-cessful after six months, his chances of persuading the business-man to lend him yet more money are higher than before, because the businessman has more to lose. And if he persuades him to lend yet another lot of money, his chances of getting a third loan are higher still, for the businessman will realise that the pump has got to be primed until it *is* giving water.

Gurdjieff used the same principle in his teaching. He made his pupils pay immense sums, knowing that this was the first step in getting the fullest concentration out of them; the more they paid, the more effort they would put into getting value for their money. Anything we acquire easily bores us after a while, because we do not *put the effort* into appreciating it; there is a failure of subconscious intentionality.

I have invented a useful concept called 'the robot'. I have a robot in my subconscious mind, and when I learn some difficult activity, like typing or driving a car, I first of all acquire it painfully and consciously, and then my robot takes it over, and does it much more efficiently than I could do it by thinking about it. In fact, if I try thinking about it once the robot has taken it over, I simply mess up the robot. I have a friend who cannot let go of a dart when he is playing, and this is because someone once asked him 'How do you hold a dart when you throw it?' He tried thinking about it—and ruined his darts style.

Now if I put an immense amount of effort into learning some new skill, the robot is impressed by its importance, and will always do it thoroughly. If I learn something too easily, the robot takes it over in a casual, bored manner, and puts less energy into repeating it. And if he has to repeat it too many times, he goes on strike. And at this point, the planarian worm lies down and dies, or chooses the dark passage out of sheer perversity.

I had thought that the 'robot' is restricted to the higher animals. But obviously not; even the planarian worm has one.

This emphasises an interesting point. In Husserlian psychology, there is no such thing as 'instinct'; there are only acquired habits, intentions that have been passed on to the robot. My acquired taste for olives, my sexual response to a pretty girl, and my watering at the mouth when I am hungry and I smell food cooking, are all 'habits'.

But what about the moments of visionary intensity, which are obviously the key to human evolution? According to Wordsworth, the 'glory and the freshness' of the dream begin to fade as we get older, and it is inevitable. According to the theory I have just outlined, they fade for the same reason the half-trained planaria got bored: because we haven't made enough effort. According to this theory, there is no more reason why visionary ecstasy should not become a habit than why driving a car or smoking shouldn't. It did with Ramakrishna.

It is all a question of understanding our mental mechanisms, the workings of the robot. At the moment, our lives tend to be purely conscious. 'The wakeful life of the ego is a perceiving,' says Husserl. We fail to utilise these vast subconscious resources that could completely alter our lives. An emergency brings them forth automatically, as an alarm call goes straight through to the robot, yet I cannot use them for creative purposes, because 'creation' is not an emergency; in fact, it becomes a habit after a certain point, and loses its edge, as can be seen with Shaw. This wouldn't happen if we could tap the great energy tanks, what has been called 'the source of power, meaning and purpose' inside us. At the end of Greene's *Power and the Glory*, a novel for which I have great temperamental antipathy because of its defeatism, the whisky-priest, who has been an utter weakling, is about to be shot, and suddenly has the realisation that 'it would have been so easy to be a saint'. But it took a firing squad to make him realise it. What a *waste*. If he could have realised it earlier, his life would have been ten times as creative. And I am here asserting that, according to this new psychology I have outlined (I call it 'the new existentialism') it should become possible for human beings to *consciously* utilise these resources that at the moment can only be drawn forth by emergency.

Obviously, this is not really the point to end this book. It should be the point to begin it; but it is already too long. For several years now, a great many people in Europe and America have been working slowly towards an 'evolutionary psychology'. Viktor Frankl came up with some profound insights in a death camp under the Nazis, and his ideas are the cornerstone of a new 'existential psychology'; others of equal importance in this respect are Medard Boss, Erwin Straus, Ludwig Binswanger and Eugene Minkowski; in America, Rollo May and William Glasser (the founder of 'reality therapy') have done important work. Hadley Cantril's transactional psychology should also be mentioned in this context.

For some years now, I have been working on the details of an 'evolutionary psychology' in association with two close friends, Abraham Maslow and Robert Ardrey. Each of us has approached the problem from a totally different angle: Ardrey as a zoologist interested in 'territory', Maslow as an existential psychologist trying to base his psychology upon positive rather than negative Freudian concepts; myself as a novelist and existential 'philosopher', trying to break away from the nihilistic existentialism of Sartre and Heidegger. It would be impossible to exaggerate my debt to both Ardrey and Maslow. It was Ardrey who first told me about the 'dominant 5%' in 1962 (neither of us knew that Shaw already knew about it). The 'dominant 5%' applies to animals as well as to human beings.

Perhaps I should try to explain briefly why this 'dominant 5%' concept is so important. It must first of all be understood that it does *not* imply that 5 per cent of human beings are men of genius, or even talent. The dominant 5 per cent includes Mozart and Einstein; it also includes the Great Train Robbery gang, and all pop singers, film stars, politicians, business executives, army officers and N.C.O.s. Every mindless bully belongs to it.

The interesting thing is that most of the dominant 5 per cent *require other people* to express their dominance. A Napoleon needs his armies, a politician his electorate, an actor his audience, and so on. This means that the men of highest genius differ from the rest of the 5 per cent *in kind*, because obviously, a Newton or a Beethoven does not necessarily need other people to express his dominance. Newton cared so little for other people that he left the *Principia* in manuscript for years; *the work was enough in itself.* That is to say, men of the calibre of Mozart, Beethoven, Newton belong to a new group of higher evolutionary types *whose sphere of dominance is Teilhard's 'noosphere'.*

And it is at this point that we encounter the problem of the Black Room, evolved by the Chinese for brainwashing. A man who is placed in a totally black and silent room gradually loses all sense of his own purpose and identity, and will go insane if left in it for long enough. Maslow discovered that the 'higher evolutionary types', whom he calls 'self-actualisers', can stand the Black Room longer than most people—at least, if they are integrated personalities. And this is what we would expect; the higher evolutionary types inhabit the 'world of the mind', the noösphere, to some extent; what destroys most people in the Black Room is that they are normally geared to the physical world, and in the Black Room, there is nothing to do with their energies. It is rather like that torture devised by Tiberius, of tying up a man's genitals with string so he couldn't urinate, and then forcing him to drink heavily.

The trouble is that even the self-actualisers cannot stand the Black Room for more than a few days. Man is not yet truly a creature of the mind. If someone could devise a method for training men to withstand the Black Room, this would be equivalent to finding a way in which man could take his evolution into his own hands. The higher evolutionary types among the dominant 5 per cent must somehow make that 'evolutionary leap' to the control of the subconscious energy tanks.

My own view of the process of evolution can be expressed very simply. Animals possess powers that human beings have lost. For example, as Ardrey points out, there is the mystery of the 'homing instinct', which seems to prove that animals are on some kind of universal radar. And many dog owners could testify to examples of 'extra-sensory perception' on the part of their pets. (Hugh McDiarmid, the Scottish poet, has a dog that always knows when he will return from a journey, and sits at the end of the lane for several days before he is due home.) Men have *deliberately* lost this instinctive power, allowed it to atrophy; for the development of consciousness tends to destroy it, and they prefer consciousness and the efficiency it brings. However, they have reached a point where they have so far developed the conscious mind that they have lost touch with the subconscious source of power and purpose. They are *trapped in consciousness*, and the result is often neurosis and sickness.

But while consciousness traps them in a daylight world, far from the universal radar that forms the bond between animals and nature, they have developed a compensatory power to which we apply the inadequate word 'imagination'. If I take a psychedelic drug, it can plunge me back into my animal sense of oneness with nature, the universal radar; but this isn't what man is aiming for; this is going backwards. He wants the animal breadth of perception, the exciting sense of multiplicity, *combined with* the sharpness and control of consciousness. When the young H. G. Wells became almost drunk on scientific knowledge, the fascination of astronomy and physics and biology, he was exercising a *different kind* of universal radar from the animal kind. It possessed all the sharp clarity of consciousness that man has developed over two million years, together with the power to touch his creative springs, the subconscious energy tanks.

Some years ago, Sir Julian Huxley remarked to me: 'Never underestimate the importance of art and poetry in human evolution.' I asked him to explain exactly what he meant, but he only said, 'Think about it.' I now see exactly what he meant. If one thinks of the sense of oneness with the universe that mystics have experienced, it can be seen that it is closely connected with the animal 'radar' that enables Hugh McDiarmid's dog to anticipate his homecoming. When we allowed that 'sixth sense' to atrophy, we became trapped in consciousness. But when I am moved by poetry or music or painting, I have not abdicated my human ability to 'focus'—as I do if I take a psychedelic drug— and yet strange feelings flow over me; my consciousness expands beyond the present. *Art is the distinctively human way of compensating for the loss of the animal radar*. But then, anyone who has read the tenth volume of Arnold Toynbee's *Study of History* will recall the passages in which he describes how history suddenly became for him a kind of mystical experience. Clearly, *all* intellectual activity has the same purpose as art, although scientific and mathematical thinking lack the instantaneous magic of great music. (Is that why such a high percentage of mathematicians love music?) All the activity of what we call the 'imagination'—using it in its broadest sense of scientific as well as artistic creativity—is man's attempt to develop *a new faculty* to compensate for the loss of animal radar. It has only just begun to develop, but all the evidence indicates that we are on the point of a *leap* to a new stage, and that this leap will be the result of conscious effort. When man has fully developed this new faculty—foreshadowed in art and music—he will possess the ability to move freely from mystical consciousness (or direct *vision* of his over-all purpose) to the kind of narrow concentration required for everyday purposes. 'Instinct' in the animal sense will become almost unnecessary. I am also inclined to believe—as I have suggested in *The Philosopher's Stone*—that this new control of consciousness will automatically entail the longevity that Shaw prophesies in *Back to Methuselah*.

Shaw's evolutionary vision was a kind of dawn, in which new things become visible in the half-light. Since then, the light has grown stronger, and it becomes possible to see an answer to the question: What shall we *do*? Psychology is not simply moving away from the old Freudian determinism; it is actually uncovering the practical mechanisms of evolution in human beings.

One more point about these 'mechanisms'. We know that the moments of intensity, of poetry, are due to an 'opening up' of the subconscious mind. 'Bored consciousness' is empty, flat, dull; and then something happens, some relaxation, some key symbol dropped into the depths, and a warm glow of energy begins to flow from 'below', consciousness begins to glow, takes on a bubbling, champagne-like quality. What is more, I know this is 'intentional'—*I am doing it myself.* It is as if I have overcome some amnesia, and suddenly know how to awaken my subconscious instinctively just as I know how to swim or drive a car. Animals, I have said, never *get* this far separated from their subconscious powers; separation is the price we have paid for this laser beam of focussed consciousness. So is there nothing *practical* we can say about that 'intention' that re-establishes contact between our upper regions and our depths?

There is, and I suppose I would regard this as my key insight. I observed first of all that a man who is bored by pleasure or comfort can still be stimulated by pain or inconvenience, and I gave to this discovery the arbitrary name of 'the St Neot margin', for reasons I have explained elsewhere.* 'There is an area of consciousness that is indifferent to pleasure, but that can be stimulated by pain or inconvenience'—that is 'the St Neot margin'. The next stage was to consider the mechanism of this 'awakening-due-to-inconvenience'. What *happened* when Ramakrishna despaired of finding the Divine Mother, and was about to run himself through with a sword? The sudden expectation of pain and annihilation caused a spasmodic 'clenching' of the whole being, like a fist closing. This clenching, *followed almost immediately by relaxation*, had the effect of syphoning up from the subconscious the immense waves of energy that he described as 'samadhi'. It is a simple double-action, like working the handle of a pump up and down. Wordsworth told De Quincey that his moments of 'poetry' came when he suddenly concentrated his mind on something *that has nothing to do with poetry*, and then allowed it to relax.

We possess a *muscle* in the brain, so to speak, whose purpose is to keep consciousness flooded with vitality. But man is, after all, 99 per cent an animal, whose 'living' is merely a series of responses to stimuli from the external world. The 'muscle' responds automatically to crisis, but it is extremely difficult for us to move it by an ordinary process of intentionality. However, once we recognise its existence, we know that it *can* be done. Half the trouble with a man who is bored or exhausted or in a state of despair is that he thinks that what his consciousness tells him is the *whole* truth. Therefore he remains passive in his despair. A

* Appendix to *The Outsider,* Pan Books and Dell.

sudden crisis can flood his being with energy. But if he knows of the existence of the 'muscle'—the hot-line to the subconscious, so to speak—he doesn't have to wait for a crisis; in spite of his sense of purposelessness, there is a direction in which he can move. It is a matter of a simple piece of *information*, the grasping of a *fact*, nothing else. Gurdjieff's legend of the magician and the sheep is relevant here. If you wanted to keep a flock of sheep in a field without a fence, a good way would be to persuade them —perhaps by hypnosis—that there is *nothing outside the field*, at least, nothing of interest. This will be all the easier if the field, like human consciousness, is surrounded by hills that prevent the sheep from seeing anything beyond. But if once some enterprising sheep breaks the spell, wanders over the hilltop, and realises how fascinating is the world beyond, nothing can now stop it. It *knows* there is a world beyond.

The ideas I have sketched above do not amount to a developed evolutionary psychology (although I have tried to develop them elsewhere*). But what should be clear is that they constitute a *real* beginning, a beginning in the sense of a direction, a scientific direction. The Shaw-Wells conflict has at last been transcended, with Shaw declaring his belief in an active evolutionary force, and Wells answering that this is contrary to the spirit of science.

I am not, course, asserting that all the scientists and psychologists involved in this revolution would call themselves evolutionists. Sir Karl Popper and his follower Michael Polanyi believe themselves to be concerned simply to undermine the old deterministic philosophy of science. Arthur Koestler's *Act of Creation* and *The Ghost in the Machine* are brilliant attacks upon psychological determinism that take great care to avoid anything that sounds like 'vitalism'. Sir Alister Hardy describes himself as an orthodox Darwinian biologist; yet in his Gifford lectures *The Living Stream* and *The Divine Flame* he advances views that would

* In the six volumes of my 'Outsider cycle', and in *Introduction to the New Existentialism*. The psychological aspects are more closely examined in a work in progress called *The Self Image*.

have struck even Lamarck as wildly mystical. Sir Julian Huxley, who introduced the work of Teilhard de Chardin to English readers, also believes that he is a strictly orthodox Darwinian. Ardrey regards himself as a thoroughly sceptical student of animal behaviour; he was insistent that I remove certain references to the inheritance of acquired characteristics from a chapter in *Beyond the Outsider* on the grounds that everyone knew it to be unscientific nonsense. The late Maurice Merleau-Ponty demonstrated the inadequacy of behaviouristic psychology in *The Structure of Behaviour*, yet he was in many ways an orthodox Marxian. I know of no existential psychologist, from Frankl to Maslow, who would be happy to be described as a Shavian evolutionist. And it is unnecessary to point out that the whole philosophy of existentialism, which began as a revolt against scientific systematising, has become an assertion of the ultimate meaninglessness of human existence in the mid-twentieth century. A revolution may not be aware of its objectives.

But what I *am* here pointing out is that Shaw grasped the objective of the revolution fifty years before it began to emerge into more general consciousness; and when the revolution is completed, I believe that Shaw will be seen as its original prophet as Marx was the prophet of the Russian revolution. Shaw aroused a great deal of hostility by his assertions that he was the most far-sighted man of his time, that he was born a hundred years ahead of his age. And now, slowly, we are beginning to see the joke: that he was telling the truth. I believe that Shaw was right when he said that human beings are on the point of outgrowing 'tragedy', and that a certain optimism and sense of intellectual purpose can prolong human life far beyond its present limit. 'Wellsian man', the intellectually creative portion of the '5%', will then have to recognise that the way forward lies through world government, through some degree of genetic control, and through a careful attempt to devise means of creative self-expression for every one of the rest of the '5%'. But, far more important, a new psychology that recognises the importance of human will and optimism will devise means of investigating and exploring the capacities of that will. A hundred years ago, man did not suspect that he had the power to fly and to watch Olympic Games taking place on the other side of the world. To Shakespeare, or even Dickens, such powers would have seemed pure magic or witchcraft. What new 'magic' powers might he not discover when psychology has taught him a new control and understanding of his inner being? Whether you, now reading these words, or I, now adding the last words to this book, accomplish the 'break-through' or not, it *can* be accomplished, and will be. The prophets of decadence and the 'decline of the West' were wrong. We are living in one of the most important epochs in human history.

For more than three years now, in the writing of this book, I have lived with and thought about Shaw almost constantly. Teaching courses on him in American universities has not helped particularly, for one became aware that the old Beecham view of Shaw—as amusing but emotionally shallow—is a hydra with a thousand heads; it has been said so often that it seems to be accepted by everyone who has ever heard of Shaw. But thinking about him so constantly has given me an odd sense of closeness to him, as if he was the ghost of Hamlet's father, and I carrying out some last request. I am too close to the book to judge how successful it has been, but as I wrote the words about his death at the end of Chapter Ten, I had an odd sensation of the ghost nodding courteously, as if to acknowledge that I have at least done my best.

At all events, I want it to be understood that this book is intended as a partial repayment of a debt that can never be cleared.

Mevagissey, 1965–8

INDEX

Works by Shaw in CAPITALS AND SMALL CAPITALS; works by other authors in *italics*.